D0044503

EMINENT VICTORIAN SOLDIERS

EMINENT VICTORIAN SOLDIERS

Seekers of Glory

BYRON FARWELL

W·W·NORTON & COMPANY
New York   *London*

Published simultaneously inn Canada by Penguin Books Canada Ltd., 2801 John Street, Markham, Ontario L3R 1B4
Printed in the United States of America.

The text of this book is composed in Aster. Composition and manufacturing by the Maple-Vail Book Manufacturing Group.

First Edition

Library of Congress Cataloging in Publication Data

Farwell, Byron.
   Eminent victorian soldiers.

   Bibliography: p.
   Includes index.
    1. Marshals—Great Britain—Bibliography. 2. Generals—
Great Britain—Bibliography. 3. Great Britain. Army—
Biography. I. Title.
DA68.32.A1F37 1985   355'.0092'2   84–29601

ISBN 0-393-01884-9

W. W. Norton & Company, Inc., 500 Fifth Avenue, New York, N.Y. 10110
W. W. Norton & Company Ltd., 37 Great Russell Street, London WC1B 3NU

1 2 3 4 5 6 7 8 9 0

For

Jill Farwell
and
Mervyn Lewis

Contents

———

Illustrations

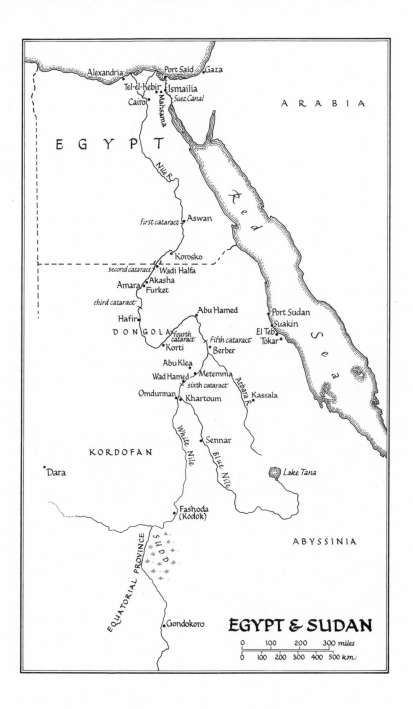

Alexandria · Port Said · Gaza
Tel-el-Kebir · Ismailia
Cairo · Mahsama · *Suez Canal*

ARABIA

EGYPT

Nile R.

first cataract · Aswan

· Korosko

second cataract · Wadi Halfa
Amara · Akasha
· Furket

third cataract

Hafir ·
· Abu Hamed
· Port Sudan
Suakin ·
El Teb ·
DONGOLA
fourth cataract
· Korti
fifth cataract
· Berber
Tokar ·

Abu Klea ·
· Metemma
Wad Hamed ·
sixth cataract
Omdurman · *Athara R.*
· Khartoum · Kassala

Red Sea

KORDOFAN

White Nile
· Sennar
Blue Nile

Dara ·
· Lake Tana

· Fashoda
(Kodok)

ABYSSINIA

SUDD
EQUATORIAL PROVINCE

· Gondokoro

EGYPT & SUDAN

0   100   200   300 *miles*
0   100 200 300 400 500 *km*

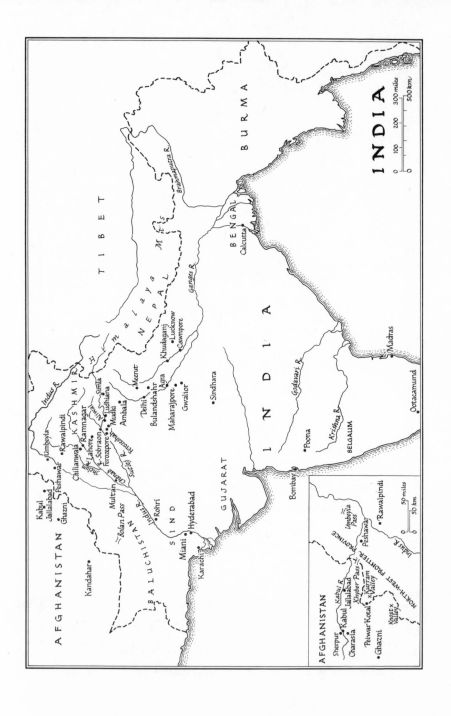

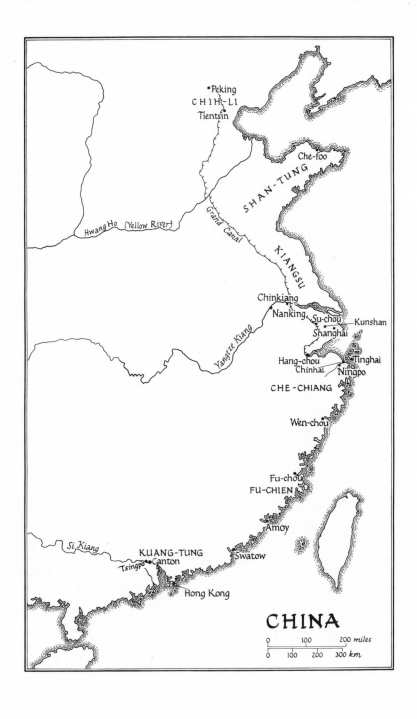

Peking
CHIH-LI
Tientsin

Che-foo

SHAN-TUNG

Hwang Ho (Yellow River)

Grand Canal

KIANGSU

Yangtze Kiang

Chinkiang
Nanking
Su-chou
Shanghai
Kunshan

Hang-chou
Chinhai
Tinghai
Ningpo

CHE-CHIANG

Wen-chou

Fu-chou
FU-CHIEN

Amoy

Si Kiang
KUANG-TUNG
Canton
Swatow
Tsingpo
Hong Kong

CHINA

0   100   200 *miles*

0   100   200   300 *km*

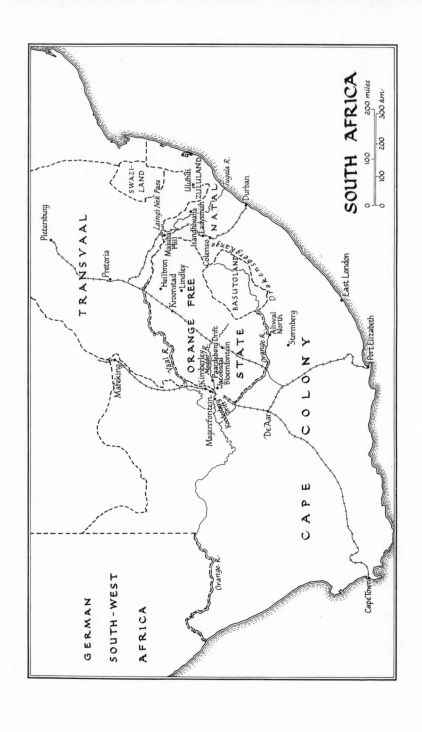

Author's Note

I t is a popular but absurd belief that the Victorians enjoyed a simple, shared set of moral imperatives and that they were hypocrites because they failed to live up to their moral code. Truth is, however, that Victorians were in many ways more diverse, honest and realistic than people today. The middle classes did indeed aspire to a higher and more rigid moral code, and they were perhaps no more successful than we are today in achieving their moral aspirations. But each age has its own conventions and its own treasured myths, and it would be wrong of us to deny them theirs. If we see them with different eyes, they should none the less be held only to their own standards of conduct.

Although millions of men still make careers in armies, few today readily admit to a love of war. Such was not the case in the last century. The general attitude of all the soldiers presented here, and probably of most soldiers, was: War is a terrible thing, but we love it. Officers would travel great distances at their own expense in the hope of being allowed to take part in campaigns. Ian Hamilton thought war was life's greatest experience, barring a honeymoon. Redvers Buller actually interrupted his honeymoon to fight in Egypt. Soldiers were honestly eager for war and counted themselves fortunate to live in an age that provided them with battles in such profusion.

'The story of the human race', Winston Churchill once said, 'is war'. Certainly wars have been the most persistent

non-biological activity of mankind, and it is only in this
century that anti-war movements have sprung up – without, however, causing any notable decrease in the number
or the ferocity of wars. There was not a single year in Queen
Victoria's long reign, from 1837 to 1901, when her soldiers
were not fighting and dying somewhere in the world. In
this century, in spite of Britain's retreat from empire, the
pattern has changed remarkably little, except in 1968 when,
mirabile dictu, no British soldier was killed in action anywhere.

In this collection of Victorian military heroes, all reached
at least the rank of local major-general and five died as
field marshals. All were knighted for their services, and four
were raised to the peerage. None attended a university, and
only two, Sir Evelyn Wood and Lord Roberts, went to a
public school. Six of the eight were sons of soldiers, and
Wood, although his father was a clergyman, had an uncle
and grandfathers who were admirals. Five of the eight were
born or brought up in Ireland. As Correlli Barnett has
remarked, the Anglo-Irish constitute the closest thing the
British have to a *Junker* class, and its men were always well
represented in Victorian armies. All eight men were devoted
to their profession and sought glory at the cannon's mouth.

My title must inevitably call to mind Lytton Strachey's
Eminent Victorians, that savage attack on the age of his
father through biographies of four admired personages:
Cardinal Manning, Florence Nightingale, Dr Arnold and
Chinese Gordon. Only one of Strachey's subjects is included
in this study, and readers will find the account of General
Gordon presented here in a different, more factual and, I
believe, truer form. Although I have painted these admired
Victorian soldiers 'warts and all', I have not tried, as
Strachey did, to attack them 'in unexpected places' or to
'fall upon the flank, or the rear'.

Strachey wrote in his Preface, 'It has been my purpose to
illustrate rather than explain'. Such indeed has been my
aim, but my focus on soldiers narrows my scope, and my

inclusion of twice as many lives should give a deeper insight into a vanished era where the political, economic, social and scientific landscape was vastly different, though its inhabitants included men with feelings and personalities and problems – and sometimes attitudes – that were no different from our own.

Several people have assisted me, particularly in bringing to light the truth about Hector Macdonald. Among these I should like to thank George Macdonald Fraser on the Isle of Man; Dale Walker of Texas; C.J. Sinclair of the Scottish Record Office; and Alistair Phillips, also of Scotland.

In Virginia my friends Elizabeth Moore and Henry A. Romberg, Jr., have given me invaluable help in indexing and proof-reading.

Special mention must be made of my wife, Ruth, whose keen eye, sure sense of the worth of a word and many suggestions have improved every page.

Byron Farwell
Hillsboro, Virginia

EMINENT VICTORIAN
SOLDIERS

CHAPTER

1

Hugh Gough
(1779–1869)

*'Then I'll be at them with the
bayonet!'*

1

Colonel George Gough and his wife, Letitia, were disappointed when, on 3 November 1779, Mrs Gough gave birth to a son, for they already had three and this time had hoped for a girl. The boy, whom they named Hugh, grew up on the family estate in Ireland with a sense that he was unwanted. Later in life he claimed that he had gleaned his only education by listening to his older brothers' lessons. This was not perhaps quite accurate, though it was close to the truth. Two sisters were born later, but Hugh remained neglected – or felt himself to be, which is much the same. In any case, he appears to have developed early in life a hunger for recognition and the habit of exacting attention.

His military career began early. He first wore the King's

uniform at the age of thirteen when he was commissioned in the Limerick Militia, commanded by his father. By fifteen he was adjutant of the 119th Foot, a fact that does not speak well for that regiment's internal arrangements. In 1795 the boy-officer transferred to the second battalion of the 76th Highlanders (which later became the 2nd Seaforths). As an old man he spoke of his time in this battalion as 'days of youthful enjoyment'. It was while he was with this unit that he first saw action: the fierce hand-to-hand fighting of the Highlanders who landed at the Cape of Good Hope as part of the force that seized the Dutch colony.

On his return from South Africa, Gough again transferred, this time to the 87th Foot (later the Royal Irish Fusiliers), in which he was to win his first laurels and with which he always identified. With this regiment (having only one battalion at that time) he sailed to the West Indies, where during a three-and-a-half-year stay he was in action against brigands in St Lucia and Trinidad, took part in the ill-fated attack on Puerto Rico and fought with the force that attacked the Dutch in Surinam.

About 1800 he returned to Britain. Although commissions and promotions were purchased in the infantry and cavalry, there had to be a vacancy before an officer could advance in grade, and in stable times promotion could be slow. Even with money to purchase advancement, Gough languished as a subaltern for nine years before he became a captain in June 1803. Then, in only twenty-six months, he was offered an opportunity to advance another step. Gough later spoke of the 'almost brotherly kindness' of Major E. Blakeney, 'who sold out earlier than he otherwise would have done in order that I might get his majority'. Thus, at the age of twenty-five he became a field officer and joined the newly formed second battalion of the 87th Regiment, which had been raised in the counties of Tipperary and Clare.

In the same year he met at a military ball Miss Frances Maria Stephens, daughter of an artillery general. She was instantly smitten, for she believed she had seen the slender, red-headed young officer in a dream only the night before. In July 1807 they were married; in August of the following year a daughter, Letitia, was born. Four months later Major Gough sailed with his battalion for the Iberian Peninsula to join the forces resisting the French occupation. In March 1809 he took command of the battalion while its commander served elsewhere and remained in command for the duration of his service there.

The war in the Peninsula was a far more serious affair than anything Gough had previously experienced. Not only were the physical conditions more daunting, but praise and rewards were harder to win. On 23 June 1809 Gough wrote to his father, describing the hardships suffered by his battalion and his own 'most violent fever', adding peevishly, 'The occurrences of the past few weeks have fully proved to me that War is a Lottery, and those who least deserve may be those who get the most credit'. Gough was, and ever remained, a glutton for glory. Never shy in putting forward his claims for honours and rewards, if others did not readily praise him, he praised himself. However, in an era that accustomed its fighting men to acclaim, he was exceptional only in his unabashed ambition and the exuberance of his self-praise.

Gough was certainly no coward, for he led his men in battle with reckless bravado. In the great battle of Talavera, in July 1809, he received his first serious wound when a cannon shot fractured the ribs on his right side. Nevertheless, twenty months later he led his troops in the battle of Barrosa, where they captured the brass eagle of the French 8th Regiment. (These eagles had been presented by Napoleon to his regiments, and it was considered the greatest disgrace to allow one to fall into enemy hands. Many a soldier was killed or maimed defending an eagle or attempting to capture one.)

It was at Barrosa that the 87th made an exceptionally gallant charge, which Gough described to Frances:

The French waited until we were about 25 paces from them before they broke, and as they were in column when they did, they could not get away. It was therefore a scene of most dreadful carnage. I will even own to you my weakness. As of course I was in front of my regiment, therefore in the middle of them, I could not, confused and flying as they were, cut down anyone, although I might have twenty, they seemed so confounded and so frightened.

For its courage the 87th was awarded the title of the Prince of Wales's Own Irish Regiment, and Gough was given the brevet rank of lieutenant-colonel, the first instance of brevet rank ever being conferred upon an officer for the conduct of his regiment in action.

A few months later, during the siege of Tarifa, Gough laid the foundation of his military reputation when, on 29 December 1811, the besieging French breached the wall and burst in upon the British garrison. As his battalion formed up to repel the attack at the breach, Gough ordered the band to strike up 'Garry Owen' and told his men, 'Whenever there is an opportunity, the bayonet must be used'. The French were beaten back in a short, fierce action in which Gough was slightly wounded in the head and finger. He described the battle to Frances:

Your husband and his gallant corps shone most conspicuous. . . . The scene was awfully grand; every officer and man seemed to outdrive one another in acts of heroism, and never while life is left in me can I forget their expressions and looks . . . at seeing me bleed.

In March 1812 he was given his first independent command as garrison commander of Tarifa. He had complained bitterly of the town when he first arrived there, calling it 'the most wretched village in Europe'. With his appointment it was transformed into 'this important fortress'.

Gough liked to regale his wife with the compliments he received. His men 'adored him', he said, adding modestly, 'I am also a great favourite with the Spaniards'. ('A most wrteched rabble', he called them privately.) It was undeniably true that the soldiers of the 87th admired Gough, for he was a charismatic leader. In turn, he had an enormous regard for them. On 14 October 1812 he wrote ecstatically:

> My men have astonished the Division in marching; I never saw such a set of fellows. I came yesterday seven and twenty miles over a most wretched road, and it raining all the time, in eight hours and a half, without having one man out of his section an inch. The Guards saw us come in to their astonishment.

Splendid the battalion may have been in October, but six months later it was reduced by half through sickness and privation. The men who remained were broken in spirit and starving. Gough, too, was dispirited. In addition to his troubles in Spain, there had been tragedy at home: his only son, Edward, born on 9 December 1810, had died. It was a hard winter.

Spring brought reinforcements and fresh supplies to the army in the Peninsula and also a victory, at Vittoria in 21 June 1813, where men of the 87th again distinguished themselves. To Gough's delight, General Sir Charles Colville exclaimed before a group of officers, 'Gough, you and your corps have done wonders!' And, as Gough confided to his wife, the general had not seen half the actions in which his battalion took part that day.

At Nivelle on 9 November 1813 the first stage of Gough's military career came to an end when he was seriously wounded in the hip. He had by that time commanded a battalion in the Peninsula longer that any other British officer. In spite of a splendid constitution he could still only hobble about on crutches seven months after receiving his wound, but he found comfort back in Britain, where he was given some of the rewards he craved. In 1815 he was knighted and allowed a pension of £250 (later increased to £300), and his brevet rank of lieutenant-colonel, which he had held for six years, was made substantive.

When the Napoleonic wars ended, the army was reduced, and on 1 February 1817 his battalion was disbanded. Gough, at the age of thirty-seven, went on half pay. For the next eleven and a half years he lived the life of a country squire in Ireland, serving for a time as magistrate for the counties of Cork, Limerick and Tipperary. It was during this period that most of his children were born: another son and three more daughters. Those who have read George Meredith's *Diana of the Crossways* will remember Lord Larrian, for whom Gough was the model.

When the 48-year-old Gough returned to active duty, he held various commands in Britain, in one of which he spent three years 'suppressing outrages in Ireland', where, he said, 'every passion of a misguided and infatuated Population was let loose on the Land'. He continued to advance up the Army List, even when he was on half pay, becoming a full colonel in 1819 and a major-general in 1830. (The rank of brigadier or brigadier-general was not then substantive.) In 1834, when the colonelcy of the 87th Regiment fell vacant, he was bitterly disappointed that the honour was not conferred upon him, and he talked of resigning. Then, in 1837, he was offered, and accepted, the command of the Mysore Division of the Madras army, headquartered in Bangalore.

He took his family with him to India and spent three years there, a peaceful period that ended abruptly when Lord Auckland, then governor-general, offered him the command of the British expeditionary force in China. For a year an unsatisfactory, desultory war had been in progress against the Imperial Chinese government, which, for reasons the British failed to understand, objected to the importation of opium from India. Gough, now sixty-one but trim and vigorous and as eager as in his youth to achieve

Viscount Gough when commander-in-chief of the English forces during the Chinese war, 1840–42 *(Photo: BBC Hulton Picture Library)*

distinction, embarked upon a second active military career. Ahead of him lay four more wars, in which he was to be in command in sixteen battles.

2

Lord Auckland sent Gough off to China with the expressed hope that he would not ask for more troops, but one of Gough's first acts on reaching Hong Kong in early March 1841 was to request two more battalions, one British and one Indian. They were in fact needed. In a letter to Archibald Arbuthnot, his son-in-law, he wrote, 'I cannot think that Lord Auckland will withhold them'. Indeed he did not; the troops were sent.

Gough's first task in China was simply to give such support as he could to the naval forces engaged in reducing the forts guarding the great commercial city of Canton. He had plenty of time to initiate one of those unpleasant controversies that were to mark the remainder of his military career. This one was with Captain Charles Elliot, RN, Britain's plenipotentiary in China, whom Gough described as being as 'whimsical as a shuttle-cock'. Gough argued for a vigorous forward policy: he wanted to occupy Canton and then attack Amoy. Elliot believed Britain could achieve its desired aims – the cession of Hong Kong, the resumption of trade (including trade in opium) and the payment of an indemnity of six million dollars – through diplomacy.

Gough fumed, cursed Elliot and appealed to Lord Auckland. At last he prevailed, and a joint army – navy operation, 3,200 sailors and marines under Captain Sir Le Fleming Senhouse and 2,200 soliders under Sir Hugh, got under way. It was hoped that Canton could be taken by 24 May, Queen Victoria's twenty-second birthday. This proved impossible, but Gough celebrated the day by landing troops at Tsingpo, on a creek four miles west of Canton, and a royal salute was fired from the warships.

There was no opposition to the landing, and Gough,

without bothering to make a reconnaissance, recklessly advanced on the outlying forts protecting the metropolis, bringing his infantry under cover just out of range, where it waited until the rocket battery and six heavy guns could be brought up. By eight o'clock on the morning of 25 May the artillery was in place; after an hour's bombardment he sent his infantry charging forward, with bayonets bared. By the end of the day the protecting forts had been subdued and the British were at the city's gates, ready for a frontal assault at first light, but dawn revealed a white flag floating over the ramparts. Under a pouring rain, tents were hurriedly erected between the lines for a parlay, but Gough refused to treat with anyone other than the commanding general. As no Chinese general was willing to appear, the tents were struck and a four-pronged attack on the city was prepared. It was never launched, for while Gough laid his plans the Chinese appealed to the plenipotentiary, and Elliot, without consulting either Gough or Senhouse, arranged a deal.

Within the next few days the Chinese paid five million of the six million dollars demanded and gave security for the remaining million. Holding Canton ransom gave the expedition something of a buccaneering aspect, as Gough noted, but the old soldier was delighted to be again on campaign, and he wrote exuberantly to Frances of his 'deep unaltered gratitude to that Being who in my old age enables me to serve my country'.

Soon after Canton's capitulation, Gough received the good news that he had at last been appointed colonel of the 87th Regiment and that he had also been named commander-in-chief of the Madras army, though he was asked to stay put until the war was over. There were at this time significant changes in the high command in China: Sir Le Fleming Senhouse died on board a ship off Hong Kong and was replaced by Rear-Admiral William Parker. To Gough's delight, Captain Elliot was replaced as plenipotentiary by Sir Henry Pottinger. Under the new triumvirate a campaign against the island city of Amoy was undertaken with complete success.

Throughout the China campaign Gough exhibited a clear understanding of the rough, unprincipled nature of his soldiery and a fine regard for the lives and property of noncombatants. In general orders he reminded his troops, 'Britain has gained as much by her mercy and forbearance, as by the gallantry of her troops. An enemy in arms is always a legitimate foe, but the unarmed, or the suppliant for mercy, of whatever country or whatever colour, a true British soldier will always spare'. Before the attack on Amoy he warned, 'Private property must be held inviolable; the laws of God and man prohibit plunder; and the individual appropriation of the goods of others, which in England would be called robbery, deserves no better name in China'. His exhortation was unheeded. When his troops entered Amoy, they rampaged through its streets in a frenzy of destruction. In a letter to Frances he wrote, 'The moment a house is broken open . . . every article is destroyed. The wanton waste of valuable property is heart-rending, and has quite sickened me of war'.

British successes made little impression on the Emperor of China, for he was under the pleasant illusion that his armies were winning the war. The charming skill of the mandarins in ingeniously presenting defeats as victories in their dispatches kept him pacified. Amoy had fallen because his forces had burned and sunk five of the barbarians' warships and a steamer, they explained. 'The south wind blew the smoke in our soldiers' eyes and Amoy was lost'.

From the ransacked Amoy the expedition moved northward on 5 September 1841 to attack Tinghai, on the south shore of Chu Shan Island at the mouth of the Yangtze Kiang River. Gough and Admiral Parker worked well together, and the combined sea and land assault on the city walls was a complete success: 100 iron guns, 36 brass cannons, and 540 gingalls (heavy muskets or light guns mounted on swivels) were captured for a loss of two killed and twenty-seven wounded. The expedition then moved on to capture

Chinhai, on the left bank of the Ningpo River.

Although in every battle the British were outnumbered by their opponents, they were better armed and, more importantly, better disciplined. Invariably the Tartar and Chinese troops were forced to give way before their resolute assaults.

Honours were not slow in coming to the victorious commanders: Parker was promoted vice-admiral; Gough was given the local rank of lieutenant-general and raised to the dignity of Knight Grand Cross of the Order of the Bath.

The war was not popular in England; it seemed unduly protracted. Lord Ellenborough, who had replaced Lord Auckland as governor-general of India, feeling the pressure of opinion at home, rashly promised Queen Victoria that the expeditionary force would be in the Emperor's palace by her next birthday; Gough was then pressed to fulfil his quixotic pledge.

Gough was often accused of being reckless, but never of being dilatory. With Admiral Parker, he planned and carried out an expedition farther north: a 200-mile advance up the Yangtze Kiang River. After several smaller actions near the river's mouth, the expedition, now heavily reinforced by fresh troops from India, occupied Shanghai. From here Gough and Parker launched an attack upon Chinkiang (then called Chinkeangfoo), the fortified town that protected Nanking, forty-five miles upriver. Chinkiang was stormed on 21 July 1842. British casualties totalled only 114, of whom the dead numbered 3 officers and 31 other ranks, who were either killed in battle, died of their wounds or were felled by the intense heat of that summer in China. Chinese casualties were equally light, but in his dispatch Gough described the horrors he and his men discovered on entering the town, mute testimony to the terror that the advance of the British barbarians had struck in the hearts of the Chinese, and particularly their Tartar rulers:

Dead bodies of Tartars in every house we entered, principally women and children thrown into wells or otherwise murdered by their own people. A great number of those who escaped our fire committed suicide after destroying their families; the loss of life has been appalling, and it may be said that the Manchu race in this city is extinct.

And he wrote home, 'I am sick at heart of war and its fearful consequences'.

In spite of an outbreak of cholera, the British army advanced on the great city of Nanking, second city of the Empire, while Parker's ships disrupted the normally busy river commerce. Gough was preparing to assault the town's walls when the Chinese capitulated. The Treaty of Nanking was signed on board a British warship on 29 August 1842. Under its terms the Chinese agreed to the cession of Canton, Amoy, Fu-chou, Ningpo and Shanghai – cities that became known as the treaty ports. The treaty made no mention of the opium trade, although six million Chinese dollars of the indemnity was given in compensation for the destruction of the opium stores of British merchants at Canton.

With the end of the war in China, Gough returned to India. For once he could find no cause for complaint in the recognition given him for his services. He was rewarded with a baronetcy and given the thanks of both houses of Parliament: the Duke of Wellington himself praised both Gough and Parker in the House of Lords.

Not long after his return Gough was appointed commander-in-chief in India, an appointment that, Wellington assured him, was 'one of the highest, if not the highest situation which an officer in Her Majesty's service can hold'. It was indeed a high military command, and none was higher paid, but it was perhaps not as grand as its title suggests. British India was ruled by a Court of Directors of the Honourable East India Company in London, which was, in turn, watched by the government Board of Control, whose president was, in effect, secretary of state for India. In India itself, supreme authority rested with the governor-general, who was appointed by the Court of Directors with the consent of the Crown. British India was divided into three 'presidencies' – Bengal, Bombay and Madras – each with its own governor and each with its own commander-in-chief, but the governor-general was also governor of Bengal, generally considered the most important presidency, and the commander-in-chief of India actually had only the troops of the Bengal army under his direct control.

3

While winning victories in China, the British army had suffered one of its most humiliating disasters in Afghanistan, where an army under an aged and incompetent general was demolished piecemeal while trying to retreat from Kabul. Although another contingent of the British army marched back and wreaked vengeance by destroying a few of the city's public buildings and carrying off some beautiful temple gates, the impression was left in the minds of the rulers of several Indian states that perhaps the British were not, after all, invincible.

Shortly before Gough took over his new duties in Bengal, Sir Charles Napier had, in February 1843, broken the treaties with the amirs of Sind, conquered their armies and annexed their lands. Such high-handed actions not unnaturally aroused distrust of British intentions. This, together with the perceived weakness of the Indian army, led the rulers of some states to reassess their ambitions.

On Bengal's borders two Indian states cast covetous eyes on British territory: the Marathas in Gwalior and the Sikhs in the Punjab. Both had large and powerful armies that had been trained by European officers, and both possessed ruthless, ambitious men in positions of power. Macaulay in his 'Essay on Clive' (1840) wrote, 'The highlands which border on the western seacoast of India poured forth . . . a race which was long the terror of every native power and which, after many desperate and doubtful struggles, yielded only to the fortune and genius of England'. He spoke of the Marathas.

Both Clive and Wellington had fought the fierce Marathas and had torn from them the cities of Delhi and Agra, together with all of their possessions in Hindustan. Yet the Marathas still controlled a large, though scattered, empire, with a number of minor princes ruling the individual states, the largest of which was Gwalior. The Maratha succession process was complex, and at Gwalior it was made even more so by palace intrigues. Such was the case in 1843, and British administrators and soldiers, aware of the disorder, itched to take over and sort things out in proper English fashion. Lord Ellenborough, for his part, was aware that the Marathas were potentially hostile, and, declaring that 'a hostile Government at Gwalior would be inconsistent with the continuance of our permanent influence in India', he placed an 'Army of Exercise and Observation' (12,000 infantry and cavalry, plus artillery) on Gwalior's border.

The army was already deployed when Gough reached Calcutta, and Lord Ellenborough at once directed that he go to Cawnpore and take command. He went with alacrity and almost immediately recommended that a second army be formed on the Sutlej River, the boundary between the British and Sikh territories. He also increased the Army of Observation on Gwalior's border to 20,000 men, split into two forces, one at Agra, the other at Bundelkhand.

In August 1843 Lord Ellenborough invoked the long-neglected Treaty of Burhanpur (1804), by which the British had agreed to aid the Maharaja of Gwalior in maintaining 'a settled government'. In order to create this settled government, two British armies invaded Gwalior territories from different directions and on the same day won battles against separate Maratha forces at Maharajpore and at Punniar. This war, lasting only forty-eight hours, was the shortest in British history. The victorious British suffered a loss of only 6 officers and 100 other ranks killed and 34 officers and 650 other ranks wounded.

Lord Ellenborough *(Photo: BBC Hulton Picture Library)*

On the field at the battle of Maharajpore was the governor-general himself, who came to see the battle with a party
of ladies: Lady Gough and her youngest daughter, the 18-
year-old Miss Frances Gough; Juana Marie, the beautiful,
Spanish-born wife of Colonel Harry Smith; and a Mrs Cur-
tis, wife of the commissary-general. Gough had suggested
that Lord Ellenborough and the ladies – all mounted on

elephants – take up a position at the rear of the reserve battery, a point from which he believed they could safely observe the battle, but the little party and its cavalry escort proved to be conspicuous on the field and soon drew considerable fire. Nevertheless, they gamely stayed until, near the end of the battle, their elephants, terrified by the explosion of a nearby powder magazine, bolted with them. They were rescued by the gallant Major Patrick Grant (who soon after married Miss Frances Gough and eventually became a field marshal).

Toward the end of their exciting day the governor-general and the ladies were preparing to take tea in a tent pitched for the purpose on the battlefield in what had been the Maratha lines when, without warning, a party of British soldiers descended upon them and rushed them away. They looked back to see their tent blown to bits by a mine. When Sir Charles Napier heard of this incident, he wrote in a jocular vein to Sir Harry Smith, 'How came the ladies to be in the fight? I suppose you all wanted to be gloriously rid of your wives.* Well, there is something in that, but I wonder that the women stand such an atrocious attempt. Poor things! I dare say they too had their hopes'.

The Gwalior campaign was largely ignored in Britain, where passions ran high over the Corn Laws debate and the trial of Daniel O'Connell, the Irish politician charged with 'creating discontent and disaffection among the liege subjects of the Queen'. Nevertheless, Gough was given the thanks of the government of India, and handsome medals, made from the metal of captured guns, were issued to all participants. Lord Ellenborough gallantly presented to each of the ladies who shared with him the excitement at Maharajpore a commemorative medal similar in design to that given the troops.

A few critical voices were raised in Indian newspapers.

---

* Lord Ellenborough had already rid himself of his wife, by divorce for adultery, and she, after going through three other husbands, settled down happily as the wife of a bedouin sheikh in Syria.

Some said that Gough, without any idea of where he was going, had merely blundered into the enemy. Others charged him with having dangerously and recklessly divided his forces in the face of a numerically superior foe. He had certainly not been reckless, Gough assured the Duke of Wellington, for he felt confident at the time that *either* wing of his army could have defeated the entire 22,000-man Maratha army. This may have been true, but he later confided to his son that he had been misled by the political officers: 'The Politicals entirely deceived me. I thought I should have a mob without leaders, with the heads at variance. I found a well-disciplined, well-organized army, well-led and truly gallant'.

In the winter of 1843–44 there were two small mutinies in India; both were clashes over pay and allowances. Troops under Sir Charles Napier in Sind had been paid extra money *(batta)* for serving on foreign soil; this was discontinued when Sind was annexed and declared a part of British India. The sepoys, finding it difficult to comprehend such a distinction, mutinied. In Bengal, troops under Gough stationed at Ferozepore on the Sutlej frontier were suborned by the Sikhs. According to Sir Charles Napier, 'The Sikhs collected a great number of beautiful wives and it was by their agency they seduced our sepoys'. In any case, when the Company's troops learned that Sikh soldiers received twelve rupees a month while they received only eight and a half, they did not need pretty women to urge them to mutiny.

Napier and Gough disagreed as to the best way of handling the mutineers. Napier wrote, 'He and I quarrel sadly: not personally but about the mutiny. When it broke out I was going to seize the ringleaders and shoot them . . . being resolved to let no man escape, especially officers who might be in fault'. Gough would not hear of this. He favoured clemency for those who repented and punishment only for those who persisted in mutiny, and, as he was senior to Napier, his view prevailed. Gough and Napier, frequently regarded as rivals, were often in disagreement, though each had a high regard for the other. Napier wrote to Gough after the Gwalior campaign, 'I think between China and Gwalior you have made a good base for a pyramid of glory. You have now only to clap the Punjaub on the top and your edifice of fame will be complete'. Gough set about to do just that.

4

In the 'hump' of north-western India lies the Punjab, an area comprising about 100,000 squre miles and known as the 'land of the five waters', because of the five rivers that drain the mountains of Kashmir and Jammu into the mighty Indus (from roughly north to south, the rivers Jhelum, Chenab, Ravi, Beas and Sutlej). The areas between the rivers are called *doabs*, and on these fertile lands live the Sikhs, a mixture of races whose members belong to a monotheistic Hindu religion founded in the fifteenth century. They appear always to have been martial, holding off their many would-be enemies by the might of a religious–military brotherhood, the Khalsa, 'army of the free'. Under one famous Sikh ruler, Ranjit Singh, French mercenary officers were employed to organize and drill the Khalsa on European models, with particular attention to the Sikh artillery. On Ranjit Singh's death in 1839 the struggles and intrigues that accompanied the choice of a successor threw the political capital, Lahore, and much of the country, into disorder. The British nervously watched from their perch across the Sutlej and began discreetly to build up their army until there were some 30,000 troops stationed in and around Ferozepore, Ludhiana, Ambala and Meerut.

In the summer of 1844 Lord Ellenborough was replaced as governor-general by Sir Henry Hardinge, a veteran of the Peninsula and Waterloo, and a former secretary of state for war. Gough was delighted to have a soldier as his superior, particularly as war with the Sikhs appeared more and more probable. He was receiving an increasing number of reports stressing the 'incapacity and debauchery of the Lahore Government'. The court was seething with assassinations, coups and revolts, and the anti-British Khalsa seemed to be gaining the upper hand; an invasion of British territory was feared. Gough ordered still more troops to be moved to the Sutlej, but Hardinge, fearful of provoking the Sikhs, countermanded his order. The honeymoon period between governor-general and commander-in-chief was over.

On 10 December 1845, while Gough was giving a ball at Ambala, Sikh patrols reconnoitred the east bank of the Sutlej. Finding no force to oppose them, they crossed in force and three days later invested Ferozepore. On learning of this, Gough at once set his army of 12,000 men in motion, pushing them forward with forced marches. Speed, however, with Indian armies was always relative, for they carried long columns of people and animals in their wake. Gough had in his train 40,000 camp followers − cooks and tailors; grooms, grass cutters and personal servants; water carriers and nautch girls. Three hundred camels and sixty elephants were required for the personal supplies, servants and camp equipment of the governor-general alone.

The Sikhs detached 10,000 cavalry and 2,000 infantry to meet Gough, and the two armies collided on 18 December near Mudki, a mud village twenty miles from Ferozepore. 'The country', said Gough in his after-action report, 'is dead flat, covered at short intervals with a low, but in some places thick, jhow jungle, and dotted with sandy hillocks'.

Gough's plan of attack was to silence the enemy's guns, outflank them with his cavalry and then rout them with a bayonet charge. Silencing the Sikh artillery was not an easy task, for their guns were of a heavier metal and their artillery was the Sikhs' proudest arm. The Sikh cavalry was also stronger than Gough's and threatened to outflank him. Nevertheless, the 3rd Light Dragoons made a most gallant charge and the infantry dashed forward with great *élan*. Wearing his white fighting coat and visible to all, Gough was in the forefront of the action. In his dispatch he wrote, 'Their whole force was driven from position to position, with great slaughter, and the loss of seventeen pieces of artillery, some of them of heavy calibre; our infantry using that never-failing weapon, the bayonet'. The victory was complete at a cost of 215 of all ranks killed, including two generals, and 657 wounded. Among the latter was Major Patrick Grant, now Gough's son-in-law.

Again Gough's generalship was criticized. The battle had extended into the night, and in the darkness some of the British and Indian regiments had fired into each other by mistake. Brigade commanders and their staffs were unknown to the troops and the troops to them, creating, as the governor-general pointed out in a private letter to Lord Ripon, president of the Board of Control, 'a feeling that the army was not well in hand'. There were also complaints about the long casualty list – Gough was to establish a reputation for managing bloody battles.

The 80th Foot was on the march when it heard that the war had begun, and one Captain John Cumming described in a letter to his father the plangent response of the accompanying women and children: 'On the words "The Sikhs have crossed the Sutlej!" a shout of defiance ran along the regiment, but as it died away a wail of lamentation was heard along the whole line of carts occupied by the women and children'.

On the day after the battle of Mudki, Sir Henry Hardinge did an extraordinary thing: although he was himself a lieutenant-general, and as governor-general was Gough's political superior, he offered to serve under him as his second-in-command. Gough foolishly accepted this quixotic offer. It was certainly a peculiar thing for Hardinge to do. He was a brave officer whose left hand had been shot away by grape-shot at Ligny two days before Waterloo; at Albuera he had shown daring and initiative when, as a mere assistant adjutant-general, he had on his own responsibility ordered the movement that won the day. Yet now he seemed unsure

The Sikhs' fortified camp at Ferozeshah *(Photo: BBC Hulton Picture Library)*

of himself. It was the conviction of Sir Charles Napier that Hardinge 'felt unequal to the details of command or he would have taken command; he could not wield the weapon, and his error in volunteering to be second proves he felt rightly.'Had he been master of his game he would have taken supreme command, and thrown the details on Gough'. Less than forty-eight hours after Gough accepted Hardinge's offer, the arrangement came unravelled.

In the early morning of 21 December, Gough's little army found the Sikhs entrenched near the town of Ferozeshah. Gough allowed his men a hasty breakfast at about ten-thirty and then prepared to attack. He was in fine fettle, and rode up to Hardinge, shouting out, 'I promise you a splendid victory!' Hardinge was not so sure.

Until the battle of Mudki, Hardinge had seen no action since the Napoleonic wars, but he felt that the present situation called for caution. At Mudki he had been impressed by the discipline and fighting abilities of the Sikhs, now well entrenched before him. General Sir John Littler with about 5,000 men – two brigades of infantry, one of cavalry, and twenty-four guns – was coming up by forced march from Ferozepore. Hardinge urged Gough to wait until Littler arrived, but Gough, citing the advantages of fighting in daylight and pointing out that this was the shortest day of the year, insisted upon an immediate attack. Although Hardinge had placed himself as Gough's subordinate, he could not, in fact, escape his responsibilities as governor-general of India. Believing that it was necessary for him to prevent his high-spirited commander-in-chief from a rash act that might spell the ruin of Britain's empire in India, he reverted to being governor-general and ordered Gough to obey him.

It was certainly an extraordinary situation. With the British army poised to attack and the Sikhs ready to meet them, all was suspended while these two old soldiers stood in a grove of trees and wrangled. In the end, Gough had to give way. It marked the first time in British history that a general in the field in the face of the enemy was overruled by his political superior. At about one-thirty, when Littler's force, tired and hungry after being on the march for eighteen hours, finally arrived on the field, Hardinge turned to Gough and said, 'Now the army is at your disposal'. However, it was nearly four o'clock in the afternoon before Gough had all of his troops in place and was again ready to attack. The particoloured battle line of British and Indian soldiers stretched nearly a thousand yards in a slight curve facing the Sikh entrenchments. Gough put himself in charge of the right wing, and Hardinge took the left wing; Sir Harry Smith commanded the reserve.

Weapons had changed little and tactics hardly at all since the Napoleonic wars. The battle began with an artillery duel in which the Sikhs, with nearly a hundred guns, most of heavier metal than Gough's sixty-five guns, hammered the British into the ground. A third of the British guns were disabled in their carriages, and dozens of artillery tumbrels were blown to bits. Brigadier George Brooke, commanding the artillery, reported to Gough, 'Excellency, I must either advance or be blown out of the field'. Gough's decision was made for him by a premature and unsupported advance by Littler's division on the far left of the line. (It was a costly mistake: seven officers and ninety-seven other ranks fell before a shower of grape-shot within minutes; three regiments of native infantry bolted.) Gough at once ordered a general advance of his entire line. The Sikhs, firing their guns with rapid precision, were bayoneted at their posts; the Sikh infantry valiantly held their ground until they were ridden down by the British cavalry. Conspicuous throughout the battle was Gough in his white fighting coat.

As at Mudki, the battle lasted into the night: the moon did not rise over the Sutlej until midnight, and the darkness compounded the confusion. Not all the Sikhs had been driven from their entrenchments, and there was much firing throughout the night. Lieutenant Robert Bridges Bellers of the 50th Foot wrote in his diary:

> No one can imagine the dreadful uncertainty. A burning camp on one side of the village, mines and ammunition wagons exploding in every direction, the loud orders to extinguish the fires as the Sepoys lighted them, the volleys given should the Sikhs venture too near, the booming of the monster guns, the incessant firing of the smaller ones, the continued whistling noise of the shell, grape and round shot, the bugles sounding, the drums beating, and the yelling of the enemy, together with the intense thirst, fatigue and cold, and not knowing whether the rest of the army were the conquerors or conquered – all contributed to make this night awful in the extreme.

Some of Gough's officers thought the battle lost and urged him to retreat. Hardinge, trying to assess the results, stood uncertainly under a torch amid the burning wagons, the moaning wounded and the detritus of battle. Turning to

Major Henry Havelock, he said, 'Another such action will shake the Empire'.

All awaited first light, when friend could be distinguished from foe and the tactical situation could be assessed. Gough was calm and unperturbed, at least outwardly; he later claimed, 'I saw nothing to make me despond. . . . I had not a doubt in my mind as to our success'. With the dawn, British guns opened fire on the Sikhs who had remained in their positions or had reoccupied them, and the bombardment was followed by a general onslaught of the infantry. The enemy fled in confusion, leaving twenty-three guns on the field. It was a victory won at frightful cost. The 18th Foot had lost eighteen of its twenty-three officers, leaving the regiment largely commanded by its sergeants. The 9th Foot had lost a third of its strength in killed and wounded. Other regiments, British and Indian, also suffered severely. Nevertheless, it was a victory, if a tenuous one, and Gough and Hardinge were cheered by their weary soldiers as they rode along the lines.

There was to be little rest. Late in the afternoon a second Sikh army suddenly appeared on the scene, coming up from Ferozepore with heavy columns of cavalry, infantry and artillery. It was only when he received word of the approach of this fresh Sikh army that Gough felt any doubt about his success. And this doubt he later regretted: 'I deeply deplore my want of confidence in Him who never failed me nor forsook me'. Gough never wavered in his conviction that God took a personal interest in his military career.

The Sikhs opened fire with a furious cannonade, showering Gough's soldiers with both grape-shot and round shot. The British, soon out of ammunition, could not respond for long. Under the Sikh shelling the Indian troops were shaken and the British troops reeled, but the steadfast figure of Gough in his white fighting coat, shouting out encouragement, unperturbed by the fire he drew on himself, had a steadying effect. With energy and great gallantry the British infantry and cavalry threw themselves upon the Sikhs, who wavered and then broke.

The British gained the field in what Sir Harry Smith described as 'the most glorious battle ever fought in the East, adding lustre to H.M. and the Honbl. Company's arms and to the already acquired glory of the commander-in-chief'. Still, Gough's exhausted army lacked the strength to pursue. The troops had been marching and fighting, alternately sweating and freezing, for more than forty hours. They were hungry, thirsty and emotionally drained by the excitements and anxieties they had endured.

It was indeed a victory, but Major Hope Grant of the 9th Lancers said that 'never perhaps in the annals of Indian warfare has a British army on so large a scale been nearer to defeat'. The cost was high – 694 killed, of whom 499 were British (37 officers and 462 other ranks); of the 1,721 wounded, 78 were British officers and 1,051 were British other ranks. In all, Gough lost one man in eight. The Sikhs lost an estimated 5,000 men and 100 guns. The British public was shocked by the casualty figures, and there was an outcry in the press.

Hardinge was disillusioned with his commander-in-chief, and on 30 December 1845 he wrote a strongly worded letter to Sir Robert Peel, the prime minister, demanding that Gough be recalled. He paid tribute to Gough's personal qualities, calling him 'a brave and fearless officer, an honourable and amiable man' and a 'fine-tempered gentleman', but he insisted that he had 'no capacity for order or administration' and that consequently the state of the army was 'loose, disorderly and unsatisfactory'. Gough, he said, was 'not the officer who ought to be entrusted with the conduct of the war in the Punjab'. He painted a frightening picture of the state of affairs: 'We have been in great peril, and are likely hereafter to be in greater peril if these very extensive operations are to be conducted by the commander-in-chief', for 'at this extremity of the Empire a defeat is almost the loss of India'.

Although the Sikhs had been driven from the field, they

refused to consider themselves defeated and appeared to be undiscouraged. They once again crossed the Sutlej, and on 29 January 1846 Sir Harry Smith, with 12,000 men and 30 guns, defeated a Sikh force of about equal strength at Aliwal. Smith characterized the action as 'one of the most glorious battles ever fought in India. . . . Never was victory more complete, and never was one [*sic*] fought under more happy circumstances, literally with the pomp of a field day; and right well did all behave'. Although the victory might not have been as great as Smith imagined, still, Sir John Fortescue, the great historian of the British army, called it 'a battle without a mistake' and Sir Harry's victory did relieve fears that the Sikhs would attack Ludhiana.

While Sir Harry Smith was winning the battle of Aliwal, Gough and Hardinge were debating how best to attack the entrenched camp of the Sikhs at Sobraon, a village nestled in a curve of the Sutlej. Major Henry Havelock proposed that they turn the right flank of the enemy by bridging the Sutlej near Ferozepore, but this seemed too complicated and Gough rejected it. Sophisticated tactics never appealed to him. Instead, he determined on a direct frontal attack, an action more suited to his temperament. Hardinge disliked the plan, but finally consented as long as Gough did not 'anticipate a heavy loss'. As the ever-optimistic Gough *never* anticipated heavy losses, he plunged ahead.

On 7 February a siege train arrived, and the British began a heavy bombardment of the Sikh defences. On the evening of the ninth, battle orders were issued and the troops were moved into attack positions overnight. Gough's plan was straightforward: he simply put his infantry in a line facing the enemy and gave them orders to fix bayonets. Sir Robert Dick commanded on the left and Sir Harry Smith on the right. A thick fog at dawn delayed the start of the battle but as it began to clear, the British artillery opened with a cannonade of all its guns. Two hours later a staff officer brought Gough the alarming news that the guns were running out of ammunition. To his astonishment, Gough,

The battle of Sobraon *(Photo: BBC Hulton Picture Library)*

instead of showing signs of alarm, exclaimed, 'Thank God!
Then I'll be at them with the bayonet!'

Minutes later an aide rode up to Gough with a cautious
message from Hardinge: if he was not completely confident
of success, he was to withdraw. But Gough was full of confidence. A short time later, the aide returned with the same
message, and Gough sent him back with the same reply.
The third time the hapless aide galloped up, Gough did not
wait to hear his message but burst out, 'What! Withdraw
the troops after the action has commenced and when I feel
confident of success? Indeed I will not!' Turning to his
nephew and aide-de-camp, Colonel J.B. Gough, he snapped,
'Tell Sir Robert Dick to move on in the name of God!'

It was nine o'clock when Dick received the order, and he
immediately moved on the Sikh positions, carrying them
with the point of the bayonet. In Sir Harry Smith's colourful language, it was 'a stand-up gentlemanlike battle, a
mixing of all arms and laying on, carrying everything before

us by weight of attack and combination, all hands at work from one end of the field to the other'. It was a hard fight: out of a force of about 16,000, casualties were 2,283 – nearly one in seven – of whom 320 were killed, including 13 British officers. Sir Robert Dick, another veteran of the war in the Peninsula and of Waterloo, was mortally wounded by grape-shot while leading his men. Colonel J.B. Gough was also wounded, but survived. Sikh dead were said to be 3,125, and at least three or four times that number must have been wounded.

After the victory at Sobraon, Gough crossed the Sutlej with most of his army. He had penetrated thirty-five miles into Sikh territory when the Lahore government sued for peace. Many Englishmen favoured complete annexation of the Punjab, but the Court of Directors of the Honourable East India Company ordered Hardinge to treat with the Sikhs. Charles Napier was appalled and correctly predicted, 'The result will be another war!' Nevertheless, Hardinge did as he was told and terms were arranged: the Sikhs ceded to the East India Company the Jullundur Doab (the land between the Beas and Sutlej rivers); gave up twenty-five guns; agreed to restrict the size of their army to twenty-five battlions of infantry and 12,000 cavalry; and promised to pay an indemnity of one and a half million pounds.

Gough's army then moved to Lahore and camped outside its walls. On 8 March 1846 a treaty was signed by the Sikh leaders, and at a durbar the next day it was ratified with great ceremony by Lord Hardinge. One incident stuck in the memory of all who attended: the Sikhs passed around a small tin box wrapped in a shabby cloth; it held the Koh-i-noor diamond, which then weighed its full 800 carats.

The end of the war did not stop the stream of criticism of Gough and his methods. Of Sobraon, Sir Harry Smith thought Gough chose the wrong point in the Sikh line to attack; others said he should have made better use of his cavalry; some blamed him for the shortage of artillery shells;

and he was generally damned for his 'Tipperary tactics'. Civilians in Britain thought Gough's losses in the campaign were appalling. Certainly they were higher than usual for battles in India, but few at home could realize that the Sikhs were splendid soldiers. In spite of the criticism, and although Hardinge had summoned Sir Charles Napier from Sind with the intention of having him replace Gough if London approved, Gough was not relieved of his command. Before the battles of Aliwal and Sobraon were fought, Wellington had written to Gough suggesting that he yield the command to the governor-general and subordinate himself to Hardinge. Gough had refused. He never learned of Hardinge's plan or of the demand for his recall. The war was over before Napier arrived, and it has always been difficult to sack successful generals. If Gough lost more men than he ought to have, he had, after all, won the war – and within sixty days of its beginning.

Gough found it 'rather hard' that his services in China were 'not accounted of any moment', because his victories there were won with few casualties, and now he was considered 'a reckless savage, devoid of stratagem and military knowledge', because his losses in the Punjab were severe. He tried to ignore the storm of criticism and wrote to his son, 'Let the world carp, let them call me savage, incompetent, and what they please; I am ready to bear all their taunts, rather than throw a shade over the bright laurels the Indian Army have won. Posterity will do me justice'.

Some of the criticism seems peculiar today. Many in the higher echelons of the British government thought it shocking that he had given commissions to all five of the sergeant-majors of the Queen's regiments serving under him. In his defence, Gough pointed out that battlefield commissions supplied troops with 'every stimulus to induce in future acts of daring' and that, in any case, the severe losses among his junior officers had made them necessary. That he had encroached upon the authority of the commander-in-chief of the British army, the Duke of Wellington himself, and even upon the prerogative of the Queen, had not deterred him.

His critics did not deter him, either, from complaining to Wellington that he had found the Duke's encomium delivered in the House of Lords inadequate. Wellington, practised in dealing with prickly generals, answered with one of his graceful and lofty letters in which there was praise enough for any ego:

> Great operations have been planned and undertaken and successfully carried into execution under your command, glorious Battles have been fought and victories gained, and the War has been brought to a termination by the destruction of the Army of the Enemy and the capture of all its cannon, by that under your command; and the peace has been dictated to the Enemy at the Gate of his Capital, upon terms equally honourable to the Army and to the Nation.

In truth, Gough had no reason to complain of official neglect: he and his army were given the thanks of Parliament, and he was raised to the peerage of the United Kingdom as Baron Gough of Chinkiangfoo in China and of Maharajpore and the Sutlej in the East Indies. Furthermore, on the recommendation of Sir Robert Peel the House of Commons granted him a pension of £2,000. This was in addition to the £2,000 pension conferred upon him by the Honourable East India Company.

5

Hardinge, believing that 'it would not be necessary to fire a gun in India for seven years to come', reduced the size of the Indian army by 50,000 men as an economy measure: the number of sepoys in each battalion of native infantry was reduced from 1,000 to 800 and the number of sowars in each regiment of cavalry from 500 to 420. This done, he

Sir Henry Hardinge on the cover of the march composed to celebrate the victory at Sobraon *(Photo: National Army Museum)*

retired from India. He was replaced by the 38-year-old Earl
of Dalhousie, who arrived at Calcutta on 12 January 1848.
Less than four months later his government was again on
the verge of war in the Punjab.

On 20 April two young Englishmen, an officer and a civil servant, were attacked and killed by Sikh soldiers at Multan, and their mutilated bodies were exposed on the town walls. Although a small force mustered by the British Resident at Lahore marched on the town, Gough did not reinforce it. Unsure whether the attack was the forerunner of a full-scale rebellion or an isolated incident, he was unwilling to chance provoking another war in the Punjab. Often criticized for his impetuosity, he was now attacked for failing to act decisively. In fact, Hardinge's economy measures had made it nearly impossible to assemble an army of any great size and move it to the frontier. As Gough explained to Dalhousie, 'There is no carriage whatever for these troops, the whole having been discharged; and to move without camp equipage, doolies, and ample Commissariat arrangements, through the hottest locality in India, at the worst season of the year would be certain annihilation'. Furthermore, it was the furlough season for the Indian army, and, with the reductions in force that had already been made regiments were so weakened that it was difficult or impossible for them to take the field.

Turmoil in this corner of India increased with an outbreak of violence in the Hazara District. Lieutenant John Nicholson, later to win fame as the 'Lion of the Punjab' and to die of wounds received before Delhi during the Mutiny, was sent to quell the uproar. He requested a brigade of British troops, but Gough refused, for he thought such a movement 'would be more likely to lead to a concentration of the disaffected in that wild country, than to the extinction of a rebellion'.

Unrest continued to spread throughout the Punjab. John Lawrence, one of the famous brothers who were to add lustre to the Indian civil Service, suppressed an insurrection in the Jullundur Doab, but there was trouble in the Peshawar District, and at Lahore an uneasy British Resident imprisoned a clutch of Sikh leaders whom he considered treacherous.

Gough did his best to prepare for war, but was hampered by Dalhousie, who resisted in the interests of economy. From the beginning of the difficulties in the Punjab, Gough had begged for an increase in the military establishment that would bring infantry battlions back up to 1,000 sepoys and cavalry regiments up to 500 sowars, but it was not until 13 September that the governor-general reluctantly agreed to an increase and gave permission for Gough to assemble an army on the frontier. Having finally decided to fight, Dalhousie grandly announced, 'I have drawn the sword and thrown away the scabbard'. However, the army had not yet completely overcome its logistical deficiencies. In a letter of 13 October 1848 to Arbuthnot, Gough wrote, 'Lord Dalhousie is a young man, his blood is very hot, and he speaks of walking over everything. But to walk we must eat'.

Eventually an army was assembled and moved to Lahore, arriving on 13 November. Three days later Gough took it across the Ravi River, but the political situation was murky and he did not know yet whether the war was to be waged against the Sikh durbar or in support of it; that is, whether the Khalsa was supported by the Sikh government or was at odds with it. 'I do not know', he wrote, 'whether we are at peace or war, or who it is we are fighting for'. A few days later he learned he was to fight the Khalsa, backed by the Sikh durbar.

When Gough's force joined with that of Sir Colin Campbell (later to win fame in the Crimea and the Indian Mutiny), they totalled one cavalry division, two infantry divisions and eleven batteries of artillery, two of them heavies. This army found the Sikhs posted on the right bank of the Chenab opposite the town of Ramnagar. The British infantry took up position on the opposite bank while the cavalry unwisely charged into a sandy riverbed lined with Sikh riflemen and commanded by Sikh guns; horsed guns were pushed too far forward and one was lost. The British lost 26 killed and 59 wounded in this unsatisfactory skirmish.

The Sikhs, having bloodied the British nose, slipped away. Gough prepared to pursue, but Dalhousie forbade it. There was some doubt as to Gough's ability to march very far in any case, for the commissariat arrangements had fallen into disarray. Gough openly blamed Dalhousie for this, and Dalhousie countered by abusing Gough for criticizing him. Once again, Gough was at odds with his political superior.

On 9 January 1849 Gough wrote in his diary, 'Heard from G-G that he would be glad if I gained a victory'. This was all the authority he needed to act, and he advanced at once with about 12,000 men and sixty guns to engage an estimated 40,000 Sikhs with sixty-two guns. It was midday when Gough, standing on the roof of a house in the village of Chilianwala, surveyed the Sikh position, or what he could see of it, for most of the enemy was concealed in thick jungle. In spite of the lateness of the hour, he decided upon an immediate attack. He did not attempt to turn a flank. An hour's bombardment followed by an infantry charge with the bayonet into the centre of the line was Gough's style. In spite of the simplicity of the plan, the battle became confused and there were uncoordinated attacks by two brigades in the division commanded by Sir Colin Campbell.

One of Campbell's brigades consisted of the 24th Foot (later the South Wales Borderers) and the 25th and 45th Bengal Native Infantry. The 24th Foot, led by Lieutenant-Colonel John Pennycuik, advanced between the two Indian regiments. It soon outstripped them and, unsupported, rushed forward in a wild, impetuous charge straight into the muzzles of twenty Sikh guns. Pennycuik fell dead near one of them. His son, fresh from Sandhurst, ran to him and was shot dead over his father's body. The men charged without firing, for they had been ordered to use only their bayonets. Lieutenant Andrew Macpherson, one of the survivors, wrote:

> One charge of grape-shot took away an entire section and for a moment I was alone and unhurt. On we went, the goal is almost

won, the ground clears, the pace quickens . . . the bayonets come
down to the charge. My men's pieces were loaded but not a
shot was fired; with a wild, choking hurrah we storm the guns
and the battery is won.

The 24th Foot, at nearly full strength, had carried into
battle 31 officers and 1,065 other ranks. Only 9 officers came
through unscathed; 13 were killed. Lieutenant Lloyd Wil-
liams received twenty-three sword and lance wounds – his
skull was fractured and his left hand was severed – but he
survived to live for another forty years. Total casualties were
515 men, half of the regiment.

Of the officers and men of the 24th Foot, Sir Charles Napier
said, 'Their conduct has never been surpassed by British
soldiers on a field of battle'. It was the infantry equivalent
of the charge of the Light Brigade at Balaclava, but there
was no Tennyson to celebrate their courage in poetry. Even
Gough, devotee of the bayonet though he was, called this
dreadful charge 'an act of madness'.

The cavalry, too, had its trials that day. Its commander
was an old man, infirm and half blind, who gave conflicting orders and appeared to have difficulty getting his men
to face the right direction. His soldiers had the distinct
impression that he did not know what he was doing. Gough
considered him 'quite unfit for the responsible position to
which his seniority entitled him', but such was the rigidity
of the army's hierarchical system that it was almost
unthinkable to relieve him. When some Sikh cavalry
appeared on the field, he meant to order, or should have
ordered, 'Threes right!' Instead it came out as 'Threes about!'
and the troopers wheeled and bolted. They were halted by
a determined chaplain, and rallied on his assurance that
'the Almighty God would never will it that a Christian army
should be cut up by a pagan host!' When Gough heard of
the incident, he proposed that the chaplain be made a brevet
bishop.

The battle lasted until eight o'clock that night, and it was very much a soldiers' battle. As the fox-hunting colonel of the 61st Foot put it, 'Fine fellows. Fine fellows. Couldn't stop 'em. Saw game ahead and I couldn't hold 'em in'. Under cover of night the Sikhs retreated in good order, taking with them their guns – as well as four British guns and three regimental colours. The hungry and thirsty British also had to abandon the field; they had exhausted their supplies of water.

It had been a bloody affair. British casualties were 2,357 killed and wounded, about one in five engaged. Havelock described the battle as 'one of the most sanguinary ever fought by the British in India and the nearest approximation to a defeat of any of the conflicts of that power in the East'. It was a drawn battle, but Gough called it a victory in his dispatch – and he forever maintained that it was.

The next day, when he went to see the wounded, they cheered him. A sergeant who was present said, 'Ay, and that from many a poor fellow who had scarcely a head left upon his shoulders to shout with'. Whatever the opinion of his superiors, old Gough, with his shock of white hair and his famous white fighting coat, ever present in the smoke of battle, was popular with his soldiers, and they seemed always ready to fight and die for him.

When news of Gough's 'victory' reached England, people were appalled by the butcher's bill: more than a thousand of the fallen were British. Such losses in an Asiatic war were unheard of and unexpected. There was dismay when it was learned that the British had actually lost guns and colours. The press were unanimously critical. In the words of one of Gough's biographers,* 'He was accused of having made no preparations, of having wasted too much time in preparations, of being hasty, of being tardy, of ignorance of the elementary principles of military science, of excitement amounting to mania, of folly and of inhumanity'.

---

* Robert S. Rait, *The Life and Campaigns of Hugh, 1st Viscount Gough*, vol. 2, p. 240.

William Napier, the historian, said that at this time 'Lord Gough . . . would have been stoned to death in the streets if he had appeared'.

The government agreed with the critics, and within forty-eight hours a decision was made to relieve Gough of his command. Queen Victoria wrote to King Leopold, 'The news from India are very distressing, and make one very anxious, but Sir Charles Napier is instantly to be sent out to supersede Gough, and he is so well versed in Indian tactics that we may look with safety to the future *after* his arrival'.

Had communications been swifter, Gough's career would have ended in disgrace with the humiliation of being superseded in the middle of a campaign, but it took months for dispatches to reach London and for Sir Charles Napier, then in England, to reach India. Meanwhile, Gough remained as commander-in-chief and he continued to fight.

On 22 January 1849 Multan finally fell to the besieging British forces, freeing the army there to join Gough. On 21 February, Gough, with 24,000 men, found the main Sikh army, estimated to be 60,000 strong, at Gujrat, near the Chenab River, sixty-eight miles north of Lahore. It was here that he fought his 'last and best battle', and his after-action report to Dalhousie rang out like Celtic heroic poetry as he described

a result, my lord, glorious indeed for the ever-victorious army of India; their positions carried, their guns, ammunition, the ranks of the enemy broken, camp equipage and baggage captured, their flying masses driven before the victorious pursuers from mid-day to dusk, receiving most severe punishment in their flight.

It was indeed a great battle on which to end a long military career. Fifty-three Sikh guns were captured, besides the recapture of the two guns lost at Chilianwala, and British losses were comparatively light: 96 killed and 700 wounded. On 10 March the remains of the Khalsa surrendered at Rawalpindi, and the Punjab was soon annexed to British India.

6

The battle of Gujrat saved Gough's reputation, and he knew it. To Sir John Macdonald, adjutant-general at the Horse Guards, he wrote, 'Thanks to a gracious God for not only covering my head in the day of battle, but for granting me . . . a victory, not only over my Enemies, but over my Country!' *Punch* commented, 'When Lord Gough met with reverse, *Punch* set him down for an incompetent octogenarian; now that he has been fortunate, *Punch* believes him to be a gallant veteran; for *Mr Punch*, like many other people, of course looks merely to results; and takes as his only criterion of merit, success'.

Charles Napier, carrying orders to assume command of the Bengal army 'without loss of time', was at sea when the battle of Gujrat was fought. By the time he arrived in India on 6 May 1849, Gough had humbled the Sikh Khalsa and had won the war. Napier, who had not looked forward to superseding Gough, wrote in a letter home:

> I like that noble old fellow Gough more than ever. I told him that my wish was that he would order me home; it would be a kindness, and so saying I told him the truth. . . . Again, let me express my delight with old Gough; he is so good, so honest, so noble-minded.

Arriving with Napier was the mail carrying periodicals filled with criticism written after Chilianwala and before Gujrat. Gough was hurt and for a time was bitter until later posts brought the paeans of praise for his final victory. And there were rewards, not only the compensation for his share of the Sikh booty, but another pension from a grateful government: £2,000 a year for his life and for the life of his next two heirs. He was also publicly thanked by both houses of

Parliament and honoured with a viscountcy. Queen Victoria, too, was pleased: Dalhousie had sent her the Koh-i-noor diamond taken from the Sikhs.

Charles Napier said of Gujrat that it made Gough 'the first of generals and a viscount! And it made Lord Dalhousie, who had nothing to do with the matter, a marquis! Did ever the world see the like? Not since the senate thanked Varro after Cannae'. Napier admired Gough's character but thought him a bad general: 'Everyone who knows Lord Gough must love the brave old warrior, who is all honour and nobleness of heart, and . . . were his military genius as great as his heart, the duke [Wellington] would be nothing in comparison'.

On 31 March, Gough issued his farewell Order to the Army. He praised 'the ardour, the vigilance, the endurance, the closing and triumphant bravery and discipline' of the troops. Always eager for honours himself, Gough was also careful to see that those who served him were honoured as well. When it was decided that soldiers should not be awarded a clasp to their war medal for the dubious victory at Chilianwala, he rose up in wrath, firing off letters to those responsible and demanding justice for his men. Gough as well had a personal reason for demanding the clasp: battle clasps were awarded only for victories; to deny the clasp for Chilianwala was to deny that Gough had won a victory there. The clasp was awarded.

After turning over his command to Napier, Gough rejoined Frances at Simla, where she was recovering from a fall. On 10 November, a week after celebrating his seventieth birthday and only a few weeks after hearing of the birth of a grandson, the couple left Simla, and on 8 January 1850 left India for ever.

They reached Southampton on 24 February and received a warm welcome. There was a general feeling that Lord Gough had been wronged and a desire to atone for the criticism he had suffered. In London, distinguished politicians called on him, Prince Albert received him at Buckingham

Palace and he dined with the Queen. The City of London and the Goldsmiths' Company enrolled him among their freemen, Oxford conferred on him an honorary degree and the Court of Directors of the Honourable East India Company gave a dinner in his honour at which Sir Robert Peel sang his praises. Then Gough and Frances left for Dublin and more honours and to Scotland for still more, including the Freedom of the City of Edinburgh.

Gough lived on for another nineteen years; he enjoyed an excellent constitution and outlived most of his distinguished contemporaries and many younger men, including Dalhousie. He lost much of his fortune in a bank failure, but enough remained for him to buy a handsome house in Dublin where he lived comfortably on his pensions. In May 1856 Lord Panmure, then secretary of state for war, invited him to represent the Queen in the Crimea, conferring knighthoods and decorations on the allied officers who had just successfully concluded the war with Russia. Gough accepted with alacrity this final service for the Queen he had served so long.

It is a curious custom of the British to give some of their most glittering honours to aged men who no longer serve the Crown. Thus, in retirement Gough became a full general and colonel-in-chief of the 60th Rifles in 1854, and the following year he was appointed colonel of the Royal Horse Guards and Gold-Stick-in-Waiting to the Queen. In 1857 he was made a Knight of St Patrick and a member of the Privy Council. In 1861 he was made a Knight Grand Commander of the Order of the Star of India, and in November 1862, at the age of eighty-three, he became a field marshal.

Lady Gough, in poor health during much of her life, died suddenly on 15 March 1863. Viscount Gough lived on for another seven years, doted on by affectionate children, in-laws and grandchildren. Surrounded by loving relations, he died peacefully on 2 March 1869, in his ninetieth year.

Gough's worst critics never accused him of lack of courage or lack of loyalty to the Crown. He was not the greatest strategist and certainly he was not a brilliant tactician, but he inspired men to face death and he communicated his own joy of battle to his soldiers. This counted for much when men were ordered into the muzzles of cannons with only cold steel in their hands. Gough's infantry was armed with the flintlock smooth-bore musket known as Brown Bess, not the most accurate or reliable of weapons; and his muzzle-loading cannon had a maximum range of only 1,300 yards when firing round shot and only 350 yards firing case-shot. These shortcomings do not excuse Gough's disdain for firepower and his over-reliance on the efficacy of the bayonet, which undoubtedly cost lives. It cannot be said that he was careless of the lives of his men, at least not deliberately, but his was a reckless nature, and he found battle exhilarating.

Few men of his time questioned that war, however horrible, was also glorious. There was glory to be won on the battlefield, and certainly Gough sought 'the bubble reputation even at the cannon's mouth' – and indeed he found it there. His stubborn refusal ever to admit defeat reinforced his obstinate courage, which, aided by luck, won battles and wars.

Although he often quarrelled with his superiors, he was ever courteous and gentlemanly, and many who found him exasperating still liked him. He had a complete and almost childlike confidence in an omniscient and omnipotent Deity and possessed a simple faith in the integrity of the Crown. This simplicity of outlook and character was appealing, even to those who were appalled by his military tactics.

Charles Napier
(1782–1855)

'Peccavi'

1

It was a curious family, the Napiers, and Sir Charles Napier, the Conqueror of Sind, was a worthy representative of the clan. Throughout the nineteenth century the British armed forces were filled to confusion with Napiers, many of whom distinguished themselves. They were a prolific family, and there were so many with the same first name and so many who married cousins (not to mention the numerous illegitimate offspring they produced) that quite elaborate genealogical tables are needed to sort them out. General Charles Napier (not to be confused with his cousin and contemporary Admiral Charles Napier, known as Black Charles) was the son of Colonel the Honourable George Napier, who in turn was the sixth of the ten sons of the 6th Lord Napier.

George Napier stood six feet two inches tall and was

reputed to be the strongest and most handsome man in the army. In the course of his military career he carried arms three times against revolutionaries – American, French and Irish – and it was during the American War of Independence that tragedy altered the course of his life.

Earlier in his career he had unwisely wed in Corsica a soldier's daughter 'as poor as himself' and had had by her two sons and two daughters in four years. His family sailed with him to America, and in New York his wife, both sons and a daughter died of yellow fever. Napier himself caught the disease and, at death's door, was put aboard a ship bound for England. As no one expected him to survive, General Sir Henry Clinton kindly sold Napier's commission so that his infant daughter, Louisa, would not be left penniless.*

To everyone's astonishment, Napier recovered on board ship, and he was dismayed to find when he landed in England that he no longer had a commission or a career. It was not until 1782 that he managed to rejoin the army, and then only as an ensign. On 27 August 1781, at the age of twenty-nine and with an income of only £300 a year, he married the 36-year-old Lady Sarah Bunbury (née Lennox), fourth daughter of the 2nd Duke of Richmond. By 1794 they had produced eight children, five boys and three girls, the eldest of whom was Charles James Napier, born on 10 August 1782 at Whitehall in London.

From the maternal side of Charles's family came a series of dashing eccentrics. The 1st Duke of Richmond was the illegitimate son of Charles II by Louise de Kéroualle. The 2nd Duke married off his son to pay a gambling debt. The details of the wager are unknown, but one day the son, Lord March, was brought from college, and Lady Sarah Cadogan, daughter of Marlborough's favourite general, was brought from the nursery for the marriage rite. Young Lord

---

* Officers who died in active service lost the value of their commissions, which were then given without purchase to some worthy officer in the same regiment. Thus, on news of war poor young officers would recklessly drink toasts to a bloody and pestilent campaign.

March took one look at his bride and exclaimed, 'Surely you are not going to marry me to that dowdy!' But married he was, and, as soon as the deed was done, his tutor whisked him off for a lengthy tour of the Continent.

Three years later, Lord March returned to London and spent his first night there at the opera, where he was much taken by an exquisite young woman. On inquiring her name, he was astounded to learn that all London was agog over the beautiful Lady March, the toast of the town. He introduced himself to his wife, and they fell deeply in love, living happily ever after. Sarah died of a broken heart within a year of her husband's death. Such is the tale, firmly believed by Napiers even today. It is a charming story, and – who knows, – perhaps much of it is true.

What is certain is that of this union came a remarkable daughter, Lady Sarah Lennox. As a young girl she was, said Horace Walpole, 'more beautiful than you can conceive . . . [and] she shone, besides, with all the graces of unaffected but animate nature'. King George III proposed to her when she was seventeen, but she rejected him* and later married Sir Thomas Bunbury, whose main claim to fame is that he was the owner of the first Derby winner. Bunbury spent too much time with his horses and sporting friends, and Lady Sarah ran off with Lord William Gordon, by whom she had a child, whom Bunbury generously accepted as his own. After only three months with Lord William, Lady Sarah abandoned him and fled to one of the houses of her father, now the Duke of Richmond and Lennox. Next she divorced Bunbury and six years later met and married the penniless Colonel Napier, six years her junior.

Charles Napier, their first-born, was for the initial eighteen months of his life ill-treated by an ignorant nurse, on whom he later partly blamed his poor health. She was replaced, not a moment too soon, by a warm-hearted Suffolk woman, Susan Frost, who won the hearts of all the

---

* The King's nephew did later marry one of her granddaughters.

Napier children. Charles admired his father (who died of consumption when Charles was twenty-two), but he adored his mother and his nanny, who perhaps instilled in him the touching tenderness he often displayed in adult life, in contrast with his reputation in some quarters as a bloodthirsty general.

Later in life, speaking of himself and his brothers, he told his friend Lord Byron, 'We are all a hot violent crew. . . . We were all fond of hunting, shooting, and fishing; yet all gave them up when young men because we had no pleasure in killing little animals'. It was a sentiment of which Byron approved, for he once said, 'I am serious when I say I don't believe it possible for a fisherman to be a good man'.

As long as his mother lived, Charles regularly wrote fond letters to her. On 10 August 1816 he wrote, 'Beloved mother. I cannot pass over my birthday without reflecting that for thirty-four years no benefit has accrued to me of body or mind which cannot in some way be traced to you'. Wherever he was, he sighed for her tenderness and love, suffering from what soldiers than called 'mother sickness'. He was a passionate admirer of women and was always attracted by a pretty face. At the age of twenty he fell madly in love with the daughter of Lord Gage and wrote to his stepsister, 'She looked so wicked and haughty. Her eyes are beautiful. She is to me the most charming creature ever beheld. . . . I think of nothing else, and hate any kind of company where she is not'. Yet he did not propose marriage to her or any other woman until after his mother died. He eventually married two widows in succession, each almost old enough to be his mother.

Charles was three years old when his parents settled in Celbridge, a village twelve miles west of Dublin, and there in genteel poverty he and his siblings grew up in a close and loving family – a remarkable occurrence in the aristocracy of the era. Although the grandsons of dukes, the boys attended the village school and chased pigs with the villagers' sons. Often sick, Charles was short for his age and short-sighted, but at the age of twelve he was commissioned in the 33rd Foot, then commanded by Lieutenant-Colonel Arthur Wellesley. Later to become the Duke of Wellington, Wellesley remained for ever Charles Napier's idol. Child officers were not really expected to serve, and Charles remained in school – by this time in a nearby seminary. When he was seventeen and had reached his full height of five feet seven and a half inches, he was appointed aide-de-camp to Sir James Duff, who commanded the Limerick District.

In this period he broke his leg while out hunting. It was a compound fracture, but his brother George (at fifteen an officer in the 46th Foot) and another young officer managed to set it. Doctors feared that it would be necessary to amputate the leg, but it mended, although so badly that it later had to be re-broken and reset – an early experience of the pain that was to be an almost constant companion throughout his life.

2

In 1801 Napier transferred into the 95th Regiment and, the 19-year-old subaltern wrote to his mother, 'There is a billiard table, but feeling a growing fondness for it, and fearing to be drawn into play for money, I have not touched a cue lately'. Indeed, unlike most officers of the era, he never smoked, gambled or drank, not even wine.

After the Peace of Amiens (27 March 1802) and the reduction of the armed forces, Charles was afraid he was doomed to remain a subaltern for the next ten or twelve years. However, in June 1803 he obtained his captaincy and was appointed aide-de-camp to his cousin General Henry Edward Fox, commander-in-chief of the forces in Ireland, where he saw some action against the Irish insurgents. Two years later he was promoted major and transferred to the 50th Foot. Shortly after the battle of Vimeiro (21 August 1808) in Portugal, he was ordered to join the first battalion of his regiment at Lisbon. On arrival he found that its commanding officer was on leave and that he was in command. The battalion was part of Sir John Moore's force and took part in the famous retreat to Corunna. Two of his brothers, William (who was later to write the best contemporary history of the war in the Peninsula) and George, were both regimental officers in this tragic little army.

Describing his first major battle, Napier wrote, 'I felt great anxiety, no fear; curiosity also. It was unpleasant until the fire opened, and then only one idea possessed me: that of keeping the soldiers steady and animated'. He was handicapped by his short-sightedness. In one battle he lost his glasses and, unable to see the French lines, unwittingly advanced his men almost upon them before he thought to call out, 'Do you see your enemy close enough to hit them?' A frightened Irish soldier replied fervently, 'By Jasus we do!' 'Then blaze away!' yelled Napier.

On 16 January 1808 Napier received his first battle injuries: a musket ball broke his leg six inches above the ankle; then he was bayoneted in the side and the back, was sabred on the head, had his ribs broken by gunshot and suffered severe contusions from being hammered with the butt end of a French musket. After the battle, Captain George Napier went over the field, turning over bodies, looking in vain for his brother. Charles had been taken prisoner.

The French did not have much interest in the wounds of an English officer. It was not until two days later that he found himself at the headquarters of Marshal Nicolas Soult, commander-in-chief of the French forces on the Iberian Peninsula, where he was given food and a bed and was finally examined by a doctor. The tough little man survived, and his first concern was to find a way to notify his mother that he was still alive. In 1807 he had become a Freemason, as did, throughout the nineteenth century, most British officers who wished to rise in the military hierarchy. In France, where he was transported as soon as he could travel, he found a French officer who was also a Mason and invoked

A watercolour ascribed to Charles Napier showing the bridge at Coa on which the battle was fought *(Photo: National Army Museum)*

the brotherly bond to have a letter carried across the channel.

On 20 March 1809 he was paroled, and in the following January he was exchanged for a French officer. Soon afterwards he was back in the Peninsula, and at the battle of Coa (24 July 1810) had two horses shot from under him. He was also soon wounded again, at the battle of Busaco (27 September 1810). Serving as one of Wellington's staff officers and riding in his train, the only officer in a red coat, he had just refused to don a blue cloak when a bullet struck him on the right side of his nose and lodged in his left jaw near the ear, shattering the bone. Its force knocked him

from his horse; barely conscious, he heard someone say, 'Poor Napier, after all his wounds he is gone at last'. He was being carried away when Wellington halted to ask whose body it was. Unable to speak and afraid he was about to be buried alive, Napier waved his hat. Later, his brother William, always prone to hyperbole, claimed that as he waved it he declared, 'I could not die at a better moment'. Charles, to his credit, never confirmed this – on the other hand, he never denied it either. It was, after all, in the spirit of the age, and he might have said such a thing had he been capable of speaking.

Wellington ordered that the wounded man be taken to

his quarters, but on the way his bearers were stopped by a surgeon named Kirkpatrick. Napier later described what happened:

> Setting me on the grass, he and another surgeon worked, and very disagreeable work it was; for the ball was embedded in the bone and pull as they would it could not be extracted, though they cut open my cheek for three inches. At last one put his thumb in my mouth and pushed while the other plucked and away it came tearing innumerable splinters of bone with it; I did not call out but it was very painful.

After this mauling he was carried to a nearby convent and the next day transported to Coimbra, a day's march away. From there he and his servant made their way to Lisbon, a painful ride of several days under a blazing sun. His stay there was brief: Wellington took the offensive, and Napier was eager to return to the action. He left Lisbon with his wound still open and his face swathed in bandages. He was never to recover fully, for the ball had so damaged his palate and nasal passages that he continually suffered from a feeling of suffocation. In his journal for 27 September 1849 – the anniversary of the battle of Busaco – he wrote, 'Now, thirty-nine years after, the horrid suffocation of that wound is scarcely endurable. Oh! it shakes my very soul, the horror of this feeling does!' He often felt forced to get up in the night and light a candle: 'If I remain in the dark I should go mad; the light relieves me, yet I live in terror lest it come on violently'.

Returning to the battle front, Napier encountered one after the other of his brothers being carried wounded to the rear. William's wound was feared mortal, but he recovered and went on to become a major-general and, later in life, a historian. George Napier had been hit in the hip, which led Charles to quip, 'George was hit in the stern and I in the stem. That was burning the family candle at both ends'. George later lost an arm leading a forlorn hope at Cuidad

Rodrigo, but he survived, eventually becoming the governor of Cape Colony in South Africa.

Charles found his way to Wellington's headquarters and,
in spite of his wound, took part in the battle of Fuentes de
Oñoro and was engaged in the siege of Badajos. Napier did
not yearn for honours and rewards as Hugh Gough did, but,
as he told the Prince Regent when he wrote to ask for a
lieutenant-colonelcy, 'I acknowledge myself strongly ambitious of military rank'. He was anxious for command, for
power. In this instance, Lady Sarah also wrote on her son's
behalf to the Prince Regent, and when Napier was at last
promoted lieutenant-colonel on 27 June 1811 and given
command of the 102nd Regiment, he gave full credit to his
mother: 'To you I owe it entirely', he told her. On 25 August
1811 he returned to England and spent several months with
her before assuming command of his regiment on Guern-
sey in January 1812.

3

Napier first heard of the war with the United States on 28
July 1812, when his regiment was already embarked on a
transport for Bermuda. He found Bermuda dull, but it was
there that he became a passionate gardener. He felt somewhat guilty about his gardening, wondering if he was
neglecting his profession. 'Hang mother nature for making
me love such things, and women's company, more than the
sublime pleasure of cutting people's throats, and teaching
young men to do so', he wrote to his mother, with the cyn-
ical, sometimes dark wit that pervades his letters and his
journals. When he lost a companion in Bermuda, he wrote,
"My friend Stewart is dead: I wonder how he likes it'.

Like most officers, Napier hated the flogging of soldiers
but thought it necessary. He once ordered 900 lashes to be
given a man who had robbed a comrade – or so it was
believed, for, said Napier, his conscience aquiver, 'all was
presumptive evidence'. After 200 lashes he halted the flog-

ging, hoping the man was ready to confess. To Napier's dismay, he refused, and the flogging was resumed. At 400 strokes Napier had had more than he could bear; he had the man cut down and put in solitary confinement with the promise that unless he confessed the remaining lashes would be delivered. Solitary confinement did what the lash could not. Much to Napier's relief, the prisoner confessed.

When he took his regiment to Bermuda, he swore that his young soldiers would never see a bloody back, but he found the drunkenness of his regiment beyond endurance. So he flogged them into sobriety. As he wrote from Bermuda, 'There are always some ruffians who may be flogged with satisfaction', including one who, after beating his wife for contradicting him, 'gave her a kick which absolutely lifted her from the ground, and then, before he could be reached, jumped twice upon her breast with thick shoes, leaping high up to crush her!' Napier himself, armed with a bayonet, rescued her. 'This kind of man it gives me pleasure to flog, and no regiment is without several', he said. Years later, in India, where European soldiers were flogged but Indians were not, he wrote to his brother William, 'We must have flogging restored or the Indian Army will be destroyed'.

Early in 1813 Napier took part in a raiding expedition on the American coast under Admiral Sir John Warren and Colonel Sydney Beckwith. Serving as Beckwith's second-in-command, he took part in two inconsequential battles, one at Craney Island at the mouth of the Elizabeth River just west of Norfolk, Virginia, the other at Ocracoke, North Carolina, a village on a barrier reef between Pamlico Sound and the Atlantic. Due to a lack of cooperation between army and navy, neither action was particularly creditable to British arms and little was accomplished. Napier wrote home, 'I dislike sacking and burning towns. . . . This authorized, perhaps needful plundering . . . is very disgusting. . . . Nevertheless a pair of breeches must be plundered, for mine are worn out, and better it will be to take a pair than to shock the Yankee dames by presenting myself as a *sans culotte'*. In one letter he teased, 'Tell Aunt that out of regard for her I don't bayonet many children'. As for the enemy, Napier rather liked the Americans: 'They are fine fellows, liars it is said, but so are we'.

What the Americans call the War of 1812 did not much interest the British at the time and has since been largely forgotten. The focus of everyone's attention was the war against the French, and Napier, in an effort to return to that war, exchanged in September 1813 back into the 50th Foot, which had been fighting in the Pyrenees, but by the time he reached England the war was over. In December 1814 he was placed on half pay. He and his brother William then entered a military college at Farnham where Charles studied not only military and political history but also agriculture, engineering and political economy.

When Napoleon escaped from Elba, Napier interrupted his studies to go to Ghent as a volunteer. He missed the battle of Waterloo, the most famous battle of his generation, but he appears to have seen some action, and he marched into Paris with the victorious allied armies. On his way home from Ostend, his ship sank at the harbour entrance and he was nearly drowned. He returned to his studies at Farnham until the end of 1817, then was idle until, in May 1818, he was appointed inspecting field officer in the Ionian Islands, then ruled by the British. Napier soon became interested in the struggle of the Greeks to throw off Turkish rule, and he made several visits to the mainland, where he met with Greek rebel leaders and gave them advice. In March 1822 he was appointed Resident of Cephalonia by the high commissioner, Sir Thomas Maitland, thereby beginning some of the happiest years of his life.

4

It was the curious custom of the Victorians to give lowly titles and vast powers to the officers or bureaucrats who ruled in far places. As Resident, Napier wielded a virtually dictatorial authority over the inhabitants of his little island. He was placed there to protect the peasants from the feudal oppression that prevailed, and this he effectively did, putting in its stead his own. The difference, Napier argued, was that the Cephalonian aristocrats oppressed the peasants for their own, greedy benefit while he oppressed them for their own good. He wrote to his mother, 'My kingdom is sixty thousand people and martial law exists. This is a fearful power in the hands of one man; but feeling no inclination to be unjust or cruel (except over their horrible trick of maiming animals out of spite for their owner) it does not annoy me. I even like it'. In fact, he liked it very much indeed. 'Power', he noticed, 'is never disagreeable'.

Napier introduced the hated corvée – for the people's own good. Ably assisted by Captain John Pitt Kennedy, who became his lifelong friend, he built a new prison and a lighthouse, improved the harbour, drained marshes, constructed bridges and, among other public works, covered the island with a network of roads. He developed a passion for building, and more than twenty years later, after he had achieved fame as a general, he wrote, 'I would rather have finished the roads of Cephalonia than fought Austerlitz or Waterloo'. Napier was in love with his rocky island and its sullen, passionate people: 'Cephalonia, which is so dear to me that every hour not employed to do her good seems wasted'.

He also fell in love with a Greek girl named Anastasia, who became his mistress and bore him two daughters – Emily Cephalonia and Susan. Little is known of Anastasia, but she appears to have been beautiful, turbulent, charming and irresponsible. Something of her temperament can be glimpsed in her reaction when Napier sailed to England without her or their daughters. Storming to the shore, she arranged the infants in a boat and pushed them out to sea after him. They were rescued by a fisherman. A few years later she left him and the children, to marry a Greek officer. Napier steadfastly continued to provide for her until her death in 1838, and for her parents as well as long as they lived. On his daughters he lavished all the love of a most tender hearted father.

Strange fish were cast up on the Ionian shores. One such was Joseph Wolff (1795–1862), a famous missionary and bizarre character with a curious background. The son of a German Jewish rabbi, he had studied for the Roman Catholic priesthood but was cast out of the seminary when he attacked the doctrine of papal infallibility. He had lived in the United States and there had been ordained a deacon by the Episcopal bishop of New Jersey. He liked to call himself 'the protestant Xavier'.

Napier was deeply religious, but he detested priests and pastors of all faiths (he once described a newly appointed Greek bishop as 'an excellent pious man, who formerly lived by sheep stealing, which he now calls his pastoral life'). Wolff was the exception. The two became friends when Wolff was shipwrecked off the coast of Cephalonia and was succoured by Napier. Wolff admired Napier extravagantly, considering him 'the greatest man whom not only England but all nations have for centuries had'. Nevertheless, he admonished his idol constantly for his habit of cursing. It did no good. Throughout his life Napier swore with zest.

An even stranger fish, in a way, was George Gordon, Lord Byron, who arrived on the brig *Hercules* on 3 August 1823, burning with a fierce desire to free Greece from Turkish rule. He stayed on Cephalonia for three months. Napier liked Byron, whom he described as 'a very good fellow, very pleasant, always laughing and joking . . . very compassionate, and kind to everyone in distress'. Both the poet and the soldier were philhellenes with romantic notions of Greek independence, and they shared a leaning towards sardonic humour.

Napier revitalized Byron, and Byron fired in Napier the notion that he ought to lead the Greek rebels to victory and freedom. Napier knew the Greeks, their foibles and passions; he understood, too, that politics was their national sport. Yet he was strongly tempted:

> Seeing how fit and unfit such a people were for war, I longed to lead them, and resolved to do so. I saw Greece about to rise in strength and glory and my resolve was to join her if it could be done with advantage to her just cause and honour to myself.

Lord Byron recommended Napier to the Greek committee that was busy raising funds in London, declaring, 'A better or a braver man is not easily found'. Napier made the long journey to London to talk with Robert Bowring, the committee's chairman. Money was the stumbling block. Napier spoke frankly: 'I cannot afford to lose my commission. My military means are a thousand pounds yearly; by going to Greece I lose the whole'. The Greek committee felt unable to compensate him for such a loss, and the British government, to which he appealed, refused to permit him to retain his commission while leading Greek rebels against a friendly power. Napier returned to his island. Later the committee reconsidered and offered to meet his terms, and on 14 September 1825 he wrote, 'The Greeks have offered to place me at the head of their army'. But it was too late. Their forces were now scattered, and victory seemed only a remote possibility. By this time Napier had other interests on Cephalonia and had lost some of his initial enthusiasm. 'It cost me a bitter gulp', he said, but he refused.

On the death of his mother, Napier returned briefly to England, and there in April 1827 he married Elizabeth Kelly. He was forty-four; she was nearly sixty, a semi-invalid and a widow with grown children and nearly grown grandchildren. One of her sons-in-law, Samuel Laing, was two years older than Napier. Mrs Kelly and Napier had met when he was twenty-two and she thirty-seven, and he had declared his love then, but marriage had been impossible: although her husband, Captain Francis Kelly, had deserted her, there had been no divorce. Their mother's marriage to Napier outraged her two daughters, and Samuel Laing was so incensed he demanded that Napier repay him with interest all the money he had previously supplied to his mother-in-law. Elizabeth Napier appears to have been a warm, gentle person, and she became a good mother to the two Napier girls, who when grown never failed to speak of her with affection.

With the possible exception of his liaison with Anastasia, Napier seems to have kept sex and love separate. His view of women – other than the elderly, marrying kind – was most honetly expressed when he wrote, 'I think dashing women the most agreeable for acquaintance, at least for soldiers; as to loving them that is quite out of the question, but then they are beautiful and flirts for that very reason, and have a pleasant and entertaining turn for their lovers'. He had been introduced to sex when, as an adolescent officer on General Duff's staff, he had been seduced by a housemaid. He took to the game with zest.There was a run of Limerick girls, whom he considered 'the prettiest and the wickedest in the world', and there had been many women since, some of whom caused him to 'go about all fire' – the devil himself, he said, was 'not more flaming'. At the age of sixty-three he wrote in his journal, 'Never have I wronged woman in my life. I have kissed away many a tear but never caused one'. It was a fine, proud boast, but demonstrably untrue. He was blessed with a conveniently selective memory. Near the end of his life, when living with his second wife, he wrote, 'Marriage is a drag upon military ambitions. I have done pretty well, but not half of what I could have done as a bachelor'.

Napier fascinated women, although his appearance could have had little to do with the attraction. He was short and dark, with a scarred beak of a nose that carried little wire-rimmed glasses, through which he peered at the world with weak but determined eyes. At about the time of his first marriage he described himself as being 'so thin, so sharp, so black, so Jewish, so rascally, such a knavish looking son

Sir Charles Napier *(Photo: National Army Museum)*

of a gun'. His wound from Busaco still plagued him and gave him a nervous facial twitch; his old leg injury induced a jerking limp; and it was on Cephalonia that he felt the first signs of the liver disease that eventually killed him. It is perhaps understandable that his aches and pains made him often irritable and intractable.

Napier usually quarrelled with his superiors, and on the Ionian Islands he quarrelled with Sir Thomas Maitland; when Maitland was replaced by Major-General Sir Frederick Adam, a hero of Waterloo, Napier quarrelled with him too. His differences with the latter proved serious and resulted in a long and bitter wrangle: Adam's notions of domestic administration differed radically from Napier's, and Adam ordered him to reduce expenditure and, specifically, to proceed with his road building only on a 'moderate scale'. But moderation was foreign to Napier's nature, and construction of the roads was the work that satisfied him the most.

In February 1830 Napier took leave to carry his sick wife and his daughters to England. During his absence Adam halted all road work, seized Napier's public papers and filed seventy charges of misfeasance and malfeasance against him at the Colonial Office. Napier was not permitted to return. He responded angrily by writing a book that was a major attack upon Sir Frederick: *The Colonies: Treating of their Value Generally – of the Ionian Islands in Particular.*

5

Although Napier was offered the Residency of Zante, another Ionian island, eight miles south of Cephalonia, he refused it. He was next offered a post in Canada, but he feared that the Canadian climate would be too severe for his wife's precarious health. A few months later, on 31 July 1833, Elizabeth died. With nothing more than his half pay he found England too expensive, and, like many another half-pay officer, he emigrated to France. He settled in Normandy with his daughters and turned his attention to supervising their education and to writing.

In the next six years he wrote numerous political pamphlets and a book on military law. He also tried, without success, to write a novel. He continued to seek employment and applied unsuccessfully for the governorship of Jersey. In 1834 he was offered the governorship of an Australian colony and for some time had high hopes, high ambitions, and dreams of doing grand things. But his schemes were expensive and his terms were too stiff; the offer was withdrawn. He was bitterly disappointed and years afterwards confided that having given up Australia often tormented him.

In 1835, in the middle of the negotiations and when the outcome still appeared hopeful, he married again. His bride, Mrs Frances Alcock (née Philips), widow of a navy captain, was, like his first wife, much older than he. He wrote of her unsentimentally: 'I saw she had a good head and no humbug and this, I thought, would suit the kangaroos'.

Two years after his marriage he was promoted major-general. The following year he was knighted. In April 1838 he at last returned to active duty and was given command of the troops in the Northern District of England, the eleven northernmost counties. Chartism was rife; there were frequent demonstrations (then called 'outrages'), and Napier, although engaged in preserving law and order, had strong sympathies for the disaffected poor. Over and over again in his journal he expressed his sentiments. In the hard winter of 1840–41 he wrote, 'The people are starving and the government do nothing . . . a fearful day, the cold is terrible. God help the poor people in their dreadful suffering'. He believed that 'manufacturers produce corrupt morals, bad health, uncertain wages and dependency on foreign markets'; they were, he said, 'uncontrolled despots and corrupted by power'. He considered factories to be 'hotbeds of ill-health, wretchedness and rascality', and he once declared that the road to hell 'may be paved with good intentions but it is assuredly hung with Manchester cottons'. He worked hard to prevent bloodshed, but there were wild moments in the streets as soldiers confronted mobs. 'This is dreadful work', he wrote. 'Would to God I had gone to Australia'. He blamed the politicians: 'Would I had been saved this work, produced by Tory injustice and Whig imbecility'. Yet he stayed on, and his firmness and his impartiality in upholding the law may well have prevented a revolution.

In the midst of trying to keep the peace in the North with a mere 5,000 troops, Napier suffered a bad attack of shingles and an inflammation of the eye so severe that doctors feared he might become blind. While he was struggling for personal health and public peace, he bombarded his superiors with pleas for better, more hygienic barracks for his troops. This was a cause for which he fought, with mixed results, both in England and, later in India. The barracks of the time were indisputably unhealthy; Napier pronounced them absolutely disgusting.

6

In April 1841 Napier was offered a command in the Bombay presidency, but he was unenthusiastic about going to India as he was *'terribly afraid* of a sea voyage'. He also worried about the health of his wife and daughters, for he thought 'life in India bad and dangerous for a woman' and had a low opinion of the Honourable East India Company. Still, he badly needed money (he had recently lost £8,000 in an unwise investment in the United States and could not get life insurance because of his wounds and ill health), and the pay in India was higher than anywhere else. So on 16 June 1841 he accepted. He had little hope of furthering his career. To a friend he wrote, 'If a man cannot catch glory when his knees are supple he had better not try when they are stiff. All I want is to catch all the rupees for my girls; and then die like a gentleman. I suppose if I survive I shall do this'. He calculated that in his time in India he ought to be able, by living frugally – and he always lived frugally – to save £10,000.

In the week before he sailed in October he endured rheumatism so painful that he found sleep impossible. He had just enough money to get himself and his family to India: 'At Bombay the purser received my last money, a bill for £500 in payment for the voyage from Suez, and returned two pounds!' Then his baggage was ransacked, and he lost about £400 worth of goods. At the end of December 1841 he took up his command at Poona – a 60-year-old major-general in wretched health, without prospects of promotion or gain and without any means of support other than his pay. His days of glory and happiness were all behind him – or so it seemed.

7

The year 1842 was an unfortunate one for the British Empire. It saw one of the most appalling disasters ever suffered by its army when troops in Afghanistan were virtually annihilated trying to retreat from Kabul to the safety of India. Some 16,000 British and Indian soldiers, officers' families and camp followers were massacred or taken prisoner in the snow-clogged passes of the Safed Koh range. Only a single Englishman, an army surgeon, reached the safety of the British cantonment at Jalalabad with news of the catastrophe. British prestige in India was at a low ebb.

It was at this point that Lord Ellenborough arrived in India as governor-general, succeeding Lord Auckland. The colourful Ellenborough was a man after Napier's heart – outspoken, brilliant, headstrong and contemptuous of bureaucratic folly. As president of the Board of Control he had been ever critical of the policies and operating methods of the Honourable East India Company: its monopoly of the China trade, its resistance to all reforms and the failure of its Court of Directors to recognize that they were, in fact, no longer merely a commercial company but the rulers of a vast country. He had even argued for the transfer of administrative control of India to the Crown.

News of the disaster in Afghanistan greeted him as he disembarked in Madras after a tedious five-month voyage.

Next was a report that the sepoys of the Madras army were on the verge of mutiny. As he was already aware, the war in China, then being pushed forward by General Hugh Gough, was draining India of some of its best troops. Nevertheless, he sent off reinforcements to Gough and called on Napier for a assessment of India's military situation.

British India was separated from Afghanistan by the Sikh-controlled Punjab to the north and by Sind, the valley of the Indus, in the south. When Alexander Burnes entered Sind in 1831 during his exploration of the Indus, a wise inhabitant told him, 'The evil is done. You have seen our country'. Indeed, such was often the case with the British: to see was to desire, and to desire was to take. Sind was ruled by several amirs (ameers or mirs) of Baluch descent with whom the British had made a treaty concerning trade, unrestricted traffic on the Indus and the deployment of troops. Regarding the relation between the Honourable East India Company and the amirs, Napier wrote, 'Our mutual friendship has been cemented by a treaty which kindly relieved them from the inconvenience of independence: they have signed but do not like this treaty, have broken it in every petty way, and are much alarmed'.

In August 1842 Ellenborough ordered Napier to take command of all the troops in Sind, 'from the Kojuck pass to the Indus at Bukkur, and down to the sea', and he sailed from Bombay on 3 September. This new assignment began badly. Cholera swept the ship, and sixty-four lives were lost. Napier escaped the cholera, but shortly after their landing, at a demonstration of some rockets to troops in Karachi, a rocket exploded prematurely, severely wounding him in the calf.

In spite of his injury he set off up the Indus to inspect his troops and to confer with some of the amirs. While complaining, 'I am too old and the climate is not invigorating', he was at the same time excited by his new command: 'To try my hand with an army is a longing not to be described; yet it is mixed with shame for the vanity which gives me such confidence'. Just before leaving Bombay, he wrote in his journal, 'Charles! Charles Napier! Take heed of your ambition for military glory; you had scotched that snake, but this high command will, unless you are careful, give it all its vigour again. Get thee behind me, Satan!'

He soon had even more power in his hands. In every frontier district and attached to every command was a political officer or agent who was responsible for relations between the British and the native chiefs, rajas, amirs or other rulers. Frequently there was friction between the 'politicals' and the soldiers, even though the former were themselves often serving officers. Lord Ellenborough felt that this division of responsibility tended to make the military commanders lax and the politicals irresponsibly bold. He therefore abolished the political establishment – a step that made him unpopular with the civil servants and also with the Court of Directors of the Honourable East India Company, whose members saw their patronage reduced.

In Sind, Napier took over the political responsibilities of Major (later Lieutenant-General) James Outram (1803–1863). He had formed a high opinion of Outram in the short time he had known him and thought him 'a good fellow'. On 5 November 1842 at a farewell dinner given in Outram's honour at Sakkar and attended by one hundred officers, Napier, full of goodwill, proposed an extravagant toast:

> In the sixteenth century there was in the French army a knight renowned for deeds of gallantry in war and wisdom in council . . . indeed so deservedly famous was he, that by general acclamation he was called the knight 'sans peur et sans reproche'. The name of this knight, you may all know, was the Chevalier Bayard.* Gentlemen, I give you the Bayard of India, *sans peur et sans reproche*, Major James Outram of the Bombay army.

The encomium 'the Bayard of India', hung from him like a medal, and although he and Napier later indulged in a

---

* Pierre Terrail de Bayard was born in 1473 and died in battle at the Sesia River in Italy in 1524.

long and venomous quarrel, which poisoned the lives of both, that flattering appellation, given to him by the man who became his most bitter enemy, was carved on his tombstone in Westminster Abbey. Napier later regretted the toast and grumbled, 'When I called him Bayard I knew little of him, and took that little on report'. It was the unfortunate tendency of both men to exaggerate the best and the worst in others.

In 1842 their feud lay in the future, albeit the near future. As Outram was about to board his ship at Bombay for an extended leave in England, he was detained by an offer of Napier's to return to Sind as a 'commissioner'. Napier thought Outram could be useful in convincing the amirs that they ought to sign the new treaty; it is not clear why Outram, who considered the new treaty odious, accepted the new post. Perhaps he imagined that he could soften the terms.

Outram felt that he understood the amirs, and, in general, he trusted them. With some of them his relationship went beyond the formal friendship required by his duties as political officer: one dying amir had confided to him the care of his son. Napier had quite the opposite view: he considered them treacherous rascals whose rule was a 'government of low intrigue'. In a burst of rhetoric he called them 'these tyrannical, drunken, cheating, intriguing, contemptible Ameers'. One, whom Outram described as a 'venerable old man', Napier characterized as 'old and silly before his time by drunkenness and debauchery'. He soon began to think of deposing them. On 7 October 1842 he wrote in his journal, 'They are tyrants, and so are we, but the poor will have fairer play under our sceptre than under theirs. . . . We have no right to seize Scinde, yet we shall do so, and a very advantageous, useful, humane piece of rascality it will be'.

Napier began to turn the screws on the amirs by insisting that they keep to the letter of the treaty they had signed. 'We break treaties', he said, 'but that is not a reason for letting others do the same'. The amirs tended to ignore the more onerous aspects of the treaty, particularly the clause that prevented them from levying tolls on river traffic. Napier's spies had secured letters indicating that the amirs were conspiring to attack the British forces in Sind and to throw out the Company's army. Napier believed them to be genuine; Outram thought them forgeries.

The new treaty that Ellenborough drew up on the basis of Napier's reports was even more onerous than the first. Under its terms the amirs were required to yield large chunks of territory to the British, cease minting their own money and, among other equally odious conditions, allow the crews of British boats on the Indus to chop firewood in the amirs' hunting reserves. To their remonstrances Napier replied with threats. He even marched a small force across the western desert to seize the fortress at Imamghar, long a safe haven for the amirs in time of danger. If it had been held by resolute men, he could never have taken it, but he found it abandoned and took advantage of his good fortune by blowing it up. Much to Napier's gratification, this little expedition among the sand dunes was praised by his hero and military exemplar, the Duke of Wellington.

Although Outram's sympathies were with the amirs and he thought it wrong to impose a new treaty on them, he met them at Hyderabad and made an attempt to convince them they must yield to the inevitable. Most of them promised to sign, but none did. Instead, an outraged mob of Baluchi warriors, estimated to be 8,000 strong, attacked the British Residency where Outram was housed. He had only one company of the 22nd Foot to protect him, but they fought their way to the river and the safety of the boat waiting for them. Napier blamed the amirs, but Outram refused to believe they were responsible, preferring to think they had simply been unable to control their irate tribesmen.

Napier made extensive use of scouts and spies and so received a steady flow of messages (concealed in quills carried in the rectum of the messenger) bearing word that the tribal warriors were assembling. There seemed every reason to believe that the amirs were preparing to attack, and he was determined to strike first without delay. Time would only allow the amirs' forces to swell, and the odds against him were already fearful. Outram begged for a delay, but Napier was convinced that 'rapid movement and boldness [would] do the work', and he set his army in motion.

On 16 February he found the Baluchis entrenched on the banks of the Falaili River near Miani (Meeanee), and at nine o'clock the following morning his troops were drawn up in order of battle: twelve guns and 2,200 men faced an enemy with eighteen guns (directed by an Englishman in the amirs' pay) and at least 22,000 warriors. Outram, at his own suggestion and with Napier's approval, took 200 men to set fire to a forest on the enemy's flank and so took no part in the battle.

Distraught with worry over his beloved nephew John, an officer in his command, who lay seriously ill, perhaps dying, Napier found it difficult to summon his old optimism. Just before the battle was joined, he wrote, 'I ought to have quiet thoughts and cannot, but I am throwing myself and my troops into a desert, and must not think of John or I may involve all under me in disaster and disgrace. This is a hard trial for an old man of sixty; it shakes me to the foundations'. He himself was far from well, suffering from diarrhoea and painful rheumatism. In addition, he had broken or badly sprained his hand when dealing a blow to the head of a camel driver whom he had found abusing an animal: 'His head was like an anvil', he complained. During the battle his injured hand tormented him: 'The pain was terrible, almost past bearing. . . . In agony I rode, holding my reins with a broken hand'. In his other hand he carried his father's sword.

William Napier later described the battle in his usual, colourful prose:

The battle of Miani *(Photo: BBC Hulton Picture Library)*

Thick as standing corn and gorgeous as a field of flowers were the Beloochies in their many coloured garments and turbans. They filled the deep bed of the Fullaillee; they were clustered on both banks, and covered the plain beyond. Guarding their heads with dark shields, they shook their sharp swords, gleaming in the sun, and their shouts rolled like peals of thunder as with frantic gestures they dashed against the front of the 22nd [Regiment]. But, with shrieks as wild and fierce, and hearts as big and strong, the British soldiers met them with the queen of weapons, and laid their foremost warriors wallowing in blood. . . .

It was indeed a bloody affair, and in his after-action report to Lord Ellenborough, Napier wrote, 'I regret to say we could not take prisoners; the overwhelming numbers, and all the combatants being hand to hand, made it impossible to spare; it was a butchery such as I never beheld; no quarter was given on either side. . . .' To his brother Henry he confided, 'I saw no safety but in butchery: It was they or we who must die'. Even so, he had made an effort to save an exhausted though unyielding chief, but a British soldier, too quick for him, drove his bayonet into the Baluchi's breast. 'This day, General, the shambles have it all to themselves', he said. To his friend John Kennedy, Napier marvelled, 'How I escaped heaven knows, I do not. We were for three hours and a half only one yard apart, man to man'.

The enemy's losses were estimated at between five and eight thousand. British losses were remarkably light: 6 officers killed and 13 wounded; 3 Indian officers wounded; 54 other ranks killed and 177 wounded. Riding over the battlefield the next day, viewing the carnage and listening to the moans of the wounded and the shrieks of pain from men whose limbs were being amputated in the hospital tent, Napier asked himself, 'Am I guilty of these horrid scenes?' The thought was untenable. He quickly absolved himself.

Some time later it was reported to him that the amirs, certain of victory, had decided before the battle that all the British soldiers would be slaughtered on the field except Napier, who was to have had an iron ring thrust through his nose with a chain attached by which he could be led.

Only a few miles from the Miani battlefield was the encampment of one amir who had either deliberately held back from the fighting or been unable to reach the field in time. Known as the Lion of Mirpur, he had an army of 10–12,000 men. Napier planned to attack him at once, but Outram persuaded him to try diplomacy. Letters were exchanged, and the Lion slunk off to his lair to make war another day. On 24 March, near the village of Dubba, Napier defeated a force of some 26,000 men with eleven guns. On the night before the battle he wrote in his journal, 'God bless my wife and children: if I fall it will I hope be in a way to make them glory in my name'. He was untouched, although a musket ball hit the hilt of his sword, his orderly's horse was shot from under him and he was dangerously close to an enemy powder magazine when it exploded.

There was a general reluctance to christen the battle 'Dubba', for this was the local word for 'skins of grease'. Although bleeding profusely, Major Montague McMurdo (soon to marry Miss Susan Napier) gallantly rode about the countryside looking, without success, for a village whose name might be more acceptable. Lord Ellenborough finally settled the matter by naming it after the nearest major town, and it became the battle of Hyderabad. Again, British and Indian casualties were light: 39 killed and 231 wounded.

It was, and still is, the custom in the British army for the general to list in his after-action reports the names of officers who distinguished themselves. Such officers were said to have been mentioned in dispatches. After his battles in Sind, Napier not only gave the names of officers who had been particularly brave but also, for the first time in British history, listed the names of men from other ranks, both British and Indian, who had performed valiantly.

8

Sind was conquered, and *Punch* invented for Napier a one-word telegram: 'Peccavi' (I have sinned). Many found the pun apposite.

Persuaded that the amirs (now referred to as the fallen princes) had been unjustly robbed of their countries, some people joined in an outcry, led by Outram, against what they considered unnecessary high-handedness on Napier's part. Nevertheless, Napier was created a Knight Grand Cross of the Order of the Bath, and Sind was annexed. No one suggested giving it back. However, no guns were fired in Britain to ·celebrate the victories, and until 1844 Napier was denied the official thanks of Parliament. In the parliamentary debates on the conquest, Lord Howick and others charged that he had provoked an unnecessary war merely to win prize money. Napier was incensed and wrote in his journal of 'the insolence, the injustice, the falsehoods of men like Lord Howick', but he added, 'I forgive all of them. . . . I never feel angry in my heart against any one – beyond wishing to break their bones with a broomstick!'

Napier's relatives and friends believed he should be given

a peerage, but he wrote to his sister, 'No power on earth would make me take a pension, and a peerage would therefore ruin me'. Nevertheless, he was nettled when Harry Smith was made a baronet for Aliwal and Gough was created a baron after the First Sikh War.

The conflict between Outram and Napier now sharpened and became increasingly bitter as the *Bombay Times* weighed in on Outram's side and as William Napier published a book apotheosizing his brother. The charges by each and by their advocates grew more and more personal and vitriolic. What had started as a difference of opinion as to what ought to have been done and what had been done in Sind swelled into campaigns of defamation, and the feud, which gained a momentum of its own, went on for years – continuing even after Napier's death.

Napier certainly had not waged war for prize money; still, there was a large amount of treasure taken from the amirs (all of which was placed in the hands of prize agents), and the story spread that in the pursuit of prize money Napier had stripped the amirs' helpless wives and concubines of their ornaments and that he had even taken a bed from under one poor woman who was in labour. Major John Jacob added fuel to the flames by reporting that he had seen prize agents auctioning children's cots and household crockery. The charges against Napier were proved to be fabrications, and Jacob was known to be a staunch friend of Outram, but there was still enough evidence that the prize agents had indeed been over-zealous to delay the distribution of prize money, and there was an attempt by the Court of Directors to deny Napier his share. It was 1849 before the final distribution was made. Napier's share of £70,000 made him a rich man.

Although Napier never pressed for personal honours, he fought for the award of campaign medals to those who had fought at Miani and Hyderabad. The Queen added her voice to his and wrote to Lord Stanley on 24 June 1843, 'The Queen is much *impressed with the propriety* of a medal being

given to the troops who fought under Sir Charles Napier. . . .'
Two years later the medals were awarded. On 7 November
1845, in a letter to the governor-general, Napier commented dryly, 'We have received our medals, sent to us
amongst commissariat stores as a bale of goods, and without ribands or any means of hanging them on our breasts!'

9

On 31 March 1843 Napier learned to his delight that Lord
Ellenborough had appointed him governor of Sind. That
night he exulted in his journal:

> This is glory! is it? Yes! Nine princes have surrendered their
> swords to me on fields of battle, and their kingdoms have been
> conquered by me and attached to my own country. I have
> received the government of the conquered provinces, and all
> honours are paid to me while living in mine enemy's capital!

He had all the instincts of a benevolent dictator and was as
exuberant as a schoolboy at the chance to govern one of the
British Empire's more remote provinces. In high good
humour he confided to his journal, 'I strive to curb pride
and vanity. Get thee behind me, Satan! But it is not easy
to make Satan obey when one is a conqueror'. On 5 April
he declared, 'I have done with war! Never again am I likely
to see a shot fired in anger. Now I shall work at Scinde as
at Cephalonia, to do good, to create, to improve, to end
destruction and rise up order'. He had not yet seen the end
of war, but for the time being he revelled in being a ruler
in his own special way – a way not popular with the Honourable East India Company's bureaucrats and directors.
  Napier had his own notions of justice. He was impatient
with lawyers and their legal quibbles: 'The substituting Acts
of Parliament for the Articles of War . . . while some whip-
per-snapper boy, as judge advocate, takes the whole proceedings into his hands and lays down the law. . . . I have

shortened my life trying to break down this system'. He complained that courts martial in India had 'become so legal and wise that there [was] not the slightest chance of convicting the greatest scoundrel'. As he told one young judge advocate, 'My object is to have sentence passed according to the real conscientious conviction of the judge, and not what is required in an English court of justice'.

Now, as governor, Napier set about providing justice according to his own lights. He had always favoured the underdog and the weak – the Chartists in northern England, the peasants in Cephalonia. He listened with a fine scepticism to complainants, for he believed that in such situations all men are liars, although he was also convinced that 'no set of wretches ever complain without a foundation'. He described his own system as follows:

> On all these occasions my plan was an unjust one. For against all evidence I decide in favour of the poor; and argue against the arguments of the government people so long as I can. . . . My formula is this. Punish the government servants first and enquire about the right and wrong when there is time! This is the way to prevent tyranny, and make the people happy, and render public servants honest. The latter know they have *'no chance of justice'* if they are complained against, and in consequence take good care to please the poor. If the complaint is that they cheat the government, oh! that is another question; then they have fair trials and leniency: we are all weak where temptation is strong.

In spite of the Honourable East India Company's policy of non-intervention in religious customs, he abolished suttee, the practice of burning widows on the funeral pyres of their husbands. When Brahmin priests complained of this intrusion into their ancient religion's rites, Napier told them brusquely, 'This burning of widows is your custom; prepare the funeral pile. But my nation also has a custom. When men burn women alive we hang them, and confiscate all their property. My carpenters shall therefore erect gibbets on which to hang all concerned when the widow is consumed. Let us all act according to our national customs'.

He found it difficult to convince his subjects that women were not mere chattels. 'I hanged a Beloochee lately, to the astonishment of his chief', said Napier. ' "What? hang a Baloochee for killing a Scindian woman?" The life of a Scindian woman under the [amirs] . . . was worth about 200 rupees'. To his brother Richard he wrote, 'There is only one crime I cannot put down – wife killing! They think to kill a cat or a dog is wrong, but I have hanged at least six for killing women: on the slightest quarrel she is chopped to pieces. . . . I will hang 200 unless they stop'. To his brother William he wrote, 'I feel very low and distressed at putting so many men to death. . . . but it must be done'.

Whenever he could, Napier gave government posts to brother officers, whom he trusted, rather than to civil servants, whom he called 'civil-villains'. He believed that the victors deserved the spoils: 'It was only fair that those who won the land should have the fatness'. Civil servants he considered overpaid and too interested in their perquisites. He himself never learned Hindustani, and he distrusted old hands who boasted that only those who had lived long in India were capable of governing it. They were 'full of curry and bad Hindustanee', he wrote, 'with a fat liver and no brains, but with a self-sufficient idea that no one *"can know India"* except through long experience of brandy, champagne, grain-fed mutton, cheroots and hookers [hookahs]'. (Like many who eat little and neither drink nor smoke, he tended to attach greater value to these negative virtues than they deserve.) He attributed much of the sickness that befell Europeans in India to over-indulgence. That he himself was frequently laid low did nothing to alter his opinion.

'Scinde is quiet as any country in the world', Napier crowed. 'The great receipt for quieting a country is a good thrashing first and great kindness afterwards: the wildest chaps are thus tamed'. Quite a few were not. Numerous small expeditions had to be mounted to put down rebellions, and the western part of the country was plagued by robbers from the hills, necessitating a full-blown military campaign led by Napier himself.

There were internal problems as well. Napier was not entirely a free agent, for he served the Honourable East India Company and there were annoying directives from Bombay, Calcutta and the Court of Directors in Leadenhall Street. In his journal entry of 3 November 1844 he wrote bitterly:

> Confound the luck that makes me a general and not a sovereign! All the trouble, all the thought of a sovereign, but responsible to fools instead of to God! . . . Well, such is our fate; he is weak in whom regret finds a port. There are two things necessary in this life: patience and perseverance. Some little of both belong to me. . . . All I do will be upset by fools after me, and the land will again be in misery.

The directors of the Honourable East India Company, those 'ignominious tyrants', incensed him: 'They are miserable wretches these directors,' he said, and 'the Court of Directors had shewn its usual folly and supreme ignorance of government. . . .' When Lord Ellenborough was replaced as governor-general by his brother-in-law, Sir Henry Hardinge, Napier lost his most useful supporter in the hierarchy, and he felt an increase of pressure and a waning of confidence in him from his superiors. He was particularly outraged when neither the Court of Directors nor Lord Ripon, then president of the Board of Control, supported him in his feud with Outram. Of Lord Ripon he wrote, 'I detest Ripon. I could not do so more if he was a rascal, his good-natured drivelling is worse than if he spit in one's face'. He was increasingly annoyed by petty quarrels with the Bombay bureaucrats. In a letter to his brother William he wrote indignantly, 'They have at Bombay tried to make me pay *forty pounds sterling* for my breakfast and dinner, every day while on board a steamer on the public service!!' He characterized the Bombay government as 'a model of tyranny and mischief'. To his brother Henry he wrote, 'I am constantly annoyed in some way; about trifles, indeed, but these trifles are designed to irritate, and they do irritate'.

His temper was not improved by his many aches and pains. He suffered from sunstroke, dyspepsia, colic, dysentery, haemorrhoids, his old wounds and the effects of a series of accidents. He complained of his eyes, of the effect of the cold, of rheumatism in his hands, of the failing strength of old age and always of the suffocating feeling caused by his Busaco wound.

There were also disappointments. When the First Sikh War began in the Punjab, he received orders to assemble an army of 15,000 men with a siege train at Rohri. He entered upon this task with enthusiasm and submitted his own plan for an invasion of the Punjab from the south. Instead, Hardinge ordered Napier to join him, intending that he would take over Gough's command, but by the time he arrived Gough had fought the battle of Sobraon and won the war. Napier argued that the Punjab should be annexed; when this was not done, he correctly predicted that 'the tragedy must be reenacted in a year or two'.

Napier's disappointments, the harassments by rebellious and larcenous subjects, the exasperating bureaucratic quarrels, and his aches and pains were all swept into insignificance by the cholera epidemic that raged through Sind in 1846. When it reached Karachi, where Napier had taken up residence with his family, it spared Napier himself but struck down many of those he loved. On his staff was his nephew John, son of his brother George, who, with his wife and infant daughter, lived with him. In July 1846 John's little daughter died. Less than forty-eight hours later, John – 'he who from his infancy I had saved and cherished, and whom I loved' – was also stricken. To his brother William he wrote:

> My boy John has fallen! He was struck by cholera about three o'clock yesterday as we were sitting down to dinner, and at ten

he no longer existed. I have seen many die, but not one in such dreadful agonies until half an hour before dissolution when he became tranquil, and then expired. My heart is almost broken William. . . . I have now to tell his wife . . . she is on the eve of child-birth: if she dies!

In the midst of his grief over personal losses, he did what he could to protect his troops, whom he scattered into the desert. Thousands of civilians fled from Karachi in wild desperation; many found miserable deaths on the roads. In all an estimated 60,000 died.

No one knew the cause of such dreaded diseases as cholera and malaria. Curiously, although Napier believed malaria was caused by bad air, he hit upon the correct source of the disease and the right remedy. Noting that 'the quantity of bad air . . . generated [by stagnant water] is in proportion to the surface covered by the water, and the number of people made ill is in the same proportion'. he recommended in a letter to Hugh Gough 'filling up all hollows containing stagnant water'.

Depressed by the deaths of John Napier and the little girl, weighed down by his own ill health and becoming increasingly disenchanted with the Honourable East India Company, he resolved to resign, a step the severe illness of his wife led him to take several months earlier than he had intended. To William he wrote on 4 July 1847, 'I have resigned. My wife has nearly died. Seventeen days and nights I nursed her. She must not stay'. Lord Hardinge kindly sent a steam frigate to take him and his family directly to Suez. When at last he reached Nice, he wrote to William on 15 December, 'I am more ill than ever I felt before, sinking, dying'. He had 'excruciating pain, passage of blood' and he complained, 'The cold piercing my marrow makes me feel well across Styx'.

10

The Napiers lingered in southern France until Charles had recovered enough to complete his journey home, where he

A toast to General Sir Charles Napier at the London Tavern *(Photo: ILN Pic. Lib.)*

was greeted as a hero. Excited crowds cheered him in the streets, and a round of banquets was given in his honour. Although he protested that he hated 'these effusions of fish and folly', his letters and journal clearly express his pleasure.

When news of the excessive casualties at the battle of Chilianwala reached England, there was an outcry against Gough and a demand that he be recalled. The Court of Directors acceded and asked the Duke of Wellington to name a new commander-in-chief in India. Wellington chose Sir Charles Napier, a decision at which the directors balked. Asked to make another selection, the Duke named Sir George Napier, but brother George stoutly refused the appointment. The next person to be offered the post was General Sir William Maynard Gomm, who accepted and set sail from Mauritius, where he had been governor. However, before he reached Calcutta his appointment was cancelled, for popular opinion – which more than once has selected British generals for particular posts – demanded Napier. The Court of Directors yielded with bad grace, pettishly insisting that he could not, as was customary, also have a seat on the Supreme Council in Calcutta. As Napier refused to go under these conditions, they were forced to back down.

Napier left England on 24 March 1849 and reached Calcutta on 6 May. For the second time the leisurely transport of the day had allowed Lord Gough to win a war before he was superseded. Napier was of two minds, as he often was, about becoming commander-in-chief in India. He hated the idea of relieving old Gough, whom he liked personally, but he had no respect for Gough's generalship: 'My God! what numbers of lives I could have saved had I been master in this Sikh War! I think there never was a such a galaxy of blunders since war was war!' he wrote.

When he first arrived Napier stayed with Lord Dalhousie, who was then governor-general, and the two men took an instant liking to each other. 'I never had a more agreeable inmate in my house', Dalhousie said, and he was full of admiration for the old soldier: 'What a life he has led, what climates he has braved, how riddled and chopped to pieces with balls and bayonets and sabre wounds he is'. For his part, Napier declared happily to William, 'I like Lord D so much'. This pleasant relationship did not last long. Napier was soon speaking of Dalhousie as 'the good but weak creature' he had to deal with, and then as 'this poor little pig'. By 7 July 1850 he was writing in his journal, 'I am now at war with Lord Dalhousie, who is a poor petulant man, cunning and sly, ill-conditioned, and ready to attack any but those he serves. . . . This little goose is quite unfit for his place'.

Napier was soon disillusioned with his job as well, for he found that he had far less authority than he had expected and that the abuses and deficiencies in his armies were too entrenched for him to correct. On 15 August 1849 he wrote, 'I am quite tired of this command; no power, no power, and great responsibility. This is a silly game to play, and I will not remain at the table'. Three weeks later he wrote, '[What] a very low-bred, miserable, sneaking, toad-eating post it is: I am not commander'.

In November 1849 the 66th Native Infantry at Gorindghur turned mutinous. Napier disbanded the regiment and gave its number to the Nasiri Gurkha Battalion, which meant that the Gurkha mercenaries from Nepal would henceforth recieve the higher pay given to sepoys in line regiments. About the same time, he suspended the introduction of a new regulation that would have reduced the sepoys' allowance on the North-West Frontier, a regulation he believed would encourage mutiny. For these actions he was given a severe formal reprimand by Lord Dalhousie. This was the last straw for Napier. He resigned. On 16 November 1850 he left Simla and was back in England by March 1851.

In a short time he settled comfortably on a small property on the Hampshire Downs near Portsmouth and busied himself writing about military matters. He continued his quarrels with Outram, Jacob, Ripon, Dalhousie and other old adversaries, and he found new men to hate, even in the country, including a neighbour who shot his dog. His health continued to deteriorate, particularly after he caught a chill while serving as a pallbearer at the Duke of Wellington's funeral. Early in June 1853 he took to his camp bed, and on 29 August he died, surrounded by his family, grieving servants and a few old veterans who had served under him. The death scene was dramatic. As he was breathing his last, Montagu McMurdo, his son-in-law, was inspired to seize the old colours of the 22nd Regiment, which had been carried at Miani and Hyderabad, and wave them over the dying conqueror of Sind.

CHAPTER

3

Charles Gordon (1833–1886)

'Too Late!'

1

Like Gough, Napier and many other Victorian soldiers, Charles George Gordon was the son of a British officer. He was born the fourth of the eleven children of Lieutenant-General William Gordon and his wife, Elizabeth (née Enderby). Charles was not a bright student; his teachers found him obstreperous and his classmates thought him a bully. He entered the Royal Military Academy, Woolwich, at fifteen; after being set back several months for unruly behaviour, he passed out in 1852 as a sub-lieutenant in the Royal Engineers. A year later he was duly promoted lieutenant and late in 1854 was sent to the war in the Crimea, where he built huts for the troops and laid out trenches. In spite of the cruel climate and execrable living conditions, he enjoyed the war, finding it 'indescribably exciting'.

He was a slight young man, five feet five inches tall, with

light blue eyes and a small head crowned with tight brown curls. His hands and feet were small, even dainty, and he presented a trim, wiry figure bursting with nervous energy. He was already a heavy cigar smoker, and, with or without a cigar, he gesticulated widely. When excited, he spoke too rapidly and stammered. Unlike most men who served in the Crimea, Gordon never complained of the physical hardships. He told his mother not to believe 'all the atrocious fibs . . . of our misery'. Admittedly the men in the ranks suffered, but this was 'partly their own fault, as they [were] like children'. It was remarked upon that he was exceptionally cool under fire and appeared to have no fear. He was wounded on 6 June 1855 but was able to take part in the famous attack on the Redan twelve days later. He was deeply religious and wrote regularly about religious matters to his sister Augusta, a spinster twelve years older than he.

After the Crimean War he spent two years with a boundary commission, laying out the new frontier between Turkey and Russia. He passed the winter of 1857–58 in England and then returned to Armenia in April 1858. On the voyage to Constantinople a 'fairy-like young lady' tried in vain to attract him, but women never appealed to him; he was more interested in his young servant, a handsome Russian boy he had brought home from the Crimea – the first of many boys who attracted his attention over the years. In England, when Ivan cast loving eyes on a housemaid who apparently wanted to claim him, Gordon declared, 'I do not mean to allow it, as he belongs to me'.

The dull work on the Armenian frontier kept Gordon from service in the Indian Mutiny, but he was working his way up the promotion ladder, for advancement was by seniority in the artillery and engineers. In 1859, at the age of twenty-six, he was promoted captain. The following year he volunteered for active service in China. On the long voyage the only excitement was furnished by a passenger who accused an attractive young steward of taking money from his cabin. Always drawn to young men in distress, Gordon made good the money and settled the affair by taking on the culprit as his servant.

The fighting was all but over by the time he arrived in China; the last battle was being fought near Peking the day after he landed in Shanghai, and he wrote home disconsolately, 'I am rather late for the amusement'. Once again Gordon was employed in building huts, this time for the troops at Tientsin, about fifty miles from Peking. The army was to stay until the indemnity was paid. He also took part in the sacking of the Summer Palace – some 200 buildings housing China's oldest books and historical treasures and finest works of art. The French and British troops were turned loose: as Gordon wrote, 'Everybody was wild for plunder. . . . but these places were so large, and we were so pressed for time, that we could not plunder them carefully'. Most of the pictures, books, statues, ceramics and tapestries were torn, smashed or slashed. It did not matter. Whatever was not carried away, Gordon and his men burned. In a letter home he said, 'You can scarcely imagine the beauty and magnificence of the palaces we burned'. Gordon's share of the prize money came to just over £48 – in addition to the throne he managed to carry off.

In March 1862 he suffered a mild case of smallpox: a clear warning from God, he thought, that he had sinned, and he determined to curb his quick temper and his lust for battle. 'I am glad to say', he wrote to Augusta, 'that this disease has brought me back to my Saviour, and I trust in future to be a better Christian than I have been hitherto'. Not long after his recovery, he was sent to Shanghai, where destiny awaited him.

2

About 1835 a young Chinese schoolteacher named Hung-sen-tsuen fell under the influence of an American Baptist missionary with a somewhat hysterical view of Christianity. Hung became an enthusiastic convert, fasting, preach-

Taiping officers and soldiers *(Photo: Mary Evans Picture Library)*

ing and handing out tracts. He denounced all pleasures of
the flesh and urged his friends and relations to cast aside
all gods but his own. After a brief stint of scriptural study
under another Baptist missionary, he struck out alone,
preaching his own brand of Christianity. Like Gordon, he
was brought by sickness to a closer examination of his religious beliefs, and in a vision it was revealed to him that he
was actually the younger brother of Jesus Christ. After God
presented him with a sword, a seal and a book, he took the
title of Tien Wang, or Heavenly King, and began to issue
decrees: the Sabbath was sacred; the Bible was to be trans-
lated into all Chinese languages; and eighteen churches were
to be built in each town. His followers were soon numbered
in the tens of thousands, and he proclaimed Taiping, or the
Great Peace, throughout China.

Sizeable armies proved helpful in creating the Great
Peace. The temptation to convert by force those who resisted
persuasion proved too strong, and the Heavenly King soon

had sufficient soldiers to increase his flock of believers. The Imperial government finally moved to suppress Hung in 1850, but it was too late. The Taiping rebels cut the Imperial army to bits and went on to capture the great city of Nanking, where they massacred the entire Manchu population of some 28,000 people. Like locusts, the Taipings swept across the land, plundering, murdering, burning, leaving desolation in their wake. Prisoners who failed to convert with sufficient speed and fervour were crucified, beaten to death or flayed alive.

Among Europeans there was at first considerable sympathy for the Taipings: many saw tham as noble Christians battling against the heathens. But as the Heavenly King's decrees grew increasingly outrageous and the behaviour of his followers more barbarous, sympathy turned to dismay and then to alarm. In 1860 the Taiping hordes, having captured most of the southern provinces, moved northward and lapped at the gates of Shanghai, a principal centre of European trade in China. The merchants there, aware of the feebleness of the Imperial government, determined to create their own army to keep the Taipings at bay, and hired an American adventurer, Frederick T. Ward, to raise a mercenary military force, optimistically named the Ever Victorious Army.

The British government, much concerned about the China trade, sent an envoy to the Heavenly King, but Hung by this time had discovered the delights of the flesh and was preoccupied with wives, concubines, exotic foods and other entertainments. The management of his government and the command of his armies was entrusted to loyal lieutenants, whom he called *wangs* (kings). The British envoys found the *wangs* generally uninterested in trade treaties, though they were eager to continue purchasing arms from British traders.

Ward and his ill-disciplined army at first enjoyed some small successes, but he overreached himself, was trounced and was forced to fall back. Ward himself was wounded

five times, and another American soldier of fortune, Henry
Andrea Burgevine, took command. The Ever Victorious
Army, plagued by desertions after its defeat, quickly deteriorated. Burgevine was a brave man, but he lacked military and administrative abilities; he was also hot tempered
and quarrelled with Li Hung Chang, the Imperial governor
of Kiangsu Province. His career ended when he struck a
mandarin and used some of his troops to steal from the
merchants he was hired to protect. When dismissed, he
decamped with a number of his officers and soon afterwards joined the Taipings.

The official British policy was one of non-intervention in
the fight between the Imperial Manchu government and
the Taiping rebels, but when Shanghai was threatened, the
merchants begged for a British officer to take charge of their
Ever Victorious Army. Colonel Charles Stavely, in command of the British forces in Shanghai, permitted Gordon
(promoted to major in December 1862) to be appointed a
general in the Imperial Chinese army and commander of
the Ever Victorious, which now consisted of about 3,000
Chinese mercenaries and a handful of European officers,
mostly renegades, fugitives and deserters from the Royal
Navy and adventurers from Europe and the United States
who, like their men, served solely for the pay and the prospect of loot. Burgevine had been a popular commander,
and the officers looked scornfully on the trim little regular-
army major who arrived to command them.

One of Gordon's first acts was to design a uniform for his
army: black boots, bright green turbans, green jackets and
knickerbockers. As his personal bodyguard he appointed
three hundred of the smartest men, whom he dressed in
bright blue uniforms with red facings.

Almost immediately he began a quarrel with Li Hung
Chang. Li had his own Imperial troops in the field commanded by a General Ching. Two French observers of
Ching's army quipped that his soldiers treated 'friends and
enemies with most perfect impartiality, plundering all alike'.

Gordon made it clear at once that he would give reports to the Shanghai merchants who paid his bills and, as a courtesy, to Li but that under no circumstances would he serve under or take orders from General Ching. He considered the army to be *his*, to be used to fight in his own way. To make plain that these were his terms, he refused to take a salary from the Imperial government, informing Li, to his astonishment, that he would accept nothing, not even, he said, a 'shoe latchet'.

With his uniforms designed and his position made clear, Gordon turned his attention to the enemy. The merchants had indicated that they would be content if he could keep the Taipings thirty miles from Shanghai; Gordon entertained grander schemes. In his first action he marched his army eighty miles and captured a Taiping town without the loss of a single man. His battle plan was simple but effective, and he used it over and over again: after a careful survey of the town to be attacked, he brought up artillery during the night and opened a bombardment at dawn. It seldom took long to breach the mud walls that usually surrounded the towns, and when a breach was sufficiently large, Gordon, a cigar between his teeth and a rattan cane in his hand, led his men in the attack. The cane, his only weapon, soon came to be called his 'magic wand'.

Town after town capitulated to the Ever Victorious Army, and their Taiping defenders either fled or changed sides. The Imperial Chinese government recognized Gordon's worth, and he was able to write to his mother, 'I am now a Tsung Ping Mandarin (which is the second highest grade) and have acquired a good deal of influence'. He was pleased with himself and posed for his portait, standing stiff and expressionless in complete mandarin regalia, his Scottish face, with its bright blue eyes and neat moustache, startlingly incongruous beneath a mandarin cap.

Although he had astonished Li Hung Chang by refusing to take any money from the Imperial government, he later consented to accept a modest salary of £260 a year, for he found that he needed money for his personal charities. Although his contempt for money was real, he relished the drama created when he refused it. This was not an attitude shared by his officers and men. They were appalled by his indifference to plunder and exasperated by his desire to be continually in the field, which left them little time to dispose of their loot or to enjoy the pleasures it opened to them. They were discontented – and they made it known – but Gordon had what is today called command presence, and the little man who led attacks armed with a cigar and cane was not to be intimidated by his own soldiers.

When his officers all sent in their resignations, Gordon simply marched his army a few miles away and sent word that he expected them to join their men by the next afternoon. They did. When his artillerymen mutinied and issued a proclamation threatening to blow up the camp unless their demands were met, Gordon ordered their non-commissioned officers to parade and demanded to know the name of the author. When no one spoke up, he pulled a corporal from their ranks and ordered his bodyguard to shoot the unfortunate man on the spot. He was prepared, he announced, to continue shooting one in every five unless someone revealed the ringleader. Not surprisingly, all agreed it was the dead man. The mutiny was over.

Gordon's successes in battle were bitter to General Ching, who found it intolerable that the foreigner and his mercenaries had accomplished what he and his regulars could not. The matter came to a head after the capture of the town of Kunshan, in which the two were supposed to have cooperated. A violent quarrel erupted over which army had actually captured the town. Both men wrote violent letters to Li in which each denounced the other in extravagant terms. Ching's men fired on the Ever Victorious; Gordon threatened to kill Ching. Li Hung Chang, in a masterly piece of understatement, remarked, 'Reports from each of them regarding the other indicate an ill-feeling'.

Li supported Gordon and had the greatest difficulty in

cooling the wrath of Ching. Gordon, in a fit of rage, nonetheless accused him of plotting to put the Ever Victorious
under Ching's command, and threatened to resign. Li, who
had done his best to understand Gordon, found his British
general inscrutable:

> General Gordon demands the respect of those who are inferior
> to him in rank, and he believes in strong measures to maintain
> discipline. Why, then, does he not accord me the honours that
> are due me as head of the military and civil authority?

Li was only one among many who puzzled over this tal-
ented military eccentric who seemed to create his own logic
as he went along.

It was hard to harm or to reward a man who cared nothing for wealth or women and who appeared to scorn honours. Gordon found pleasure only in battle – and in
roistering with a group of small Chinese boys, mostly
orphans, he had gathered around him. To superiors and
inferiors alike, Gordon was an *enfant terrible* to be treated
warily, but his boys could tease him and disobey him without fear of reproach. He clothed and fed them, gave them
pet names and showered them with affection. One naked
little boy, whom Gordon carried away from a battle in his
arms, was educated at his expense and grew up to be a
senior police officer in Shanghai.

In December 1863 the key city of Su-chou was captured,
thanks to arrangements worked out by Gordon with the
disaffected Taiping *wangs* in the city. Gordon promised that
if a city gate was left open and unguarded, there would be
no looting and the lives and property of the *wangs* would
be spared. All went according to plan, but when the city
fell Ching's men plundered it, and the *wangs*, probably on
Li's orders, were executed. Gordon, who felt his honour
violated, was beside himself with rage. Clutching a *wang's*
severed head, he went in search of Li with murder in his
heart. But Li had wisely bolted. Gordon resigned on the

spot and, carrying the *wang*'s head with him, he stormed back to Shanghai, where he sulked in his quarters for two months.

Li did all in his power to woo this Achilles from his tent. On 1 January 1864 a procession led by a mandarin appeared at Gordon's door bearing open boxes filled with silver and a letter written by the Emperor of China himself. Gordon scornfully refused the silver and was unmoved by the letter. In an effort to please him, Li paid bonuses to the Ever Victorious Army and presented handsome sums to its wounded. Gordon was adamant. It was not until Li issued a formal proclamation exonerating Gordon from all complicity in the murder of the *wangs* that he was moved to reflect that, after all, if he did not return, the Taipings would probably win back all the towns he had wrenched from them, the rebellion would drag on and thousands of people would be needlessly killed. In fact, he found the excitements of war too intoxicating to give up for long.

On 19 February 1864 Gordon, now thirty-one years old, resumed his command as general of the Chinese mercenary army. When his troops threatened to mutiny because he forbade them to sack a town, he again snatched one man from the ranks and had him shot. Gordon now plotted his strategy for completing the destruction of the Taipings. In the next few months he did indeed repeat his earlier successes. Except for two minor reverses and a wound in the leg for Gordon, all had proceeded with bloody efficiency as the Ever Victorious marched on the Taiping capital of Nanking. There was no further trouble from General Ching, for Ching had been killed in battle. Gordon cried when he heard the news.

In a letter dated 10 May 1864 Gordon described the campain to his mother:

> The losses I have sustained in this campaign have been no joke: out of 100 officers I have had 48 killed and wounded; and out of 3,500 men nearly 1,000 killed and wounded; but I have the

satisfaction of knowing that as far as mortal can see, six months will see the end of this rebellion, while if I had continued inactive it might have lingered on for six years. . . . I know I shall leave China as poor as I entered it, but with the knowledge that through my weak instrumentality upwards of eighty to one hundred thousand lives have been spared. I want no further satisfaction than this.

The day after writing this letter Gordon fought his last battle in China. His fifteen months as a Chinese general ended when the British government withdrew permission for its officers to serve in Chinese armies. Gordon, convinced that no one but he could command the Ever Victorious Army and unwilling to turn it over to anyone else, disbanded it – against the wishes of the Shanghai merchants and even of the British minister. However, it no longer mattered: the back of the rebellion had been broken and the Imperial forces, without Gordon's aid, fought their way into Nanking. In the Taiping palace they found the Heavenly King hanging by the neck from a silk cord. Around him hung all his wives.

From this time on Gordon was known to the press and the public as Chinese Gordon. The Chinese made him a Ti Tu mandarin, the highest military rank, and rewarded him with a gold medal, a yellow jacket and permission to wear a peacock's feather. He declined another small fortune that was offered him. His own government was less generous. He had been promoted lieutenant-colonel on 16 February 1864 and now was made a Companion of the Bath. Gordon's feelings about honours and rank were ambivalent: 'I had rather be dead than praised', he once said. Still, such protestations were always most vehement when he felt neglected.

In January 1865 Gordon returned to England – and to six years of routine postings and obscurity. In fact, in the next twenty-one years the War Office never entrusted him with the command of British troops on active service.

Chinese Gordon *(Photo: National Army Museum)*

3

In 1865, after a restless seven months' leave at home, Gordon was appointed Engineer Commanding at Gravesend, where he spent most of his time superintending the construction of forts for the defence of the Thames. The passion with which he had pursued war was now directed towards religion and the care of young boys.

He read the Bible daily, paying particular attention to his favourite part, the Book of Isaiah, which he was fond of quoting, though he appears never to have considered beating his sword into a ploughshare. He prayed a great deal, and in a special book he kept a list of all his enemies, for whom he prayed most fervently. He handed out religious tracts or left them where they might be found; when travelling by train, he tossed them out the window. When his sister Augusta came to visit him, they prayed together and had long discussions concerning the vileness of their bodies and of the glory that would be theirs when their souls were released from the prison of the flesh. Still, he had no qualms about killing in war, nor did he ever for long deny himself the pleasures of cigars and brandy. And he found nothing unwholesome in his delight in young boys.

Gordon's religious beliefs were idiosyncratic. He believed in predestination: 'I believe that not a worm is picked up by a bird without the direct intervention of God'. Yet he also believed in man's free will. He recognized the conflicting nature of these beliefs, but said simply, 'I cannot and do not pretend to reconcile the two'. At the same time he developed a fatalism, often punctuating his writings with 'D.V.' *(Deo volente):* he would be 'home by Christmas (D.V.)'.

He did not hesitate to quiz others. 'Do you believe in Jesus?' he frequently demanded of total strangers, and at least once of a Catholic priest. If his victims answered yes, he pressed on: 'Then do you know that God lives in you?' A mini-sermon often followed. Gordon could be tiresome.

At Gravesend he took in boys off the streets and waterfront, turned his home into a school, hospital and church for them. He fed and clothed them, preached to them, mothered them, played with them and, when they grew older, found work for them, often berths on merchant ships; over his mantelpiece he hung a map of the world with pins indicating where his boys – 'kings', he called them – were located. On a visit to Scotland he wrote to Augusta, 'I believe there are many Kings (red-haired) about, but I cannot get at them with facility'. When he became depressed, as he frequently did, the arrival of a new boy would wipe away the gloom, and he would hasten to write to Augusta about him. ('A country lad of our Lord, a Hebrew, fourteen years old, has fallen to me'.) He sometimes bathed new boys himself, and after scrubbing them vigorously would stand them naked before a mirror to observe themselves while he delivered a homily on the beauty of joining a clean mind to their freshly clean bodies.

From time to time newspaper articles appeared suggesting that more active employment be found for Chinese Gordon – after all, there was not a year in Queen Victoria's long reign when her soldiers were not fighting someone somewhere – but the government paid no heed. In October 1871 he was appointed to a commission to study ways and means of improving the mouth of the Danube and then to a committee that reported on the condition of British cemeteries in the Crimea. On 16 February 1872 he was promoted colonel. Returning from the Crimea in the summer of that year, he met at Constantinople Nubar Pasha, a shrewd Egyptian diplomatist and politician who three times became prime minister of his country. Wolseley once described him as 'a cunning old fox who is striving to run with the hare and hunt with the hounds'. Nubar asked Gordon to recommend someone to replace Sir Samuel Baker as governor of the Equatorial Provinces of the Sudan. The ever-impulsive Gordon immediately recommended himself. A year later the British government gave its approval; in September 1873 the Khedive of Egypt formally offered him the post; and on 28 January 1874, his forty-first birth-day, Gordon set off for central Africa.

4

Egypt had conquered the Sudan, more or less, in the 1820s. It was a vast land of almost a million square miles, mostly swamp and jungle in the south and desert in the north. The south, filled with primitive peoples, was the haunt of Arab slave hunters from the north; indeed, capturing, buying and selling slaves was the principal occupation of those inhab-itants who were not themselves slaves. Even some slaves were involved in the business, for armed slaves were used to hunt down potential slaves.

The governorship of the southernmost provinces was hardly a plum appointment, but it paid well: £10,000 a year. Gordon created a stir by refusing to accept that much, say-ing that £2,000 was quite sufficient. He created another commotion when he arrived in Cairo and arranged for Abu Saud, a notorious slaver and confirmed rascal, to be released from prison and appointed to his staff. Abu Saud had caused endless difficulties for Gordon's predecessor, Sir Samuel Baker, who had taken some pains to put him behind bars, and an astonished and indignant Sir Samuel wrote an angry letter to *The Times* protesting his release; Gordon ignored the tempest.

Abu Saud was not the only queer fish Gordon added to his staff. Among others were Lieutenant-Colonel Charles Chaillé-Long, an American explorer, soldier and adven-turer; Romolo Gessi, an Italian revolutionary who had served with Garibaldi; E. Linant de Bellefonds, son of a distinguished French engineer; and John Russell, son of William Howard Russell, the famous war correspondent. Young Russell, a drunkard and a sponger, was probably the worst of the lot; even his father said of him, 'I fear he is beyond help and have little hope. . . . the same story – idle-ness, self-indulgence, gambling and constant promises'.

Gordon was never a good judge of men.

Chaillé-Long described how he was recruited. While eating a late supper after the theatre in Cairo, he was brought a note: 'Will you come with me to Central Africa? Come and see me at once. Very truly, C.G. Gordon'. Chaillé-Long left his supper and joined Gordon, who offered him a brandy from a bottle standing beside an open Bible. 'You are to go with me as chief of staff', Gordon said brusquely. 'You will command the soldiery. I don't want the bother'.

Chaillé-Long was full of questions, but Gordon answered curtly with obvious impatience and announced that they would leave the following night. Chaillé-Long protested that he could not possibly leave so soon, as he had no kit. Gordon, annoyed, threw him a pair of boots, insisted that he try them on, declared them a perfect fit and seemed to feel that the problem was solved. With difficulty Chaillé-Long held out for one more day to collect his kit before Gordon hustled him out with orders to hurry.

As he and his staff made their way south, Gordon was sanguine. He anticipated no problems with slavers or with the natives or with his work. Critics and carpers in London and Cairo did not bother him at all, for he had come to believe more and more that, whatever trouble he might get into, God would take him out of it – an attitude that eventually led to his destruction.

Instead of travelling by the most direct route up the Nile, Gordon chose to take himself and his staff by the longer but in many ways easier route, sailing round to Suakin on the Red Sea and from there making their way with an escort of 200 Egyptian soldiers across the desert to Berber and then south to Khartoum, capital of the Sudan, which they reached on 13 March 1874. Ismail Ayub Pasha, the governor-general, greeted Gordon and his staff warmly and entertained them with a lavish dinner. This was followed by a performance by nubile dancing girls wearing nothing more than bangles and a thin strip of leather around their waists. One of Gordon's officers, carried away by the wine and the undulating flesh, flung himself into the dance. Ayub Pasha delightedly jumped to his feet to join what promised to be an orgy, but a disgusted Gordon abruptly pushed back his chair and strode out of the room.

Gordon paused only a week in Khartoum, but from there he issued his first decree, proclaiming that henceforth the ivory trade was to be a government monopoly and that it was now forbidden to import gunpowder or to recruit organized armed bands, such as the ones slavers employed, in the Equatorial Provinces. He then made his way by pad-die-steamer through the wild, sweltering swamplands, the Sudd, to his own provincial capital at Gondokoro. He was so eager to reach it that the leisurely progress of the steamer enraged him. He demanded more speed, and then more. When the captain at last protested that his ship had reached its limit, Gordon slapped him in the face.

Gondokoro was in the heartland of the slave hunters' preserve. Gordon, who saw his primary mission as the suppression of the slave trade, found his work beset with difficulties. He was appalled by the steaming climate, the pulsating insect life and the wretchedness of the people. To Augusta he wrote:

> What a mystery, is it not, why they are created! – a life of fear and misery night and day! One does not wonder at their not fearing death. No one can conceive the utter misery of these lands – heat and mosquitoes day and night all year round. But I like the work, for I believe that I can do a great deal to ame-liorate the lot of the people.

To do good work in such a land with so few trustworthy lieutenants to help him proved almost impossible. Eight European members of his staff died, including a nephew, Willie Anson, in the first year. The Egyptians he had brought with him proved to be cowardly, deceitful, incompetent, idle and corrupt; one captain sold six of his own men into slavery. Gordon dashed futilely about his barbarous province freeing slaves, building forts, trying to create some useful public works, trying to correct long-standing abuses and trying to inculcate Christian morals in people to whom such notions were alien.

There were entrenched interests in the southern Sudan – slave traders, tribal chiefs, Egyptian officials, witch doctors – and he managed to alienate them all. Not surprisingly, he often felt discouraged; failures bore heavily on a man prone to severe depression. When Chaillé-Long came to complain about one of Gordon's rash acts, Gordon said quietly, 'I've been very low, old fellow. Don't be hard on me. This is a terrible country'.

The bitterest pill of all was his failure to suppress the slave trade. When he found gangs of slaves, he struck off their chains – that much was simple – but the freed slaves often did not know the way back to their homes; spoke only their tribal language and were frequently in wretched physcial condition. It was a puzzle to know what to do with them; they often became, in effect, the slaves of his own government. They merely changed masters. The women held no interest for him – 'They are all black and uncouth creatures, they do not like anything but themselves' – but he did acquire for himself two slave boys. It was an annoying but indisputable fact that the ablest, most intelligent people in his province were the Arab slavers. After imprisoning them for a suitable time, he often tried to enlist them, and this aroused the distrust of the local tribes whose confidence and trust he had been striving to cultivate. Abu Saud had to be thrown in prison; he was soon released, but then was imprisoned again, for he was hopelessly corrupt.

Gordon's temper, ever short, became shorter. A hasty, seemingly ungovernable temper was a lifelong failing. To the Sudanese his edicts and behaviour seemed bizarre; even loyal European members of his staff found it difficult to work for a manic–depressive governor who viewed himself as God's servant in a pagan land. He ignored all advice he found unpalatable. When he had decided upon an action, it never occurred to him that any discussion was possible; he was firmly determined – until he changed his mind.

In this slow, backward province, where only violence was swift, terror reigned. There were fears of slavers, of the climate, of wild animals and ferocious insects and of the nameless diseases in all their varied horrors. For those few who, like Gordon, were not tormented by fear, despair usually displaced terror. Gordon often shut himself in his tent or hut, setting outside an axe with a flag attached as a sign that he was not to be disturbed. Brandy and the Bible provided support. He was a poor administrator; he could not delegate; he complained, insulted and nagged. He was often unreasonable and usually domineering. Faced with a problem, he would consult the Prophet Isaiah for guidance or simply open the Bible at random and seek a solution in what he read there. Little wonder that his staff and his subjects found him inscrutable.

He alternately raged at his officers and officials and begged their forgiveness for his rudeness. He quarrelled vociferously with those around him and by letter with his superiors in Khartoum, Cairo and London. He threatened to resign but did not; he resigned and then withdrew his resignation. He found it impossible to go on, and impossible to admit failure. It took three years for him to arrive at the only solution that would both release him from an impossible situation and satisfy his *amour propre:* he wondrously concluded that he could succeed only if he was promoted to governor-general of the entire Sudan. When the Khedive refused to consider such a thing, Gordon resigned and at the end of 1876 left for England. Behind him were his meagre accomplishments: a bit more territory explored, a few miserable forts, several thousand bewildered, homeless, freed slaves – and still the thriving slave trade he had found when he arrived.

5

Gordon's return shocked the British public. Anti-slavery sentiments were popular, and his attempts to suppress the slave trade had been much admired. Consequently, his accomplishments had been exaggerated in the press and his failures unremarked. In a short time both the British government and the Khedive were pressing him to return. He refused; he had made his terms clear: he would be governor-general of the entire Sudan or nothing. The Khedive surrendered. Gordon had been in England only about two months when he was offered the post he had demanded. His orders set forth three objectives: improvement of communications, suppression of the slave trade and settlement of a border dispute between the Khedive and King Johannis of Abyssinia. He decided to tackle the latter problem first.

His orders from the Khedive were brief and suitably vague: 'Il y a sur la frontière d'Abyssinie des disputes; je vous charge de les arranger'. Gordon's solution to the Egyptian–Abyssinian frontier problems was a rough and ready one. Instead of negotiating a treaty with King Johannis, he helped Walad el Michael, a contender for the throne, to establish a separate government – an arrangement sure to keep the two occupied with each other and not with the affairs of Egypt in the Sudan. Gordon Pasha (as he was now styled) then set off for Khartoum and was formally installed there as governor-general on 5 May 1877.

Gordon was a dreamer, a religious fanatic and an eccentric; he was often foolhardy, but he was not a fool – at least not always. His greatest concern and desire were to suppress slavery, but he was realistic enough to understand that slavery was the keystone of the economy of the Sudan and that any tampering with it had to be carried out with caution in order to avoid ripping apart the social fabric of the country and ruining the economy. He made no attempt to interfere with domestic slavery, and when he learned that Catholic missionaries were in the habit of giving asylum to runaway slaves, he ordered them to stop doing so. When they refused, he wrote directly to the Pope, asking him to restrain his priests from interfering with his government. Forced to accept domestic slavery, he could and did strike out against slave hunters. These he refused to tolerate.

Unlike his predecessors, Gordon had a conception of his duties that went beyond sitting in Khartoum and issuing edicts. He dashed about suppressing minor revolts, settling disputes between tribes, rebuking corrupt Egyptian officials and attacking the camps of slave raiders. He was an impatient man in a hurry. Inaction was intolerable. 'It is lamentable work', he wrote, 'and over and over again, in the fearful heat, I wish I was in the other world . . . this inaction, with so much to do elsewhere, is very trying indeed to my body. It is such a country, so worthless, and I see nothing to be gained by its occupation'.

In the westernmost reaches of the Sudan, Suleiman Zubair, pretender to the ancient sultanate of Darfur, threatened to raise the standard of revolt. He had grown rich and powerful through slave hunting and slave selling. Some 6,000 slaves were enlisted in his private army or as personal retainers, and with these he raided and plundered with impunity. Gordon could never rule the entire Sudan until Suleiman Zubair was brought to heel. It was typical of Gordon's thinking to believe that this could best be done by a direct, face-to-face encounter with the slaver.

He set out by camel through Kordofan with an escort of 200, whom he frequently outstripped, for he hated the normally slow pace of the camel:

> I got to Dara about 4 p.m., long before my escort, having ridden eighty-five miles in a day and a half. About seven miles from Dara I got into a swarm of flies, and they annoyed me and my camel so much, that we jolted along as fast as we could.

Upward of 300 were on the camel's head and I was covered with them. If I had no escort of men, I had a large escort of these flies. I came upon my people like a thunderbolt. As soon as they had recovered, the salute was fired. My poor escort! Where is it? Imagine to yourself a single, dirty, red-faced man on a camel, ornamented with flies, arriving in the divan all of a sudden. The people were paralysed, and could not believe their eyes.

This was typical Gordon drama. He vastly enjoyed the astonishment he created by such unexpected arrivals. The very next day he repeated his performance in perhaps the bravest, or most foolhardy, act of his career. He rose at dawn, arrayed himself in a dazzling dress uniform and with a small escort burst into the camp of Zubair's son – 'a nice looking lad of twenty-two years' – and rode straight to his tent. Later Gordon delightedly described the event to Augusta:

There were about 3000 of them – men and boys. . . . the whole body of chiefs were dumbfounded at my coming among them. After a glass of water, I went back, telling the son of Sebehr [Zubair] to come with his family to my divan. They all came, and sitting there in a circle, I gave them in choice Arabic my ideas: That they meditated revolt; that I knew it, and that they should now have my ultimatum, viz.: that I should disarm them and break them up. They listened in silence, and then went off to consider what I had said. They have just now sent in a letter stating their submission, and I thank God for it.

This was Gordon theatre at its best.

His excursions and surprises engrossed him, while in Khartoum the machinery of government sputtered along. Gordon made no attempt to direct the bureaucracy or to delegate executive authority. He was incapable of either. On the other hand, the Sudanese admired courage and dash; Gordon was their kind of leader, and he earned their respect as no bureaucrat ever could. They admired him for what he was rather than for his accomplishments, which, in truth,

were minor and transitory. Curiously, this was also true of
his own countrymen. Evelyn Wood summed up the opinion
of many of those who knew Gordon when he said, 'I think
his heart is better than his head'. But it was also Wood who
in old age wrote, 'Gordon was certainly the nearest approach
to a saint that I have met in a long life, in spite of his many
mistakes'.

Off on the Abyssinian frontier, Walad el Michael was
causing trouble, and again Gordon went to deal with him,
riding straight into his camp, trusting to God, surprise and
his own audacity. He was on his way back to Khartoum by
way of Suakin when he received a curious message from
the Khedive, who asked for his help on a serious and immediate problem. It had occurred to the Khedive, always
plagued by debts, that the man who seemed to be so successful in sorting out the tangled intrigues in the Sudan
might also be able to sort out his tangled financial affairs.
Would Gordon come to Cairo and settle his British and
French creditors as he had settled the slavers, rebels and
wild chiefs of the Sudan?

Gordon knew absolutely nothing of finance, personal or
public; he had neither an interest in nor an understanding
of money; he could not even keep straight his personal
finances. Nevertheless, with that supreme confidence he
never lost, he had no doubt that he could handle the Khedive's finances, and he accepted the challenge. He had no
fear of financiers and diplomatists, but he did dread the
social life of the Egyptian capital: 'The idea of dinners in
Cairo makes me quail', he wrote. His worst fears were realized. No sooner had he arrived in Cairo than he was whisked
straight from the railway station to the palace, where dinner with the Khedive awaited him.

6

Gordon was appointed to a commission of inquiry into
Egypt's finances. It was hoped that this commission would

be able to recommend solutions to the country's problems. Gordon agreed with the Khedive that the villains were the four European Commissioners of the Debt (British, French, Italian and Austrian), who were responsible to the holders of European bonds for the collection of the annual seven per cent interest, which ammounted to five-sixths of the country's tax revenues. Like many Third World countries today, Egypt was so deeply in debt and its bureaucracy was so hopelessly corrupt that it could never hope to reduce the principal; it was an annual struggle to find the money to pay the interest. Gordon was soon caught up in a web of diplomacy, intrigue and high finance – little of which he understood.

It was at this time that he first met Sir Evelyn Baring (later Lord Cromer), British agent and consul-general with plenipotentiary rank, who was to achieve fame as the maker of modern Egypt. Gordon correctly summarized their relationship: 'When oil mixes with water, we will mix together'. Baring was astute, sensible and analytical; Gordon was impulsive, heedless and decisive. Gordon considered Baring to be 'pretentious, grand and patronizing'. Baring at once saw that Gordon was 'not fitted to conduct any financial inquiry'. But it was Gordon who cut through all arguments with a straightforward solution: suspend payment of the next instalment of interest, reduce the rate to three per cent and send the debt commissioners packing. Such a resolution hardly seems radical today, but in those times, when it was still universally believed that countries as well as individuals should pay their debts, it was shocking. (It would be only another fifty years before both France and Great Britain entirely repudiated their war debts to the United States.) The Khedive felt himself unable to accept Gordon's recommendations in the face of the many pressures upon him, particularly from the British government. Gordon went back to the Sudan, and the Egyptian fellahin were lashed to pay the taxes needed to satisfy Egypt's creditors.

Back in Khartoum, Gordon found that Zubair had revolted, and he dispatched an expedition under Romolo Gessi to put down the uprising. Gessi succeeded: Zubair was exiled, and his son was captured and executed. Gordon continued to dash about from place to place, but the exertions of his life were beginning to exact their toll. In three years he had travelled nearly 8,000 miles on camels. Among other ills, he was suffering from angina pectoris. When he learned that the Khedive Ismail had been deposed and replaced by the Khedive Tewfik, he resigned and on 24 August 1879 arrived back in Cairo.

He had several meetings with the new Khedive and, to his surprise, he liked him. Khedive Tewfik asked him to undertake another mission to Abyssinia. King Johannis was becoming belligerent, and the Khedive wanted Gordon to cobble together a peace without yielding Egyptian territory or compromising Egyptian interests. Gordon accepted the challenge and set off on the journey, an arduous one over difficult terrain among unfriendly peoples. For many nights he slept out in the open in all sorts of weather. He suffered from boils, prickly heat and 'palpitations of the heart'. Along the way he was subjected to insults and arrest, and – almost worse in his opinion – he was forced to endure long interviews with Abyssinian generals and officials. When he and King Johannis at last met, the two men, alike in so many ways, detested each other on sight. At their first meeting Gordon found to his exasperation that he had been seated some distance from the King. Without a word and to the scandal of the court, he picked up his chair and moved it closer to the throne. 'Do you known that I may kill you for this?' Johannis asked. Gordon replied coldly; 'I do not fear death'. Like Gordon, Johannis was a religious fanatic and had his own notions of justice: he cut off the noses of those caught taking snuff and the lips of those caught smoking. Gordon described him as 'of the strictest sect of Pharisee – drunk every night, at dawn he is reading Psalms'.

The mission accomplished nothing. By 2 January 1880

Gordon was back in Cairo. He stayed less than a week, but in that time he picked a quarrel with Sir Evelyn Baring, curtly refused Khedive Tewfik's request that he return to the Sudan, embarrassed Sir Edward Malet, the British consul, by appearing unexpectedly as the thirteenth guest for a dinner party, and threatened to challenge Nubar Pasha to a duel for having made a disparaging remark about H.C. Vivian, the former British consul. Vivian, like Gordon, was a Companion of the Bath, and Gordon stormed, 'I will not permit anyone to speak in such a way of a man who belongs to the same order of knighthood as I do'. Malet and others tried to calm him, but he was obdurate; there would be an apology or a fight. To the relief of everyone except Gordon, Nubar Pasha apologized.

On 10 January Gordon sailed for England. British and Egyptian officials and diplomatists were not sorry to see the back of this peculiar soldier, a living anachronism who still entertained medieval concepts of chivalric orders.

7

Gordon, man of boundless energy, was now idle. He visited his family, prayed with Augusta, quarrelled with various bureaucrats, took his nephew to Switzerland and then accepted a post for which he possessed neither the talent nor the temperament: that of private secretary to Lord Ripon, the new viceroy of India. Five days after his arrival in Bombay he resigned and, against the advice of the War Office, set off for China, where he attempted to prevent Li Hung Chang from starting a revolution and to dissuade the Manchu government from going to war with Russia. He next considered going to Australia, or perhaps to Borneo or Zanzibar; instead he went back to England.

In London he plagued the War Office and assorted politicians by bombarding *The Times* and other periodicals with sundry letters on the Irish famine, irregular warfare, the need for conscription to meet the German threat (then recognized by no one) and events in Afghanistan (of which he knew little). On a sudden impulse he volunteered for an assignment that promised to satisfy neither his military nor his religious aspirations: the command of the Royal Engineers on Mauritius. There in loneliness he fought his battles against the temptations of the flesh, struggling without success to give up cigars and brandy. As usual, his emotional life was one of tortured conflict. Augusta received regular reports.

Within a year he was promoted major-general and shortly afterwards took up a command in South Africa, where a Basuto rebellion was brewing. At Cape Town he started out badly. He told Augusta about it: 'I dined with Sir Hercules Robinson [the governor], trod on Lady Robinson's train going in to dinner, called her Lady Barker on going away – a person she hates – and spoke evil of several people in Hong Kong and elsewhere who have been kind to me'. Three weeks later, with his customary haste in leaping to conclusions, he decided that the Basutos had been wronged, that the British government had broken its word to them and had violated a treaty – a point of view unpopular with both British officials in South Africa and politicians at home. He was soon on his way back to England.

He paused only seven weeks in England before setting off on his own for Palestine. He wanted to withdraw from the world, to meditate and to study the topography of the Holy Land with his engineer's eyes and his Bible in his hand. In Palestine he was, for a time, completely absorbed: he located – at least to his own satisfaction – the boundary between the tribes of Benjamin and Judah and the exact sites of Golgotha, Zion and Tophet. In a more complex cosmogony, he fixed the point to which the devil fled: the furthermost spot on the globe from the throne of God. It was, he calculated, at 31°47'S, 144°45'W, close to the Bass Isles, south of Tahiti and not far from Pitcairn, where the mutineers from the *Bounty* had settled: the antipode of Palestine.

After a year of this religious engineering, Gordon suddenly accepted another unsuitable position: as second-in-command to Henry Morton Stanley, who was creating a private empire in the Congo for King Leopold II of Belgium. Gordon went to Brussels to confer with the King, and then to London, where he sent his resignation to the War Office. Wolseley, then adjutant-general, wrote to him saying, 'I hate the idea of your going to the Congo. Our very best man burying himself among niggers on the Equator. If ever I have the power, the first man I shall ask to take employment will be yourself'. There can be no doubt that two such strong-willed characters as Stanley and Gordon would not long have worked harmoniously together and that Gordon's stay in the Congo would have been brief, but this relationship was never put to the test.

Momentous events had taken place in the Sudan, which had passed, as had all of Egypt, under British control. A religious fanatic calling himself the Mahdi (Messiah) had gathered to himself an immense following and had declared himself the ruler of the province. He and his followers, known as Dervishes, had defeated the Egyptian armies sent against him, and the British government under Gladstone, faced with the responsibility of deciding whether the Sudan was worth the struggle required to keep it under Anglo-Egyptian control, had determined to abandon it. There remained the problem of evacuating the European and Egyptian soldiers and officials, many with families, who would be stranded there.

The day after sending in his resignation, Gordon was interviewed by W.T. Stead, the enterprising editor of the influential *Pall Mall Gazette,* and was asked his opinion of the government's decision. Gordon had a good deal to say – all off the top of his head, with little knowledge of the current state of affairs in the Sudan. He refused to believe that the Mahdi was a religious leader. The Sudanese, he said, were 'very nice people' who only needed good government to be content. 'You cannot evacuate', he said firmly. 'You must either surrender absolutely to the Mahdi or defend

Khartoum at all hazards'. He was confident that if Khartoum was properly fortified and stoutly defended the rebellion would quickly collapse. The interview was published under the heading 'GORDON ON THE SUDAN' and accompanied by a leader recommending that Gordon be sent at once to put matters right. Almost immediately there was a popular clamour. It suddenly seemed obvious to all that Gordon should be sent to save the Sudan. *The Times* and other important newspapers took up the cry 'Gordon for the Sudan!' Queen Victoria quite agreed and wondered why he had not been sent long ago.

Lord Grenville, the foreign secretary, having been told that Gordon 'always exercised a very remarkable influence over wild, uncontrollable, uncivilised peoples', arranged a meeting with him, to which he invited several other members of the Cabinet. Although in his interview with Stead Gordon had forcefully expressed himself as being opposed to abandoning the Sudan, he now, only ten days later, agreed to go to Khartoum to see how it could be accomplished. The Cabinet, whatever reservations some members may have had, gave him their blessing, but neglected to give him complete and precise instructions.

Gordon spent his last evening in London visiting friends and playing in the nursery with the baby of Viscount Esher. He was in a carefree mood, buoyant and bubbling. Later that evening he took a cab to Charing Cross station, where, under the gaslights, he was met by Lord Granville, who bought his ticket for the boat train; by Lord Wolseley, who gave him his own gold watch and all the cash he had in his pocket (Gordon had forgotten to bring money); and by the Duke of Cambridge, who opened the carriage door for him and helped him inside. And so, with the aid of these distinguished well-wishers, and swept up by his own volatile ideas, his conceit, the confidence of government, the tide of public opinion and the drama of it all, Gordon set off for the Sudan.

A few hours later, in a calmer moment, Granville asked

General Gordon and Colonel Stewart take leave of the Duke of
Cambridge and Lord Wolseley on their departure for the Sudan
(Photo: ILN Pic. Lib.)

a colleague, 'Are you sure we did not commit a gigantic
folly?'

8

'I never had such hard work, neither was I ever in a position of such difficulty, or in one involving such a continu-
ous strain on the mind, the nerves, and, I may add, the
temper, as during the first three months of the year 1884',
wrote Sir Evelyn Baring (by then Lord Cromer) on looking
back on an official career of nearly fifty years, of the time
when Gordon arrived to save the Sudan, or Khartoum, or
the Egyptians and Europeans there – it was never quite
clear in anyone's mind, least of all Gordon's.

Although Baring, as British agent, was the virtual ruler
of Egypt, he was not a sovereign, and he was responsible to
his own government in London. Left to himself and know-

ing Gordon, he would never have sent him back to the Sudan, but great pressure was put on him by Gladstone and Granville until reluctantly he gave way.

In Britain the dispatch of Gordon to the Sudan was universally acclaimed. Newspapers throughout the country gave their approval. Gladstone in the House of Commons called him a hero with a genius for handling oriental peoples. Lord Cairns in the House of Lords evoked cheers when he called him 'one of our national treasures'.

Perhaps everyone was so sanguine because each – Gordon, Baring, Gladstone and Granville included – entertained a different notion of what Gordon was supposed to do. Initially, the government had been cautious: Gordon was merely to report on the situation in the Sudan and recommend a method for the evacuation of the foreigners. This concept of his mission rapidly changed, not officially and not because of any new developments, but simply because everyone hoped for more. The stage was set for misunderstanding at best and catastrophe at worst.

Perhaps no one had higher hopes for the success of Gordon's mission than the Queen, who wrote to Gladstone, 'We must not let this fine and fruitful country, with its peaceful inhabitants, be left a prey to murder and rapine and utter confusion. It would be a *disgrace* to the British name, and the country will *not* stand it'. The Queen was perhaps the only person ever to call the Sudan fruitful or its inhabitants peaceful, but she was right, as she so often was, in gauging the national sentiment. No one in Britain knew much about the Sudan or, for that matter, about Gordon, but the public's enthusiasm, its faith in Britain's 'soldier–saint', was such that the purpose of his mission became coloured by what the public now demanded. Gordon would save the Sudan, avenge the defeats suffered at the hands of the Dervishes, capture or kill the Mahdi, quell the rebellion and restore Anglo-Egyptian rule. How he was to do this without troops or money, simply by the magnetism of his personality, was not clear. What the public expected came to be what Gordon himself believed he could accomplish and what the British government seemed vaguely to hope for. It was all a delusion.

In London, Gordon had readily agreed to place himself directly under the orders of Sir Evelyn Baring, but as he found it difficult to obey anyone, he was even more unlikely to obey Baring, whom he personally disliked. It seems never to have occurred to him even to consult Baring before proceeding to Khartoum. He planned to go by way of the Suez Canal to Suakin and then across the desert to Berber and south to Khartoum. Evelyn Wood, then sirdar (commander-in-chief) of the Egyptian army, intercepted him at Port Said. Wood carried with him a letter from Gordon's friend Major-General Gerald Graham, VC, who had been with him at Woolwich, in Chatham and in China. Graham strongly urged him to go first to Cairo and talk with Baring: 'Throw over all personal feeling, if you have any, and act like yourself with straightforward directness'. Gordon reluctantly agreed to follow his friend's advice.

Sir Evelyn Baring was under no illusion as to his influence over Gordon. In a letter to Granville he wrote, 'It is as well that Gordon should be under my orders, but a man who habitually consults the Prophet Isaiah when he is in difficulty is not apt to obey the order of any man'. Gordon had a novel approach to orders. His own were to be obeyed implicitly; those he received he regarded as mere guidelines, a basis for discussion or something that he might or might not consider at some later date.

Gordon had drafted a memorandum outlining what he intended to do in the Sudan. This included not only the evacuation of foreigners and the withdrawal of the Egyptian garrisons but also the replacement of the Egyptian government with Sudanese rulers, restoring to power the petty sultans and chiefs who had ruled before the Egyptian invasion sixty years earlier. This mad scheme reflected Gordon's ignorance of the authority and influence of the

Mahdi, who now controlled most of the Sudan and who had his own ideas of how it should be governed. It also ignored the fact that if Egypt had the power to give the country back to the sultans and chiefs, it would also have the power to retain its own control, which it obviously did not.

No one, either in Cairo or in London, understood the nature or the power of the revolution sweeping the Sudan. In spite of the years he had spent there and his putative understanding of the people, Gordon saw the Mahdi as another Heavenly King whose Dervishes would prove to be as venal as the Taipings had been.

In Cairo, Gordon chose to be charming: when he wanted to please, no one could be more pleasant. General William Butler once wrote, 'I met two men in my life who possessed this charm of conversation, Sir Garnet Wolseley and Charles Gordon, but in Gordon the gift was the greater'. Even Baring seemed for a time to believe in the seductive fantasies Gordon wove, and he wrote to Granville, 'He is certainly half-cracked, but it is impossible not to be charmed by the simplicity and honesty of his character. . . . My only fear is that he is terribly flighty and changes his opinions very rapidly'.

As the future ruler of the Sudan, once the Mahdi had been brushed aside, Gordon fixed upon an 18-year-old boy in the family of the deposed Sultan of Darfur whose ancestors had ruled the westernmost province of the Sudan for centuries. For some years the family had been living comfortably in exile in Cairo, where the young man had acquired forty-two wives and a confirmed taste for gin. Argued out of this choice, Gordon settled for Abu Shakour, a son of the last reigning sultan. Colonel J.D.H. Stewart, who was to accompany Gordon, thought him a 'common-looking, unintelligent, and badly-dressed native'. Smartened up in an impressive gold-laced uniform and adorned with the largest decoration that could be found, he was only slightly improved.

Gordon next informed the startled Baring that he was taking back with him yet another Sudanese notable, his old enemy Zubair, whose son had been executed on Gordon's orders. Gordon had once called him 'the greatest slave hunter that ever lived', but he now found that Zubair evoked a 'mystic feeling' and that he was, or would be, 'a capital general' with a 'capacity of government far beyond any other man in the Sudan'. Baring, aware of the political impact and the reaction that could be expected from influential anti-slavery societies, was horrified by the notion that Gordon, darling of the anti-slavery movement, would put in power a man who had been one of the world's most notorious slavers. However, he reluctantly concurred and passed the idea back to London. Granville, thoroughly alarmed, was ready to recall Gordon at once, but the Cabinet, after debating the matter, decided that it was too late to recall him, though they did forbid him to take Zubair to Khartoum. Queen Victoria, wiser than her ministers, wrote to Granville, 'Having placed entire confidence in Gordon, have you now decided to throw over his advice and that of Baring and risk loss of all the garrisons?'

Without Zubair, but with the title of governor-general, £100,000 in government credit, two proclamations from the Khedive, the newly crowned Sultan of Darfur in tow and boundless confidence in himself, Gordon left Cairo for the Sudan on the night of 26 January 1884. There was some delay at the railway station, for extra carriages had to be added for Shakour's twenty-six wives and their considerable quantities of luggage. The Sultan's magnificent uniform was almost forgotten, and there was much last-minute confusion until it was located. Gordon, however, was in high spirits, his blue eyes flashing with excitement. His final words to Nubar Pasha were 'I shall save the honour of Egypt'. Baring's thoughts and feelings were different: 'My own heart was heavy within me. I knew the difficulties of the task which had to be accomplished. I had seen General Gordon'.

General Gordon *(Photo: ILN Pic. Lib.)*

9

The long trip south was dull, but Gordon's fertile mind, working overtime, was teeming with plans and ideas. Colonel Stewart noted, 'Gordon is so full of energy and action that he cannot get along without doing something, and at present he revenges himself for his enforced inactivity by writing letters, dispatches, etc., and sending telegrams'. Indeed, Baring was soon overwhelmed by a 'large number of very bewildering and contradictory messages from General Gordon'.

Baring was not the only recipient of Gordon's flurry of letters and telegrams. He seems to have written or telegraphed to everyone he ever knew, spewing out whatever came into his head at the moment. To King Leopold of the Belgians he wrote that he planned to present him with the Equatorial Provinces. To a minor Egyptian official he wrote of his intention to go directly to the Mahdi's camp and confront him, making the kind of sudden, unexpected appearance which had so confounded his enemies in the past and in which he so delighted. When Baring got word of this, he explicitly ordered Gordon to do no such thing.

Good civil servant that Baring was, he felt compelled to keep Granville informed of Gordon's many schemes, and there was a blizzard of telegrams between Cairo and London. When Gordon was temporarily silenced by a broken telegraph line, his correspondents sighed with relief and Granville confided to Baring, 'I am not sure that the stoppage of communication with Gordon for a time is the greatest of misfortunes either for himself or for us'.

At the end of the railway line, when the Sultan of Darfur understood that the remainder of the journey was to be performed on camel-back through country whose inhabitants might not always be friendly, he refused to go any farther, and nothing could prevail upon him to change his mind. Leaving him and his harem to return eventually to the comforts of Cairo, Gordon and Stewart pushed on.

Gordon bore with him a firman from the Khedive, proclaiming Egypt's intention to abandon the Sudan. The discretion to use it or not was his. At Berber he rashly revealed it – a fatal mistake. With one stroke he lost the support of those sheikhs and tribes who might otherwise have remained loyal, and whose help was essential if he was to accomplish any part of his mission, and he pushed all those who were wavering in their allegiance into the arms of the Mahdi. It appears that Gordon, who could neither read nor write Arabic and spoke it execrably, had not bothered to inform himself of the firman's exact import. In his journal he wrote, 'I showed it, not knowing well its contents'.

Another decision taken at Berber, which made sense from a practical standpoint, created a furore in Britain. In the eyes of all influential Sudanese, one of the most objectionable aspects of Egyptian rule in the Sudan was the attempt to abolish the slave trade. It was certain to regain its vigour when Egypt withdrew. Gordon, recognizing that he would have no power to control the trade, tried to turn this weakness to his advantage by proclaiming, "Whoever has slaves shall have full right to their services and full control over them'. Baring supported him, but he then had to reply to a barrage of telegrams from an angry British press and a perplexed government. He coped as best he could; Gordon was unperturbed.

When, on 18 February 1884, Gordon arrived in Khartoum, he was greeted with tremendous enthusiasm. Many saw him as their saviour, but Frank Power, the young correspondent for *The Times* in Khartoum, wrote, 'He should have come a year ago: it is now too late'.

In his oscillation between reality and fantasy, brilliance and stupidity, sensitivity and callousness, Gordon occasionally put matters into a proper perspective and behaved with intelligence and sensibility. Such was the case during his first days in Khartoum. He dramatically announced the abolition of all taxes for two years, and he ordered the public burning of the hippopotamus-hide whips, stocks and other instruments of torture that had come to characterize Egyptian rule. He proclaimed, 'I come without soldiers, but with God on my side, to redress the evils of the Sudan. I will not fight with any weapons but justice'. Indeed, he had little else.

In a crude attempt to win over the Mahdi, Gordon sent him a red robe of honour, an elegant fez and an offer to make him sultan of the province of Kordofan. The Mahdi returned the gifts with a dignified reply addressed to 'The dear one of Britain and of the Khedive, Gordon Pasha':

> Know that I am the Expected Messiah, the Successor of the Apostle of Allah. Thus, I have no need of the sultanate, nor of the Kingdom of Kordofan or elsewhere, nor of the wealth of the world and its vanity. I am but the slave of Allah. . . .

This was the beginning of a brief correspondence in which the two fanatics tried to convert or intimidate each other. Both soon realized that such attempts were useless, and abandoned the correspondence.

Khartoum is located on a triangle of land formed by the confluence of the White and Blue Niles. As the capital of the province, it contained the palace of the governor-general, all the government buildings and the homes of Egyptian officers and officials and those of the more prosperous Arabs and Sudanese. With rivers on two of its three sides, it was in a good defensive position, and it was protected by stout walls. Across the White Nile was the sprawling Sudanese town of Omdurman, larger and less prosperous. Its fort on the bank of the river was designed to help protect Khartoum.

Gordon found enough Egyptian and Sudanese soldiers to hold Khartoum against a Mahdist attack and to man the fort at Omdurman, at least for the time being. He did not, however, have enough troops to take the offensive, and certainly not enough, as he now recommended to Baring, to 'smash the Mahdi'. Still, his fertile brain could dream of calling a large army into being, and he was still in contact with Cairo. One of his more bizarre schemes involved making an appeal to American and British millionaires for £300,000, which could be used to purchase the services of 3,000 troops from the Sultan of Turkey. His request for British or Turkish troops was refused, but there was a pressing need to convince the inhabitants of Khartoum that troops were on the way – or so Gordon believed. He announced that reinforcements would arrive within a few days, a lie he was to repeat many times in the next eleven months as the Dervishes closed in on him. Gladstone was alarmed: 'Gordon assumes a license of language to which we can hardly make ourselves party'. Gladstone's concern about Gordon's behaviour was only just beginning to be aroused.

Gordon's telegrams grew wilder and more delphic. Baring characterized them as 'hopelessly bewildering and contradictory'. He confessed to Granville, 'In dealing with his proposals it is often difficult to know what he means and still more difficult to judge what is really worthy of attention and what is more or less nonsense'. Back in London, Charles Dilke remarked that the Cabinet was 'evidently dealing with a wild man under the influence of that climate of Central Africa which acts upon the sanest man like strong drink'.

On 12 March all normal communication between Khartoum and Cairo was severed by the Dervishes, and a few days later the Mahdi's artillery was throwing shells into the centre of the town. One by one the Egyptian garrisons throughout the Sudan capitulated. On 26 May, Berber fell and Gordon was completely cut off from escape or hope of quick releif. With him in Khartoum were 25,000 civilians and 8,000 unhappy Egyptian soldiers. Sir Evelyn Baring later set forth concisely the situation as it affected the British:

> It was clear that Gordon's political mission had failed, and from that moment there only remained an important military decision to decide, viz., whether a British military force should or should not be sent to the relief of Khartoum.

Baring made his view clear to Granville: 'I do not think we can leave him stranded in Khartoum if from a military point of view it is at all possible to help him'. Gladstone disagreed, but public opinion was against him, and on 12 May a vote of censure was proposed in the House of Commons on the grounds that the government had failed to assist Gordon or provide for his safety. Gladstone argued that to send troops would be to wage 'a war of conquest against a people struggling to be free'. There were cries of 'Oh! oh!' but he persisted. 'Yes, these are people struggling to be free and they are struggling rightly to be free!' On the division the government's majority was only twenty-eight.

Certainly no one was more acutely aware of the desperate plight of Khartoum than Gordon, yet curiously he seemed at first actually to enjoy his predicament. His journals reveal his delight in the drama of the situation; there were no black moods, no sinking into the sloughs of despair; the daily operations involved in preparing the town's defences absorbed him. The more hopeless the situation appeared, the more cheerful he became. When the Mahdi moved the bulk of his forces to invest Khartoum, Gordon wrote in his journal, 'Somehow this advance of the Mahdi has raised my spirit'.

He spent hours on the roof of the palace, watching through a telescope he had mounted there the enemy's movements and the progress of his own men at the town's defences. When some of the Mahdi's artillery opened fire on the palace, he was indignant: 'This always irritates me, for it is so personal', he wrote in his journal.

A few Nile paddle-steamers still brought in food, though not enough to supply the town's needs. The steamers could have been used to escape, had Gordon chosen to do so. On 9 September he sent one steamer off with all the town's Europeans, including Colonel Stewart, Frank Power and the French consul. With them he sent a load of journals, dispatches, letters and, inexplicably, his cipher books.* Nine

---

* When Wolseley discovered that Gordon had sent away his cipher books, he wrote in his journal, 'That any man could have been so idiotic is to me a puzzle'.

days after leaving Khartoum, Stewart and Power were lured ashore by seemingly friendly tribesmen and murdered.

10

In England agitation for a relief expedition grew. 'Gordon is in danger', said Queen Victoria in a telegram to Lord Hartington. 'You are bound to try to save him'. The Cabinet was divided. Gladstone dragged his feet until public pressure became irresistible. There were mass meetings in Hyde Park and in Manchester; subscriptions were launched for a private relief force; and every newspaper, led by *The Times*, clamoured for government action. At last Parliament voted £300,000 for an expedition and chose Lord Wolseley to command it.

There was considerable debate among soldiers, politicians and others as to how the campaign was to be conducted and what route it should take. Not until 5 October did Wolseley's army begin its steady but slow advance 1,600 miles up the Nile. When Gordon learned through a smuggled message that the campaign was being called the Gordon Relief Expedition, he exploded, *'I will not allow that you come for ME. You come for the garrisons of the Soudan'*.

With the other Europeans gone and communications with the outside world becoming increasingly difficult, Gordon turned to his journals, pouring into them a great hodge-podge of thoughts and emotions. He made up his mind that he would never return to England, a decision he mentioned with satisfaction more than once: 'I dwell on the joy of never seeing Great Britain again, with its horrid, wearisome *dinner* parties. . . . I hope if any English general comes to Khartoum, he will not ask me to dinner. Why men cannot be friends without bringing their wretched stomachs in, is astounding'. He complained bitterly and often that Major Kitchener, who was charged with the task of getting messages in and out of Khartoum, did not sufficiently exert himself.

April 1884 *Punch* illustration of General Gordon at Khartoum

'*Mirage*'

GENERAL GORDON . . . 'What is it that I seem to see
Across the sand waste? Is it the quick gleam
Of English steel, or but a desert-dream?
Help – or that last illusion of distress,
The mocking Mirage of the wilderness?'

(Photo: Mary Evans Picture Library)

Just as Gordon learned that a relief force was on the way, the inhabitants of Khartoum ceased to believe in its existence. As the days passed, he spent much of his time on the roof with his telescope directed down the river, watching for its arrival. On 13 October he wrote in his journal, 'It is, of course, in the cards that Khartoum is taken under the nose of the expeditionary force, which will be *just too late*'.

Taking stock of the supplies of food and ammunition, Gordon estimated that he could hold out only until the end of November, but December arrived and the red Egyptian flag still flew over the palace. On 13 December he estimated that he could last ten days longer, after which, he said, 'the game is up'. Khartoum was in desperate straits. Still Gordon hung on. The fort at Omdurman, across the Nile from Khartoum, was forced, through lack of food, to surrender on 15 January 1885. Gordon sent away his last four steamers, and these reached the advance camp of the relief force on 21 January.

In Khartoum, hundreds lay in the streets, dead or dying from starvation. The Egyptian soldiers, who had existed on a diet of raw gum arabic, boiled strips of hide and crushed cores of palm trees, were emaciated and many were too weak to perform their duties. The feeling ran through the besieged town that Gordon had deceived them, as indeed he had.

On 15 January the principal men of the city were summoned to the palace and told by a spokesman that the relief force would arrive within twenty-four hours. Gordon could not bring himself to face them, but one determined merchant, Bordeini Bey, demanded to be taken to him. He found Gordon sitting disconsolately on a divan; he was smoking and there were two boxes of cigarettes in front of him. Gone was all the cheerful optimism and the overflowing energy. When he saw Bordeini Bey, he threw his fez across the room and exclaimed. 'What more can I say? I have nothing more to say. The people will no longer believe me. . . . now they must see that I tell them lies. If this, my last promise, fails, I can do nothing more. Go and collect all the people you

The fate of General Gordon at Khartoum *(Photo: Mary Evans Picture Library)*

can on the lines and make a good stand. Now leave me to smoke these cigarettes'. Bordeini Bey, who escaped to tell the tale, said, 'I could see he was in despair, and he spoke in a tone I had never heard before'. Bordeini Bey was the last man to see Gordon alive and tell of it.

Just before dawn on 26 January the Dervishes broke through at the weakest point of the defences and swarmed into the city. There was a wild flurry of gunfire, cries of pain and alarm: in two hours it was over. Gordon was killed – accounts vary exactly how – and his severed head was shown to one of the Mahdi's European captives for identification.

Two days later, on what would have been Gordon's fifty-second birthday, Sir Charles Wilson and two steamers loaded with soldiers arrived within sight of Khartoum. Seeing that the Egyptian flag no longer flew from the palace and coming under heavy fire from the shores, he turned his steamers about and ran downstream.

Telegraph keys were soon clicking: 'Too late!' British newspapers echoed the cry: 'Too late!' Evelyn Baring recorded the reaction: 'Rarely has public opinion in England been so deeply moved. . . . A wail of sorrow and disappointment was heard throughout the land'. Gladstone was blamed for having delayed the start of the relief expedition, and Queen Victoria sent him a telegram *en clair* for all to read: 'These news from Khartoum are frightful, and to think that all this might have been prevented and many precious lives saved by earlier action is too frightful'. Gladstone refused to accept the blame, but it made no difference. He was hissed at the theatre, and crowds in Downing Street hooted and jeered at him. A popular music-hall song predicted that in hell he would 'sit in state on a red hot plate between Pilate and Judas Iscariot'. The initials by which he had been affectionately known – G.O.M., for Grand Old Man – were reversed, and he was called M.O.G., Murderer Of Gordon. Soon afterwards, some of his closest colleagues turned against him in the House of Commons, and his government fell.

Frederick Roberts
(1832–1914)

'Little Bobs'

1

Frederick Sleigh Roberts was born in Cawnpore, India, on 30 September 1832, the first child of Lieutenant-Colonel (later General) Abraham Roberts by his second wife. Lieutenant-Colonel Roberts, forty-seven years old, then commanded the Bengal European Regiment in the army of the Honourable East India Company. In the First Afghan War he commanded a brigade and led it in the storming of the great fortress at Ghazni (23 July 1839).

Abraham Roberts first married in 1820. Seven years later his wife died, leaving him with three small children. In 1830 he married again: the widow of an army officer who herself had two children. Two years after Frederick was born, the couple had another child, Harriet, a cripple. In that same year Abraham Roberts brought his family to Britain on his first home leave in nearly thirty years. When he returned to India, he left his wife behind to bring up all seven children at Clifton, where he had purchased property.

Frederick was a delicate child. As an infant in India he had nearly died of 'brain fever', which cost him the sight of his right eye. After attending a private school in England for a few years, he entered Eton at the age of thirteen. His father, knowing the poor pay of the army, hoped that his son would become a clergyman or a lawyer. 'If Freddy is clever I hope he will not think of the Army', he wrote from India. But Freddy wanted nothing else. Fifty years later it would have been impossible for him to have considered the army as a career, even as a private, for in addition to having only one seeing eye the fully grown Roberts stood only five feet three inches tall. However, in those relaxed days such matters could be overlooked in a young man of good family with solid army connections. Young Roberts was clever enough, and, more important, his father was a general and a gentleman. At sixteen he entered the Royal Military College, Sandhurst, expecting in two years' time to hold the Queen's commission, but his father, strained financially, and well aware that no officer stationed in England could hope to live on his salary, decided that he should join the Indian army. So on 1 February 1850 he entered the Honourable East India Company's own school at Addiscombe, near Croydon.

Those who passed out of Addiscombe at the head of their class were appointed to the engineers, those next highest went to the artillery and the rest to cavalry and infantry. General Roberts promised his son £100 and a gold watch if he passed into the engineers and £50 and a gold watch if he passed into the artillery. Thus inspired, young Roberts passed out ninth in a class of forty and, richer by a gold watch and £50, became a gunner second lieutenant on 12 December 1851; his commission was signed by Lord Dalhousie. It was the beginning of a career that spanned well over half a century.

On 20 February 1852 the 19-year-old officer set sail for

India. If he survived for ten years, he might hope to return to England on leave. After a journey of forty-one days, he arrived in Calcutta on 1 April. From there he went to Dum Dum, headquarters of the Bengal artillery, where he stayed for four months until General Roberts arranged for his son to join him at Peshawar on the North-West Frontier. Young Roberts spent a year with his father, serving both as his aide-de-camp and as a battery officer before ill health forced General Roberts to retire to England.

Although he was small, Roberts was sturdy and well-knit, but he suffered much from digestive ailments. A bottle of sherry, considered a sovereign remedy for such problems, stood ever ready by his bed. He also suffered from a peculiar aversion: he loathed cats and found it impossible to force himself to touch or even look at one. His colleagues, who called him 'Bobs' or 'Little Bobs', found him to be always fastidious in his dress and friendly in manner.

He decided from his first sight of the elite Bengal Horse Artillery, with their smart turn-out and picturesque uniforms, 'to leave no stone unturned in the endeavour to become a horse gunner'. In 1854 he got his wish and was posted to a battery in Peshawar. It was largely composed of Irishmen, most of whom, said Roberts, 'could have lifted me up with one hand'. He did not long remain a battery officer; it was as a quartermaster that he advanced in his career. This staff function then included not only supply but also training, intelligence and operations.

2

On 10 May 1857, when the great Indian Mutiny began in Meerut, there were 257,000 Indian and Gurkha troops and only 34,000 British troops in India. This upheaval was not, as many Indian nationalists today contend, a political revolution, but a mutiny of a portion of the Bengal army. It was nevertheless a frightening episode for the British, and it shook the Empire.

In the Punjab there were 65,000 Indian troops of uncertain loyalty and 16,000 British troops. Fortunately for the British, a number of exceptionally capable men were there, including Herbert Edwardes, John Nicholson, Neville Chamberlain (no relation to the late prime minister) and Sydney Cotton – all famous on the North-West Frontier and soon to gain wider fame when, backed by Chief Commissioner Sir John Lawrence, they saved the Punjab.

Roberts was also there, of course, and after more than five years' service was still a subaltern, but he had served several senior commanders as deputy assistant quartermaster general (DAQMG) and had begun to make a name for himself as a keen staff officer. He was not, as a staff officer, spared the rigours and dangers of campaigns, for staff officers were not then always tied to desks; their duties took them where the fighting was fiercest, and they had, if anything, a better than usual chance to distinguish themselves in battle.

When a 'movable column' was formed under Brigadier Neville Chamberlain, Roberts was delighted to be appointed to his staff. The movable column consisted of two batteries of light artillery and the 52nd Light Infantry (all British), a wing of Bengal cavalry and the 35th Bengal Native Infantry, a regiment thought to be loyal. Its mission was to descend quickly upon disaffected regiments and disarm them. The disarmed line regiments were then to be replaced by newly raised regiments of Pathans. It was always a delicate matter to disarm a regiment, and much depended upon surprise. The first troops to be disarmed were four of the five Indian regiments stationed at Peshawar, and the success in accomplishing this was a sign to the Pathan tribesmen that the British were going to be the winners in this contest and that they had better not side with the mutineers.

It would appear that the letter writers among the Indian troops believed in the inviolability of the British postal system and entertained a belief, proved to be mistaken, that

Mutineers blown from the guns *(Photo: National Army Museum)*

the English sahibs did not read other people's letters. However, acting with dispatch, the army authorities in the Punjab seized the mail, read the soldiers' letters and were therefore able to make a fairly accurate assessment of the extent of the conspiracy and to separate those regiments which were disaffected from those which were resisting the call of their mutinous comrades.

On 2 June the movable column arrived at Lahore, where some regiments had already been disarmed. Here, during the night, a loyal Indian soldier informed Roberts that the 35th Bengal Native Infantry would mutiny at dawn. Roberts promptly roused the sleeping Chamberlain, who at once ordered the regiment to parade. Two men found with loaded muskets were placed under arrest. The next day they were tried by court martial and sentenced to be blown from guns. Roberts described this awesome procedure:

The troops were drawn up so as to form three sides of a square; on the fourth side were two guns. As the prisoners were being brought to the parade, one of them asked me if they were going to be blown from guns. I said, 'Yes'. He made no further remark, and they both walked steadily on until they reached the guns, to which they were bound, when one of them requested that some rupees he had on his person might be saved for his relations. The Brigadier answered: 'It is too late!' The word of command was given; the guns went off simultaneously, and the two mutineers were launched into eternity.

It was a terrible sight, and one likely to haunt the beholder for many a long day; but that was what was intended.

Roberts was to become one of the best-loved generals of his day, recognized for his kindness and compassion, but, as Ian Hamilton said, he was 'practised to his finger tips'; he never allowed his feelings to interfere in any way with his duty – and he was never in doubt as to where his duty lay. At Lahore that day he pushed his own reactions aside to watch the response of the 35th Regiment when with a roar the cannons spewed bloody and blackened pieces of their comrades over the parade-ground:

> I watched the sepoys' faces to see how it affected them. They were evidently startled at the swift retribution, but looked more crestfallen than shocked or horrified, and we soon learnt that their determination to mutiny, and make the best of their way to Delhi, was in no wise changed by the scene they had witnessed.

The firmness of the authorities in the Punjab was not always repeated elsewhere. Many commanders of Indian regiments could not believe that their men would mutiny, and some paid for this trust with their lives. Roberts had no sympathy for the mutineers and, like many other officers, was angry with his own government when it showed them any leniency. In a letter home he wrote:

The 19th Light Infantry was disbanded . . . for gross mutiny but our imbecile Government, instead of treating the men as mutiners, paid them up, let them keep their *uniforms*!! and saw them safely across the river. The General Officer, poor fellow!! on reading the order to dismiss them shed tears!!

3

Delhi was the focal point of the Mutiny. Such forces as the British could muster had assembled outside the city, but they were not strong enough either to penetrate the defences or to invest it completely. On 8 June they seized a ridge just north of the city, and there they dug in their heels, resisting all efforts of the mutineers to dislodge them. When the word went out that artillery officers were urgently needed at Delhi, Roberts at once volunteered. When accepted, he set off immediately, leaving his tent, gear and servants to follow. He arrived at the Delhi ridge exhausted but delighted to have reached the scene of action and the place of danger:

> A good night's rest set me up. I awoke early scarcely able to believe in my good fortune. I was actually at Delhi and the city was still in the possession of the mutineers.

The famous ridge on which the little British army perched rose only some sixty feet above the plain. It was nearly bare of trees, and the army clung there for the three hottest months of the year. Almost a third of all those who lived and fought on the ridge died there. And their deaths were usually lingering and painful. To die in such fashion, wounded, lying on the ground under a burning sun, covered with dust and crawling with flies, was hardly glorious, yet to many it seemed so. Even less glorious were the deaths of those who were victims of diseases, which claimed more lives than did bullets and shells. In spite of the dangers, the wretchedness and the squalor on the ridge, Roberts, so delicate throughout his childhood, remained 'jolly and fit'.

The final successful attack on Delhi took place at the Kashmir Gate on 14 September 1857. It was led by the redoubtable Nicholson, one of the Indian army's great heroes, a man of whom Edwardes said 'that if ever there [was] a desperate deed to be done in India, John Nicholson [was] the man to do it'. Nicholson – thirty-six years old, six feet six inches tall, burly, dark and handsome – has been described as 'a violent manic figure, a homosexual bully, an extreme egotist who was pleased to affect a laconic indifference to danger'.* He had a fierce hatred of Indians; two of his brothers had been murdered in India, and he himself had discovered the mutilated corpse of one of them, a favourite younger brother. He was never known to smile and was said to have reserved all his love for his mother, to whom he was intensely attached.

When sappers blew in the Kashmir Gate, a bugler sounded the advance; with Nicholson at the head, the troops charged through and, in spite of fearful casualties, pressed on. General Sir Archibald Wilson, commanding the British forces at Delhi, was ill and irresolute. Prone to self-doubt and filled with anxiety and apprehensions of disaster, he dispatched Roberts to see how the battle was progressing. At the Kashmir Gate, Roberts found a dying Nicholson, shot through a lung, and lying on a doolie in great pain, deserted by his bearers. Roberts did what little he could to ease him and found four men to carry him back to the ridge before he went on. The fighting was slow and hard, but the British were making headway and he was able to bring back reassuring news. Wilson was dissuaded from recalling his men, and Delhi was at last won.

Nicholson lived on for nine days, long enough to learn of the British victory. Long enough, too, to see another younger

* Michael Edwardes in *Bound to Exile*.

brother brought to the field hospital with a shattered right arm that required amputation. Of Nicholson's death a modern writer* has said that he thought it fortunate, 'partly for himself and certainly for the British cause in India, that John Nicholson died at the zenith of his military glory'.

It seemed to many that with the fall of Delhi the worst was over; at least the British now felt confident that they would win. Still, there was much hard fighting to be done.

The siege had given Roberts his first wound – a slight one – and his first mention in dispatches. He was never again wounded, but he was to earn more and higher honours before the end of the Mutiny.

4

After the capture of Delhi, mobile columns were formed to go to the relief of besieged towns and to search out and destroy rebel units. Roberts was attached to one such column, serving under Colonel Edward Greathed as DAQMG. The column, composed of about 2,500 men of all arms, left Delhi on 24 September and five days later encountered a strong body of mutineers drawn up in line of battle near Bulandshahr on the Grand Trunk Road. A gallant charge by the 75th Highlanders (which later became the 1st Gordons) routed the enemy, which turned and fled through the narrow streets of the town. Roberts, on horseback, was among the pursuers. In the mêlée a mutineer levelled his musket at him and fired as Roberts tried in vain to slash his way through to cut him down. His startled horse saved his life when it reared and received the ball intended for its master. Roberts was again mentioned in dispatches. (At the end of his career it was said that no soldier had ever been mentioned so often in dispatches.)

From its victory at Bulandshahr the column moved to Agra, where the British occupied one of the strongest forts

* Major-General Frank M. Richardson in *Mars without Venus*.

in India. The authorities there, acting with a timidity that bordered on the imbecilic, had called for help. When the column reached Agra on 10 October after a hard march, there was no sign of the enemy, who, they were told, had fled at their approach. Tired from their march, they camped just outside the walls, and there, when least prepared, they were attacked. Only with great difficulty were the mutineers beaten off.

Roberts, who was responsible for intelligence, ought to have learned that the enemy was camped only four miles away. For such an oversight he might well have been dismissed, his career ruined, but the blame fell upon the authorities at Agra. Roberts was again mentioned in dispatches for his bravery. He possessed in abundance what every ambitious officer needs – luck.

The column moved on to Cawnpore and in November 1857 joined a larger force under Sir Colin Campbell, the new commander-in-chief in India. This small army, consisting of only 3,500 infantry, 600 cavalry and forty-two guns, advanced to relieve the besieged forces holding out against great odds under the leadership of Sir Henry Havelock and Sir James Outram at the British Residency at Lucknow.

With Sir Colin was Lieutenant (later Lieutenant-General) Hugh Gough,* who during the advance once shared with Roberts a perilous ride in the night to bring up more ammunition. Gough became one of Roberts's closest friends. Bobs Roberts had many friends; everyone who knew him liked him. Captain Oliver Jones, who served with him in

---

* Hugh Gough was a great-nephew of the Hugh Gough famous earlier in the century. He and his brother, Charles, both won the Victoria Cross in the course of the Mutiny. Later, Charles Gough's second son, John Edmund Gough, won the Victoria Cross fighting in Somaliland in 1903. There are only three other instances of father and son winning the VC and only four instances of brothers winning it. The Goughs are the only family ever to have won three. Charles Gough's eldest son, Hubert, commanded the British Fifth Army in World War I until he was ignominiously but unjustly relieved of his command by Sir Douglas Haig.

India, described his 'charm of cheering and [his] unaffected kindness and hospitality'. Ian Hamilton, who served with him for twenty-two years, said that 'he was never casual or inconsiderate with any human being'. Hamilton never forgot the time when as a young lieutenant he had distinguished himself in a minor skirmish on the North-West Frontier: Major-General Roberts invited him to his tent for a glass of sherry and then wrote a long congratulatory letter to his father, a retired colonel.

When the Mutiny broke out at Lucknow, capital of Oude, at the end of May 1857, the British – soldiers and civilians (including some women and children) – together with a handful of loyal Indians, barricaded themselves in the Residency and put up a determined defence. Sir Henry Lawrence, the British Resident, proved an able organizer and an inspired leader until he died of wounds on 4 July. In September, General Sir Henry Havelock and Sir James Outram, now also a general, fought their way into the Residency but lacked the strength to extricate the defenders. Not until late November did Sir Colin Campbell, after a week of hard fighting, manage to claw his way into Lucknow and bring away the gallant defenders of the Residency.

With the relief of Lucknow, all serious threats to British hegemony in India were at an end. All the great cities of Bengal were clear of mutineers, but sizeable forces remained in the country and had to be defeated piecemeal. On 2 January 1858 Roberts was riding with the column that encountered a large body of the enemy near the village of Khudaganj. After a sharp action the mutineers were routed, and he took part in the pursuit. Again he distinguished himself by his gallantry:

> On following up the retreating enemy . . . Lieutenant Roberts saw in the distance two sepoys going away with a standard. He put spurs to his horse and overtook them just as they were about to enter a village. They immediately turned round and

Lieutenant Roberts wins the VC *(Photo: ILN Pic. Lib.)*

presented their muskets to him and one of the men pulled the trigger, but fortunately the cap snapped, and the standard bearer was cut down by this gallant young officer, and the standard taken possession of by him. He also on the same day cut down another sepoy who was standing at bay, with musket and bayonet keeping off a sowar. Lieutenant Roberts rode to the assistance of the horseman, and, rushing at the sepoy, with one blow of his sword cut him across the face, killing him on the spot.

So read the citation for the Victoria Cross that this action and his generally gallant behaviour during the campaign won for him.

Roberts had distinguished himself, but the hardships of the campaign finally caught up with him and he accepted a medical certificate and fifteen months' home leave, turning over his quartermaster duties to Major Garnet Wolseley. When he sailed from Calcutta on the Peninsular & Oriental steamship *Nubia*, the young man had reason to feel proud of himself. He had won the Victoria Cross, earned seven mentions in dispatches, gained £500 in prize money and brought himself to the attention of his superiors as an able soldier.

5

The hero home from the wars was fêted by his parents and friends, and it was at this time that he met and conquered the heart of Miss Nora Bews, tenth child of a retired Black Watch officer. They were married on 17 May 1879 in Waterford; he was twenty-six and she was barely twenty. They were on their honeymoon in Scotland when he was summoned to Buckingham Palace to be decorated with the Victoria Cross by Queen Victoria. Three weeks later they sailed for India.

The young couple entered upon a life in which the routine duties of peace left ample room for the sports so beloved by the officers and for whist, for afternoons of croquet, and for the giving and attending of dinner parties. Like many officers of his time, Roberts enjoyed music. He played the flute and had a pleasing singing voice; at parties he could easily be persuaded to sing music-hall ditties. A great favourite was 'Walking in the Zoo'. He liked parties and enjoyed jokes and puns, the best of which he wrote down in his journal, together with household accounts and records of family birthdays and anniversaries.

Peacetime army duties were not without their trials. With the final suppression of the Mutiny, the British government took over the governance of India from the Honourable East India Company and replaced the governor-general with a viceroy. When Lord Canning, the first viceroy, decided to make a tour through the northern provinces to reward those Indian princes who had remained loyal to the British, Roberts was selected to be quartermaster and was made responsible for the logistical arrangements. Since Canning would be accompanied by an entourage of some 20,000 people, the tour involved the almost daily movement of a fair-sized city. It was Roberts's task to provide two tent cities for the official party, each complete with street lamps, post office and bazaar; while one was being occupied, the other was being set up on the road ahead. The tour proved to be a success; on 12 November, Roberts was promoted captain and on the following day was gazetted brevet major. But there were sorrows as well as successes. In India at this time only one out of five European children survived to the age of six. The Roberts's first child, a daughter, died within a week of her first birthday, a tragedy followed by the loss of a second child through a miscarriage.

In 1863 Roberts took part in the Umbeyla campaign on the North-West Frontier, where he once again distinguished himself. Ill health plagued him, however, and at the end of the campaign he was given medical leave to England. When he returned to duty in 1866, he was just in time to be appointed AQMG to Sir Robert Napier, who had been given command of an expedition to Abyssinia to rescue a group of Europeans who were being held prisoner by King Theodore. Roberts's duties during the campaign kept him on the coast, and he was disappointed to have missed the final battle at Theodore's stronghold at Magdala, but his work so pleased Napier that he was selected to carry the official dispatches back to London, an honour customarily accompanied by promotion, and he was duly gazetted lieutenant-colonel. At about the same time, Nora gave birth to a baby girl. It was a happy period. Unfortunately, it was all too brief.

On the voyage back to India the infant died and was buried at sea. A year later a son was born who lived only three weeks. However, in September 1870 a girl was born; two years later there was another boy; three years after that another girl; all three lived to maturity.

In this era few British officers seriously studied their profession. Most considered it sufficient to be able to ride, hunt, follow the customs of their mess and, should it be required, demonstrate their courage in battle. Few ever opened a professional book unless required to do so. Roberts was therefore unusual in seldom losing an opportunity to add to his knowledge or improve his professional skills. Once, although a lieutenant-colonel on the staff, he went so far as to enroll in a course in telegraphy so that, in the unlikely event of all the clerks being killed or disabled, he would be able to send and receive messages himself. He also wrote papers and articles on military affairs, one of which considered the steps to be taken should Russia invade Afghanistan.

In September 1871 Roberts, now a colonel, was sent to Calcutta to organize a full-scale 5,000-man expedition to rescue a little girl called Mary Winchester, who had been abducted by the Lushai, a tribe living in the forests of Assam. Because of the difficulties of the terrain and the terrible climate, it was a hard campaign, but little Mary was duly rescued and the Lushai were given a lesson in the ability of the British to project their power even into remote hills and jungles. Roberts was awarded a CB for his part and soon afterwards was named DQMG, progressing in due course to quartermaster general. However, his long years as a staff officer were now nearly over.

6

Throughout the Victorian era there was always a fear that Russia would invade Afghanistan and thus threaten India. In the late nineteenth century, Tsarist armies were indeed marching across Central Asia, coming ever closer. Tashkent was captured in 1865, Bokhara in 1867 and Samarkand the following year; the khanate of Khiva was annexed in 1873 and Khokand in 1875. By 1878 they were nudging the northern borders of Afghanistan, and their agents were in Kabul.

When the Afghan ruler, Sher Ali, refused to receive a British mission, alarms were sounded in Calcutta and London. Lord Lytton, the new viceroy, had read Roberts's paper on Afghanistan and was particularly impressed by his plan for winning the cooperation of Pathan tribes on the frontier. Lytton lost no time in dispatching Roberts to the area, where in the spring of 1878 he was given command of the Punjab Frontier Force.

He was thus the right man in the right place when, late in 1878, the British decided on a three-pronged invasion of Afghanistan. On 31 December he became a major-general and, although the most junior of generals, was given command of one of the three invading columns. At forty-six Roberts was trim and fit, but, except for one day during the Lushai campaign, he had not commanded troops in the field since he was a lieutenant during the Mutiny more than twenty years before. His sudden leap over the heads of more-senior generals was, of course, resented, but Roberts throughout his career managed to avoid the vicious quarrels with colleagues and superiors that played such a galling part in the lives of many of his fellow officers.

No general could escape all criticism, and Roberts found a bitter and vocal enemy in Colonel Henry Bathurst Hanna, a gallant officer who had served in the Mutiny, in China and on campaigns on the North-West Frontier. Roberts had won his enmity by denying him the post of quartermaster general, an appointment to which he considered himself entitled. When he retired, Hanna wrote a three-volume history of the Second Afghan War that was generally critical of Roberts. Secure in his fame, Roberts ignored him. Unlike most other generals of his day, he knew when to keep his mouth shut.

When Roberts first came to India as a young officer, he had been depressed, as well he might have been, by the prospect of the slow climb up the promotion ladder. The youngest division commander was sixty-eight years old. Wars, campaigns, his undoubted abilities, family connections and good luck had now pushed him up to general officer rank at a remarkably young age. He saw his promotion as a step in the right direction. He declared to Nora that all generals ought to be under fifty, and to his mother he wrote that 'except in a very few instances, commanders over 50 years of age cannot be as efficient as younger men'. Perhaps he came to regard himself as one of the 'few instances', for he was destined to lead troops in the field when he was seventy.

The Kurram Field Force, which Roberts commanded, the smallest of the three columns invading Afghanistan, consisted of 6,665 officers and other ranks with eighteen guns. The largest column, twice the size of Roberts's column, was the Peshawar Valley Field Force, commanded by the one-armed Lieutenant-General Samuel Browne (inventor of the famous Sam Browne belt), and the third column, the Kandahar Field Force, was led by Roberts's friend Donald Stewart, now also a major-general. In command of the cavalry with Roberts was another old friend, Colonel Hugh Gough, VC.

The mission of Roberts's little army was to advance up the Kurram Valley to within sixty miles of Kabul, destroying any enemy forces encountered, and then to turn off into the fertile Khost Valley and occupy it, thereby depriving the enemy of supplies. In late November, Roberts set his column in motion. They encountered no opposition until, on 28 November, they received intelligence that the enemy were in force at Peiwar Kotal, a narrow pass through which they would have to march. At first Roberts feared the Pathans were trying to escape an engagement, but he soon discovered that they were entrenched on heights overlooking the pass and meant to contest his advance.

He ordered a careful reconnaissance of the position while making intensive and obvious preparations for a frontal assault. Then, at dusk on 1 December, he called a meeting of his staff and the battalion commanders and announced his plans: the equivalent of a weak brigade would remain in the valley, but all camp fires would remain lit while he led five battalions of infantry and a mountain battery on a

General Roberts leads the advance at Peiwar Kotal *(Photo: ILN Pic. Lib.)*

wide swing around the left flank of the enemy's position. Roberts described the approach march:

The track (for there was no road) led for two miles due east, and then, turning sharp to the north, entered a wide gorge and ran along the bed of a mountain stream. The moonlight lit up the cliffs on the eastern side of the ravine, but made the darkness only the more dense in the shadow of the steep hills on the west, underneath which our path lay, over piles of stones and heaps of glacier debris. A bitterly cold wind rushed down the gorge, extremely trying to all, lightly clad as we were in anticipation of the climb before us. Onwards and upwards we slowly toiled, stumbling over great boulders of rock, dropping into old water-channels, splashing through icy streams, and halting frequently to allow the troops in the rear to close up.

It was a tense climb, for it was necessary to reach their attack positions before dawn. Roberts brought up the 5th Gurkha Rifles and a company of the 72nd Highlanders to lead the assault. Someone in an Indian unit fired shots, apparently in an effort to warn the Afghans, but the enemy remained oblivious to the danger they were in until the Gurkhas and Highlanders reached the final slope and, with fixed bayonets, shouting their battle cries, charged and drove them off. The Pathans counter-attacked, but the pass was carried and Roberts won his first victory as a general at a cost of only twenty killed and seventy-eight wounded. His was also the first victory of the war, and England as well as India cheered a new hero. The commander-in-chief, the viceroy and Queen Victoria herself sent congratulatory messages. Roberts was knighted (KCB) and received the unanimous thanks of both houses of Parliament.

One of the battalions in the Kurram Field Force, the 29th Native Infantry, was composed of Muslims; one company, in fact, was made up of Pathans, and many of these sepoys had little taste for this expedition against their co-religionists. It was men in this unit who had fired their muskets in an attempt to warn the enemy of their approach, and eighteen had deserted that night. When there was time, Roberts ordered an inquiry and then a court martial. The sepoy who had fired the first shot was sentenced to be executed; his comrades received lesser sentences. Roberts signed the death warrant, an unpleasant duty about which he had no qualms, for he had no doubts as to the justice of or the need for the execution, and he recorded in his journal that 'the effect of these sentences was most salutary'.

In January 1879 Roberts occupied the Khost Valley. When his camp was attacked and foraging parties were set upon, he responded in traditional fashion by burning villages and seizing hostages. Most were speedily ransomed, but six were

killed and thirteen wounded in a mêlée when a night rescue attempt failed. These incidents, luridly reported by
Hector Macpherson, a correspondent for the *Standard* who
was travelling with the column, created a stir in England.
In his zeal, he compared the killing of hostages to the Bul-
garian atrocities and the Glencoe Massacre of 1692. When
Roberts ordered Macpherson back to India, Fleet Street rose
to his defence and accused Roberts of trying to suppress
the truth and 'burke the press'. Nora was upset, but Roberts calmly assured her that such attacks would not trouble him 'in the least'. He was now 'public property', he
explained, and so could not expect that everyone would
approve of what he did.

After lengthy negotiations, the Afghans signed a treaty
by which they agreed to live 'in perfect peace and friendship' with the British. They ceded three districts, including
Kurram, and agreed to accept an envoy at Kabul. Once this
was arranged, Roberts's column remained intact in order
to occupy the Kurram while the two larger columns under
Browne and Stewart were returned to India and broken
up. This was a mistake.

7

The British envoy to Afghanistan was a political officer with
an un-English name: Major Sir Louis Napoleon Cavagnari,
the son of one of Napoleon's generals by an English mother.
He and his military escort had hardly arrived in Kabul when
they were attacked at the British Residency by a mob and
slaughtered to a man. Within hours of the confirmation of
this news, Roberts's force was renamed the Kabul Field
Force and ordered to march. Roberts was in Simla at the
time, but he speedily returned to take up his command.
Lord Lytton gave him a free hand, though with the following injunction: 'It is not *justice* in the ordinary sense, but
retribution that you have to administer on reaching Kabul.

. . . Your objective should be to strike terror, and to strike it swiftly and deeply. . . .'

It was a challenging task. He was to lead an army of fewer than 7,000 men on a sixty-mile march through unsurveyed, mountainous and hostile country to the enemy's capital. His line of communication and supply stretched back two hundred miles to India, and he was without adequate transport animals or experienced transport officers. Nevertheless, on 30 September 1880, his forty-eighth birthday, the advance began. His column was harassed by sniping and was forced into several fights but saw no major battles until it reached an area known as Charasia, about a dozen miles from Kabul. There the enemy was entrenched in force on a range of hills. A gallant charge by Gurkhas and Highlanders dislodged them and put them to flight. It was in this action that Major George White, later to command at the siege of Ladysmith in South Africa, won his Victoria Cross, and here, too, that Colour-Sergeant Hector Macdonald won his commission, first step on his path to becoming one of the few men ever to rise from private to major-general in the British army.

For the first time a heliograph was used in battle, enabling Roberts to direct the action from a distance instead of galloping about the battlefield, a development he found uncomfortable. He told Nora, 'I don't quite understand not being in the middle of the fighting myself but it is of course right that I should remain in some central place and give orders'. Even Roberts's worst critic, Colonel Hanna, later wrote admiringly of his handling of this battle:

> To watch for hours the fluctuations of a fight – so near as to be able to note individual acts of gallantry – to know that one can do nothing to determine its issue, that all the troops can give has been given, and that those left behind are too few to provide a sure refuge for themselves and their comrades in case the attack should fail, as more than once seemed likely, needs

a higher courage and stronger powers of endurance than to direct an engagement or lead a storming column; and no man could have gone through the ordeal more bravely than Sir Frederick Roberts. Racked with fear for the safety of his troops, of his sick, of his stores, of the thousands of camp followers who looked to him for protection, he attended calmly to every detail by which the peril could be lightened; sending out cavalry patrols to drive off the tribesmen, establishing strongly fortified outposts, and seeing to it that the work of putting the camp into a state of defence went on without intermission. All that he did was well done, but inexpressible must have been his relief when the danger, against which he was providing, had been dispelled, and the road to Kabul lay clear before him.

At dawn the next day the army resumed its march on the object of its vengeance and before dark made camp within sight of the famous Bala Hissar, the massive fortress whose walls, now as then, brood over the city of Kabul. Here Roberts paused for a day and collected intelligence. Learning that fresh forces were mustering west of Kabul, he sent his cavalry to lie in wait across the Afghans' probable line of retreat while he moved forward with his infantry to make a frontal attack. It was rugged terrain, and he was not quick enough; the Afghan army appeared to have dissolved. Even so, the British were able to capture more than one hundred guns, 250 tons of gunpowder, millions of rounds of ammunition and some much-needed transport. Roberts now put his army into Sherpur, a new cantonment to the north of the city.

At noon on 12 October, Roberts assembled a large number of Afghan officials and tribal chiefs at the Bala Hissar. He drew up an impressive guard of honour and announced what the future held in store: martial law to be declared, the city to be fined and any building that might hinder military operations to be torn down. On the spot he arrested a number of notables said to have been responsible for the massacre of Cavagnari and his party. The following day he made a formal entry into Kabul with his cavalry and five battalions of infantry. In the evening the convivial Roberts invited a few of his senior officers to celebrate their success. That night he wrote to Nora, 'This has been a very eventful day, and now I am King of Kabul. It is not a kingdom I covet and I shall be right glad to get rid of it, but the occasion seemed worthy of a glass of champagne'. Soon congratulatory messages arrived from the viceroy and the Queen, and Roberts, moving up half a peg on the military ladder, was given the local rank of lieutenant-general.

All were aware, however, that the war was not won. The troops were cut off from supply bases in India, and they knew that mustering somewhere outside Kabul were Afghan armies filled with tribesmen thirsting for their blood. As soon as possible a line of communication and supply was opened over the Khyber Pass, and Roberts's army was reinforced by a brigade under Brigadier-General Charles Gough.

There was work to be done in Kabul. Commissions were appointed to investigate the causes of the massacre and to bring to trial those responsible. Forty-nine men were found guilty; Roberts signed their death warrants, and they were hanged. As the great act of retribution Lytton had ordered, Roberts decided to destroy the interior of the Bala Hissar; only the outer walls were left standing.

If Roberts had any qualms about invading a country and hanging more than four dozen of its citizens, he never mentioned them and it is doubtful he felt any. When his duty was clear, he never hesitated, never quibbled about the ethics of his orders, never questioned the morality of his mission. It was perhaps a help to know that honour and fame lay in the path of duty and that Britain could be generous to successful generals. His contemporary Sir Garnet Wolseley had recently been given £25,000 for a swift, successful little campaign on the west coast of Africa. Roberts dared dream that he, too, might be awarded such a fortune – and parhaps even a peerage. In letters to Nora he speculated on his chances of distinguishing himself again: 'I can scarcely be employed again except in command and there will be Wolseley and other men in the running for berths of that sort'. Although Wolseley now appeared as an obvious rival, there were to be enough wars for both in the last twenty-five years of Queen Victoria's reign. Mars smiled upon Little Bobs.

8

Winter fell on Afghanistan and with it came snow and a cold so bitter that Roberts took his ink to bed with him to keep it from freezing. He had made adequate provision for a hard winter in a hostile land: His troops were sheltered in huts; food and firewood had been laid in; ample forage had been gathered; and the cantonment of Sherpur, although within a four-and-a-half-mile perimeter, was prepared for defence. It was just as well, for the mullahs were demanding a jihad to evict the infidel invaders, and large bodies of Afghan warriors had begun collecting in the hills. Roberts sent out forces that tried unsuccessfully to defeat them in detail, and for several days there was confused fighting around Kabul.

Realizing that he faced an overwhelming force, Roberts withdrew into the Sherpur defences, where at dawn on 23 December 1879 he was subjected to a ferocious attack by waves of Pathan tribesmen. The attacks were fended off, but nothing could dislodge the tribesmen or drive them away until Roberts ordered the 5th Punjab Cavalry and a battery of artillery to make a wide sweeping movement and come in hard on the Afghan flank. This succeeded. The enemy wavered and broke. Roberts at once unleashed his remaining cavalry in pursuit, and by nightfall not a living Afghan was to be seen. For the first time in a fortnight, Roberts undressed for bed, but before going to sleep he wrote to Nora, 'Only just time to tell you . . . the whole thing is over, the enemy have dispersed and we are masters of the situation. I am very happy and just a wee bit proud. . . .'

Lord Roberts in 1880 *(Photo: BBC Hulton Picture Library)*

His successes had been achieved with comparatively small loss of life: in the two-week period culminating with the attack on Sherpur he had lost 12 officers and 84 other ranks killed, and 15 officers and 248 other ranks wounded. These figures from the official records do not count about 30 camp followers who were either killed or wounded.

The victory at Sherpur created only a brief sensation in Britain; there was far more interest in the Tay railway bridge disaster.* The British public had had enough of Afghan affairs, and British politicians bickered without enthusiasm about the best course to pursue. Those who disapproved of Lord Lytton attacked Roberts, who had implemented his policy. He was accused of being rash and overbearing, of treating subordinates unfairly and of lacking military skill in general. His friends and relations were indignant, but Roberts was unperturbed. 'These things always come right and I am quite satisfied that I have not done anything to be ashamed of', he wrote to Nora.

On 5 May 1879 Sir Donald Stewart, who had marched up from Kandahar, fighting a small battle along the way, reached Kabul and, as he was senior to Roberts, assumed command. Stewart was a close friend; still, it hurt Roberts to be superseded, and he asked to be allowed to return to India, pleading poor health. But luck was with him, even when he made mistakes. Lord Lytton, more aware of the political situation, though about to be replaced himself by Lord Ripon, urged him 'most strongly' to stay in Afghanistan. It was good advice. Roberts was never above using his ever-precarious health as an excuse to extricate himself from undesirable situations, nor did he allow it to interfere with a chance for action. Lytton hinted of action and Roberts stayed: it gave him the opportunity of a lifetime for glory and honours.

For the time being, the tribesmen lay so low that there was very little fighting, and it required serious effort to overcome boredom. On New Year's Eve 1880 the men of the 92nd Highlanders at Sherpur had a glorious drunk and at two o'clock in the morning roused Roberts from his bed to cheer him. He wrote to Nora about it: 'I have no doubt they thought it great fun "drawing the general". They are

---

* The Tay bridge, nearly two miles long, spanned the Firth of Dundee in Scotland. It collapsed during a storm, and a mail train carrying eighty people was swept away by the river below.

such a good lot I was only too glad to do anything to make them happy'. Roberts himself was not above a bit of over-indulgence and horseplay. In a letter to Nora he described an Old Etonian party held on 5 June:

> We had a very jolly dinner here last night. 12 Eton fellows including myself dined together. . . . we were able to put a very good dinner on the table, and to drink plenty of champagne. . . . Griffin [Lepel Griffin, chief of the political staff] had a small opposition Harrow dinner . . . and as they sent us some impertinent messages we had to prove the prowess of Eton by attacking their stronghold (Griffin's mess) which we did in style, turning the flank of the Harrovians completely. Nice sort of conduct on the part of Sir Frederick Roberts!

Roberts's thoughts turned more and more toward home, and this led to thoughts about new clothes, which he liked to buy. He wrote to Nora, teasing a bit about his growing old:

> You must see how *old* gentlemen dress nowadays so as to give me some hints when I arrive. I hope turn-down collars are still in fashion. They suit me better than stick-up ones. . . . I shall require a regular outfit – boxes – umbrella – stick – dressing bag – brushes, in fact everything – Oh what fun it will be. . . .

When the prolonged negotiations between the government of India and the Afghan leaders at last produced a new amir and a new treaty, plans were made for Stewart to withdraw one division by way of the Khyber Pass and, that done, for Roberts to lead the other division out by way of the Kurram. But suddenly there came news of a disaster: at Maiwand, eighty miles from Kandahar in southern Afghanistan, on 27 July 1880, a brigade led by Brigadier-General George Burrows had been almost annihilated by Afghan forces under Ayub Khan, the most capable of the Afghan generals. It was one of the most crushing defeats ever suffered by the British in Asia. At the same time came word that Major-General James Primrose with 4,000 men was being besieged in Kandahar itself.

Stewart immediately decided that a large force must be sent to relieve Primrose. The governor-general in India agreed, and by 8 August a force of 10,000 men was ready to march. Stewart generously gave the command to Roberts and provided him with the best troops available and sufficient transport. Neither man could have foreseen the impact of this march from Kabul to Kandahar on the British public, nor could they have imagined the honours in store for its commander.

Of the 2,476 men who fought at Maiwand, 934 had been killed (310 were Britons) and 175 were wounded or missing. It was an unexpected defeat of a size to attract the attention of the public at home, and Roberts's march – perhaps in part because of the romantic, alliterative ring of the words 'Kabul to Kandahar' – captured the popular imagination as nothing else had done in the war.

It was indeed a difficult march – although, as Roberts later said, not as difficult as his march through the Kurram – through unfriendly, if not hostile, country, cut off from communications and supplies, toward a victorious enemy of unknown strength. By pushing men and animals as hard as he could, he brought his army to Ghazni, seventy-five miles from Kabul, in six days. Roberts's father had won a CB for his part in capturing this walled city forty-one years earlier. There was no need to blow in the gates now, for they were opened to him at once. But he did not linger.

On 25 August he received a message from Primrose telling him that the Afghans, aware of his approach, had lifted the siege of Kandahar and that his force was no longer threatened. This enabled Roberts to slow down somewhat. He welcomed the respite, since his men were tired and he wanted them to be in fighting trim when they arrived at the end of their long march. He, too, needed a rest, for he was so weak from fever that for four days he had to be carried along in a doolie. 'A most ignominious mode of conveyance for a general in service', he said later, 'but there was no help for it, for I could not sit a horse'. He had not been well for some time, suffering from chest pains and a feeling of weariness. Now, in addition to his fever, he suffered from violent headaches, almost constant nausea, back pain and loss of appetite. Nothing deterred him. In a diary–letter to Nora he wrote, 'I never knew how much I could stand before, or how easy I should find the command of a large body of troops to be'. On 31 August, at the end of the 320-mile march, he reached Kandahar, where the garrison turned out to meet him.

Its demoralized condition shocked him, as did General Primrose's incompetence and fecklessness. In Roberts's estimation his 4,000 soldiers and fifteen guns, protected by walls thirty feet high, had been in no danger at all. 'For British soldiers to have contemplated the possibility of Kandahar being taken by an Afghan army showed what a miserable state of depression and demoralization they were in', he wrote in exasperation. Most reprehensible of all, 'they never even hoisted the Union Jack until the relieving force was close at hand'. Only the British gunners and the Bombay Sappers and Miners had shown 'unfailing good behaviour and creditable bearing'.

Although Roberts had 940 men too sick or lame to march, and he himself was in pain and still weak from fever, he reported to the viceroy, 'The troops from Kabul are in famous health and spirits'. In any case, he wasted no time in coming to grips with the enemy, and the next day he won a stunning victory, capturing Ayub Khan's camp and all his guns. Highlanders and Gurkhas, always friendly rivals for glory, bore the brunt of the fighting, as they had in most of the battles in Afghanistan. In spite of his condition, Roberts was determined to stay on the field. Refreshed by occasional sips of champagne, he soldiered on, and at battle's end was heartily cheered by every regiment and battery. British losses were 40 killed and 210 wounded, of whom 18 died later. Afghan casualties are unknown, but in one place there were an estimated 600 corpses. 'The victory . . . was really a grand one', Roberts told Nora. At the close of the day he rode back to Kandahar, and there he collapsed, too exhausted and ill to eat. 'However', he told Nora, 'after an hour's rest and a bath I was refreshed and quite enjoyed some dinner. Then I took such a sleep and *rest*. I had nothing to think of or worry about, I awoke a different man, and now I am hourly gaining strength'.

But he was, on the contrary, a sick man. On 8 September a medical board, citing his 'torpidity of the liver and aggravated dyspepsia', decided that he must go home. He left Afghanistan by way of the Bolan Pass, and on the course of his journey he overtook, marching back to India, most of the units that had served him in the Kabul-to-Kandahar march and the subsequent final victory. As he passed, each regiment's band struck up 'Auld Lang Syne'. Years later he wrote:

> I have never heard that memory-stirring air without its bringing before my mind's eye the last view I had of the Kabul–Kandahar Field Force. I fancy myself crossing and recrossing the river which winds through the pass; I hear the martial beat of drums and plaintive music of the pipes; and I see Riflemen and Gurkhas, Highlanders and Sikhs, guns and horses, camels and mules, with the endless following of an Indian army, winding through the narrow gorges, or over the interminable boulders which make the passage of the Bolan so difficult to man and beast.

9

It had been twelve years since he had last been in England, then an obscure artillery major returning from Abyssinia. Now he was a major-general, a GCB and a hero. And to the nation's hero came a cornucopia of honours. He and Nora were the Queen's guests at Windsor; he was presented with swords of honour by Eton and the City of London; Oxford conferred an honorary degree on him; and he was given the Freedom of the Grocers' and of the Fishmongers' guilds. In addition to the Afghan campaign medal, a special medal was struck, which came to be called the Roberts Star and which was awarded to all – even his horse – who had marched with him from Kabul to Kandahar. Roberts was called upon to give innumerable speeches, and in one of these, at a dinner given in his honour by the Lord Mayor at the Mansion House on 14 February 1881, he spoke on a subject that was to preoccupy him for the remainder of his life: army reform and, in particular, the evils of short service.

In the 1870s Edward Cardwell, secretary of state for war, had introduced a number of radical reforms. Roberts was particularly disturbed by one of these: the reduction of the term of enlistment to twelve years. Known as 'short service', the policy actually reduced the time with the colours to three or seven years, depending upon the type and place of service; the remaining years were spent in the reserve. This reduced the number of old sweats, such as those Kipling immortalized in *Soldiers Three,* and gave the army, for the first time, a reserve that was almost adequate. It also made recruiting easier.

In 1871 nearly a third of the men in the ranks were over the age of thirty; twenty years later less than ten per cent were that old. Roberts contended that regiments with short-service men had not done as well in Afghanistan as those filled with old soldiers. For the rest of his life he never missed an opportunity to protest against short service, and in this campaign he was ably assisted by his friend Rudyard Kipling, who spelled out its dangers in poems and stories, most notably in 'The Drums of the Fore and Aft'. Nevertheless, short service remained in force until the First World War.

In March 1881 news reached England of a disaster in the British war against the Boers in South Africa. At Majuba Hill in Natal, British regulars had been turned out of a strong hilltop position by a party of Boer farmers, many of them either old men or mere boys, and Major-General George

Colley, the commander of the British forces there, had been killed. Roberts was at once sent out as governor of Natal and commander of all the forces in South Africa. He was still at sea when faint hearts prevailed in London and instructions were telegraphed to Brigadier-General Sir Evelyn Wood, then in temporary command, to make peace with the Boers. Although it did not seem so at the time, luck had not deserted Roberts. Wood was roundly damned for carrying out his orders – for making peace instead of fighting – and Roberts was able to return to England with his reputation undimmed.

In the summer of 1881 Roberts suffered a bitter disappointment when the rewards to those who had served in Afghanistan were announced. He and Sir Donald Stewart were made baronets, and each was given £12,500, a handsome sum, but Wolseley had been given twice that much for the Ashanti campaign, which, in the unkind words of the *United Service Gazette* (4 June 1881), had resulted only in the 'capture of an umbrella'. Also, Wolseley had been promoted; Roberts was not. He did not publicly complain, and in fact he specifically asked Lord Randolph Churchill not to make a fuss about it, but he was bruised. To a young friend, Captain Reginald Pole-Carew, he wrote, 'I was so sick of the whole business and so disgusted with the evident desire of the government not to recognize my services that I could not bring myself to fight against its illiberal and ungenerous treatment of me. . . . it goes against the grain and seems to me indelicate'.

Roberts and Wolseley had become rivals for glory. It was a gentlemanly rivalry; neither ever publicly attacked the other, but each was zealously backed by his circle of admirers and by loyal staff officers. Ian Hamilton, who had served under Roberts in Afghanistan and in 1882 became one of his aides-de-camp and served him for the next twenty years, later wrote that it was his fate 'to spend any surplus energy [he] had left after fighting the enemies of [his] country in fighting for [his] Chief against the Wolseley Ring'.

When Wolseley was being hailed as 'our only general',
Roberts was brought forward as 'our other general'.

10

In early November, Roberts once again left England, this
time with Nora and his daughters – young Freddy was left
behind at Eton – to take up the post of commander-in-chief
of the Madras army. Roberts spent the next four years in
peacetime soldiering, his leisure hours taken up with Nora
and the girls at Ootacamund, where he had his headquarters. In 1885 he was appointed commander-in-chief for India
and moved to Calcutta. Like his predecessors, he found the
job heavy with responsibility but weak in authority. However, Roberts was a team player, he was well liked, and he
did not quarrel with the two viceroys under whom he served.
He managed to accomplish much through persuasion and
good temper.

In the New Year's Honours List for 1892 he was raised to
the peerage as Baron Roberts of Kandahar, an event celebrated by Kipling in a highly popular poem:

> There's a little red-faced man,
>   Which is Bobs,
> Rides the tallest 'orse 'e can –
>   *Our* Bobs.
> If it bucks or kicks or rears,
> 'E can sit for twenty years
> With a smile round both 'is ears –
>   Can't yer, Bobs?
>
> Then 'ere's to Bobs Bahadur[1] – little Bobs, Bobs Bobs!
> 'E's our pukka[2] Kandaharder –
>   Fightin' Bobs, Bobs, Bobs!
> 'E's the Dook of *Aggy Chel;*[3]

[1] Bobs Bahadur = Bobs the Brave.
[2] Pukka = proper, genuine.
[3] *Aggy Chel* = get ahead.

'E's the man that done us well,
An' we'll follow 'im to 'ell –
    Won't we, Bobs?

If a limber's slipped a trace,
    'Ook on Bobs.
If a marker's lost 'is place,
    Dress by Bobs.
For 'e's eyes all up 'is coat,
An' a bugle in 'is throat,
An' you will not play the goat[4]
    Under Bobs.

'E's a little down on drink,
    Chaplain Bobs;
But it keeps us outer Clink –
    Don't it, Bobs?
So we will not complain
Tho' 'e's water on the brain,
If 'e leads us straight again –
    Blue-light Bobs.[5]

If you stood 'im on 'is 'ead
    Father Bobs,
You could spill a quart of lead
    Outer Bobs.
'E's been at it thirty years,
An-amassin' souveneers
In the way o' slugs and spears –
    Ain't yer, Bobs?

What 'e does not know o' war,
    Gen'ral Bobs,
You can arst the shop next door –
    Can't they, Bobs?
Oh, 'e's little but he's wise;
'E's terror for 'is size,
An' – 'e – *does – not – advertise* –[6]
    Do yer, Bobs?

[4] Play the goat = play the fool.
[5] Blue light = a reformed alcoholic or non-drinker.
[6] This is a dig at Wolseley, who many thought was too pushy.

Now they've made a bloomin' Lord
    Outer Bobs,
Which was but 'is fair reward –
    Weren't it, Bobs?
So 'e'll wear a coronet
Where 'is 'elmet used to set;
But we know you won't forget –
    Will yer, Bobs?

Then 'ere's to Bobs Bahadur – little Bobs, Bobs, Bobs,
Pocket-Wellin'ton 'an *arder* –[7]
    Fightin' Bobs, Bobs, Bobs!
This ain't no bloomin' ode,
But you've 'elped the soldier's load,
An' for benefits bestowed,
    Bless yer, Bobs!

Early in 1893 he left India for good. There was talk of his becoming viceroy, but this post was never offered him, probably because of his views regarding government-approved brothels in India.

Venereal diseases were endemic in India, and for years the authorities attempted to control their spread through special hospitals for prostitutes, called lock hospitals, and through the control and inspection of prostitutes, particularly those patronized by soldiers. Near many cantonments there sprang up what were, in effect, officially approved houses of prostitution, regulated under a series of Contagious Diseases and Cantonments Acts. All went well until a commanding officer of the 2nd Cheshires tried to requisition younger and prettier prostitutes for his men and sparked a conflagration of righteous indignation among the pious, particularly in England. As a result, approved brothels and government prostitutes were forbidden.

Most officers, concerned for the health of their men, favoured the old system of supervised brothels and registered, regularly inspected prostitutes, and there was a sus-

---

[7] Arder = a half.

picion among the righteous that some commanding officers were not obeying the prohibition. When Roberts landed in England, a newspaper reporter asked him if this was indeed so. Roberts denied that the laws were being circumvented, saying, 'That the old system is abolished is pretty plainly proved by the fact that the disease is fast spreading in our Indian army'. Did this mean that Roberts approved of the old system? 'I did not say that', he snapped. 'I merely mention a fact'.

Indeed, he was stating an incontrovertible fact. The numbers of cases of venereal disease had soared since the repeal of the Contagious Diseases and Cantonments Acts in 1886. (In Bengal, where even the lock hospitals were shut down, the venereal disease rate shot up from 210.3 per thousand in the 1875–84 period to 450.4 per thousand in 1886.) But good solid facts can sometimes make poor politics and unpalatable reading: Roberts's remarks were widely quoted in influential periodicals. Talk of the viceroyship for Little Bobs evaporated.

Nevertheless, in 1895 he was made a field marshal. Shortly afterwards he was appointed commander-in-chief of Ireland, a pleasant post to hold just before retirement. In Dublin he and Nora maintained their social reputation as charming hosts. Ian Hamilton said of his chief, 'He must know everyone's name in every room and the more information he had about their heredity and career the better'. Wolseley thought Roberts a dreadful snob – as Wolseley was himself. Certainly Roberts believed in the importance of heredity, and he always took this into account when giving appointments. As Hamilton said, 'If it was clear a man owned a good grandmother he would give him a trial'.

In October 1899 when the Boer War erupted in South Africa and Transvaal Boers invaded Natal, Roberts, sixty-seven years old and still in Ireland, was generally considered too old for active service, as was his rival Wolseley, now commander-in-chief at the Horse Guards. It seemed a war for younger men, and Sir Redvers Buller, a member of

Sir Redvers Buller *(Photo: ILN Pic. Lib.)*

the Wolseley Ring, was selected to lead a British army corps to South Africa. With him went the handsome 27-year-old Freddy Roberts, Lord Roberts's only son, a Sandhurst graduate and a lieutenant in the King's Royal Rifle Corps.

Sir Redvers had been an excellent staff officer and army administrator, but he had never commanded an army in the field and he did not do well in South Africa. General Sir George White and a sizeable field force were beseiged at Ladysmith; General Sir William Gatacre suffered a particularly humiliating defeat at Stormberg in Cape Colony; Colonel Robert Baden-Powell (later founder of the Boy Scouts) was cooped up in Mafeking; and Kimberly and its diamond mines were surrounded with an impatient Cecil Rhodes penned up inside. General Lord Methuen, pushing an army forward to relieve Kimberley, suffered a serious defeat at Magersfontein, and Buller, with the bulk of the British forces in South Africa, in a blundering attempt to relieve Ladysmith suffered a severe reverse at Colenso. It was here that Buller's chief of artillery brought his guns into action so close to the Boer positions that his gunners were swept away by rifle fire, leaving the guns standing exposed and unmanned on the veld. Several daring but disasterous attempts were made to bring them away – it was considered particularly disgraceful to lose guns – and in one of these gallant, foolhardy tries, Lieutenant Freddy Roberts was shot from his saddle mortally wounded. He died the next day.*

Before the battle of Colenso, Roberts wrote a remarkable letter to Lord Lansdowne, the secretary of state for war, in which he pointed out that 'not a single commander in South Africa has ever had an independent command in the field' and that Buller seemed to be 'overwhelmed by the magnitude of the task imposed upon him'. He went on to say:

> I feel the greatest hesitation and dislike to expressing my opinion thus plainly, and nothing but the gravity of the situation and the strongest sense of duty would induce me to do so, or to offer – as I now do – to place my services at the disposal of the Government.

Lansdowne showed this letter to Lord Salisbury, but the 69-year-old prime minister thought the 67-year-old field marshal was too old. Roberts's offer was declined. Six days later the news from the front was so alarming that Salisbury changed his mind. Lansdowne telegraphed Roberts in Dublin, asking him to come to London and be prepared to leave at once for South Africa. Roberts received this tele-

---

* Lieutenant Roberts was given the Victoria Cross; it was the first posthumous award of the medal ever made.

gram on the same day that a telegram from Buller informed him that his son had been seriously wounded at Colenso.

He made his way to London, filled with a mixture of anxiety over his son and elation at the prospect of being appointed commander-in-chief of the largest expeditionary force ever to have left England. He arrived on Sunday, 17 December, and that same day met with Salisbury, Lansdowne and other members of the government at 10 Downing Street, where he was offered the command of all the British forces in South Africa, with Lord Kitchener as his chief of staff and second-in-command. He accepted.

A few hours later on the same afternoon a telegram that had been sent to Roberts in Dublin and re-routed to London reached Lansdowne. It announced the death of Freddy Roberts. Lansdowne went in search of Roberts and located him at Mackeller's Hotel, where he broke the news to him: 'The news was almost more than he could bear', said Lansdowne, 'and for a moment I thought he would break down, but he pulled himself together. I shall never forget the courage he showed, or the way in which he refused to allow this disaster to turn him aside from his duty'.

The final week in England was busy as he assembled a staff that included a number of his favourites: Ian Hamilton, George ('Prettyboy') Pretyman and Colonel G. F. R. Henderson, author of a brilliant biography of Thomas ('Stonewall') Jackson. One of his last duties was to call on the Queen at Windsor. On 22 October she wrote in her journal, 'Saw Lord Roberts after tea. He knelt down and kissed my hand. I said how much I felt for him. He could only answer, "I cannot speak of *that*, but I can of anything else"'.

Wolseley heard with envy of Roberts's appointment and predicted grave problems, particularly with Sir Redvers Buller, who he reckoned would resign on being superseded. In fact, Buller seemed relieved at having the responsibility of being commander-in-chief lifted from his shoulders. Buller was that rare individual – a man who understood his own strengths and weaknesses. He had not wanted to be commander-in-chief in South Africa, and he had told Lansdowne this before his appointment. In most of Wolseley's campaigns he had served as chief of staff or second-in-command, and in these capacities he had performed splendidly, but he shrank from the responsibilities of commander and knew he was not a strategist.

On 23 December, accompanied by Nora and one of their daughters, Roberts boarded ship at Southampton. A great crowd had assembled to see him off on the grey, overcast winter's day. He appeared on deck in a black coat and a top hat, which he raised to the cheering crowd. A reporter for *The Times* described him as a 'little, vigorous, resolute, sorrowful man in deep mourning'. His farewells said, the ship set out to sea, and Roberts turned to pace the deck alone, perhaps to think of his son or of the problems facing him in South Africa, where lay the greatest challenge he would ever face.

11

Roberts's ship put in at Gibraltar, and Kitchener came aboard. He had recently conquered the Sudan and had been serving as governor-general there when he was offered the post of chief of staff to Roberts in South Africa. The two men were exact opposites, both physically and temperamentally: the tall and imperious Kitchener towered over the mild-mannered Little Bobs.

Roberts lost no time in shaking up the British forces in Cape Colony. He added regiments of colonials, ordered that one company from each infantry battalion be converted into mounted infantry, gathered up all the units scattered over Cape Colony on guard duties, and rearranged the transport system. He allowed Buller to stay on in Natal while he himself prepared to conquer the Orange Free State and the Transvaal. On 6 February 1900, less than four weeks after their arrival in Cape Town, Roberts and Kitchener went secretly by train to the western front.

The situation looked bleak. Roberts was told that Cecil Rhodes threatened to surrender Kimberly over the head of the garrison commander; Ladysmith was still in a state of siege, and Buller had been defeated in every attempt to relieve it; Methuen, after his defeat at Magersfontein, was sitting inactive on the Modder River with 37,000 men and 34,000 transport animals (including some draft horses from London bus companies). All his supplies had to be brought forward on a single-track railway line stretching 600 miles back to Cape Town. Many of the Boers in Cape Colony were disaffected and sympathetic toward the Boer cause, and there were fears of a rebellion in the Cape too. Roberts, however, was confident and decisive.

On 11 February, two days after his arrival at Methuen's camp, he ordered an advance, or rather a wide movement around the left flank of the positions held by the Boer General Piet Cronjé. Four days later, Roberts's cavalry division under Major-General John French (later created Earl of Ypres) dashed through the Boer lines and relieved Kimberley. Cronjé, finding his line of communication with Bloemfontein (capital of the Orange Free State) seriously threatened, abandoned his entrenched positions and began a retreat along the line of the Modder River.

British infantry, by hard marching, clung to the rear guard of the retreating Boers, and on 17 February French's cavalry came pounding up from Kimberley to block their path and prevent their crossing the Modder. The Boers, many of whom had women and children with them in their ox-carts, went to ground at a place called Paardeberg Drift, twenty-three miles south-east of Kimberley, where British infantry launched an unsuccessful attack on them. Two things soon became clear: the Boers could not escape from their laager, and the British could not evict them.

When Roberts received word of the stalemate at Paardeberg, he was lying ill at his headquarters at Jacobsdal several miles away. Kitchener was left to handle the situation. But Roberts was to have no peace, for Kitchener made

Lord Roberts at Paardeberg after the surrender of General Cronjé
(Photo: BBC Hulton Picture Library)

a hash of things, rashly throwing soldiers at the entrenched
Boer riflemen, who accounted for 1,270 British casualties.
In the end, Roberts had to climb out of his sickbed and ride
to Paardeberg. After inspecting the positions, he aban-

doned the costly infantry attacks and simply laid siege to the laager, pounding the Boers with his artillery until on 27 February – the anniversary of the battle of Majuba – Cronjé surrendered with 4,000 of his men, and uncounted women and children.

There were two other battles and a serious setback when the Boer General Christiaan de Wet made a successful attack on a large supply column before Bloemfontein was occupied on 13 March. Roberts was forced to pause at Bloemfontein, not only because of a shortage of transport but also because of a severe epidemic of enteric (typhoid) fever, largely caused by troops drinking the polluted water of the Modder at Paardeberg and by the general lack of elementary sanitary precautions in the army.

At the beginning of May, Roberts was again in a position to advance and he moved into the Transvaal on a broad front, reaching Kroonstad on 12 May and taking Pretoria, capital of the Transvaal, on 5 June, having defeated the Boers in every battle. By 1 October he had chased most of the Boer armies over the border into Portuguese Mozambique, where they were disarmed, and he was in possession of all the major cities and towns. He had lifted the sieges of Mafeking and Kimberley; the mines, factories and railways were all in his hands. Transvaal's president, Paul Kruger, had fled to Europe; Buller had finally relieved Ladysmith, and all organized Boer forces had been evicted from Natal; both of the Boer republics – the Orange Free State and the Transvaal – were now annexed as British colonies; and it appeared to most that, except for some isolated guerrilla activity, the war was over. Roberts thought so: 'There is nothing now left of the Boer army but a few marauding bands', he declared, and he left for England, leaving Kitchener to mop up. No one foresaw that the stubborn Boers would fight on for another year and a half.

In Britain, Roberts received a hero's welcome. He was named commander-in-chief of the British army, succeeding Wolseley. He was raised in the peerage to the rank of earl – with a special remainder to his daughters, as there was no longer a son to inherit the title. He was made a Knight of the Garter, the first and only general in the Victorian–Edwardian age to be so honoured, and a grateful Parliament awarded him £100,000 – a goodly sum today and a considerable fortune in 1900.

It was generally felt that Wolseley had not been a good commander-in-chief of the army, and there was widespread support and enthusiasm for Roberts's appointment. But Roberts's performance was to prove no better than Wolseley's had been. Much of the blame for this lay in the nature of the office, for, in truth, despite the lofty title, there was very little in the way of reform that the commander-in-chief could accomplish. Roberts introduced a more practical field service uniform and placed greater emphasis on more realistic training, but there was no general staff, and, accustomed as he was to the organization and methods of the Indian army, he found it difficult to adjust to the different ways of the British army at home.

In 1903 a royal commission recommended the abolition of the position of commander-in-chief, and in February 1904 Roberts resigned. For a time he remained a member of the newly formed Committee of Imperial Defence, but finding himself in disagreement with many of the government's defence policies, he resigned in November 1905 and for the next ten years devoted himself to promoting the cause of national service. He failed. So averse were the British to conscription that it was not instituted until the First World War – and even then only after the war had been raging for nearly two years. Roberts did not live long enough to see it used.

The controversy over conscription had painful personal repercussions. Ian Hamilton, his most devoted disciple and defender, disagreed with his chief and in 1911 published a short book, *Compulsory Service*, expressing his views. Roberts was incensed and deeply hurt. He spoke bitterly of Hamilton's 'defection'. His response was an angry book of his own, *Fallacies and Facts,* in which he tore at Hamilton's ideas and arguments. The First World War proved Roberts to have been right – as he usually was.

In November 1914 the 82-year-old field marshal insisted on going to France to give encouragement to the men of the Indian Army Corps who were arriving there. He accepted Hamilton's invitation to spend his last night in England with him at his London house, and the two old soldiers were reconciled, Roberts again, as of old, affectionately calling Hamilton 'Johnny'. Three days later Roberts was dead. He had caught a chill on landing in France. His body was returned to England and buried with all pomp in St Paul's Cathedral.

In 1913 Lord Roberts's youngest daughter, Ada, married Colonel F. E. Lewin and a year later produced a son who grew to manhood just in time for the Second World War. In the cloisters at Eton there is a plaque which reads:

We Praise thee O God For Three Soldier Sons of Eton
FREDERICK SLEIGH EARL ROBERTS
Of Kandahar and Pretoria Field Marshal V.C.
Royal Artillery and Irish Guards
1832–1914 St. Omer France – His Son
FREDERICK HUGH SHERSTON ROBERTS
Lieutenant V.C. The King's Royal Rifle Corps
1872–1899 Colenso South Africa – His Grandson
FREDERICK ROBERTS ALEXANDER LEWIN
Lieutenant Royal Artillery and Irish Guards
1915–1940 – Norway
AWAKE REMEMBRANCE OF THESE VALIANT
DEAD AND WITH YOUR PUISSANT ARM RENEW
THEIR FEATS. YOU ARE THEIR HEIR.

Garnet Wolseley (1833–1913)

'All Sir Garnet'

1

Garnet Joseph Wolseley was born near Dublin on 4 June 1833, the son of Major Garnet Wolseley of the 25th (The King's Own Borderers) Regiment of Foot. His paternal grandfather had fought in the Seven Years War, and the family history was liberally sprinkled with soldiers. Major Wolseley had married late in life a woman twenty-five years younger than he, who produced four sons and three daughters within seven years. His death shortly after the birth of the youngest child left his family in straitened circumstances. Young Garnet, the eldest, was educated by his mother and then at a local school in Ireland.

There was never any doubt as to his intended career, but it was not easy for a young man without means to obtain a commission. He first applied to the Duke of Wellington at the age of fourteen, requesting a commission without purchase in consideration of his father's thirty years of service. The Duke promised to consider him when he reached sixteen, then the minimum age for an officer, but his sixteenth birthday passed without an appointment. He again wrote to the Duke, and was ignored. He appealed to Lord Raglan, Wellington's military secretary, and still nothing happened. He was eighteen and his prospects seemed bleak when his mother wrote a pleading letter, begging the commander-in-chief not to forget 'a poor widow of an old officer' who had educated her son for the army but could not afford to purchase a commission. At last, on 2 July 1852, when all hope appeared to have vanished, the Duke unexpectedly presented the young man with a commission as an ensign in the 12th (East Suffolk) Regiment of Foot. As young Wolseley could not afford to live in his regiment in England, he at once transferred to the 80th (Staffordshire Volunteers) Regiment of Foot (later called the South Staffordshire Regiment) and in due course found himself aboard an East Indiaman bound for Calcutta.

Wolseley had the proper outlook for an ambitious Victorian subaltern. He knew that marriage was 'ruinous to the prospects of a young officer'; he was convinced that all proper British gentlemen were born courageous and were naturally endowed with the qualities needed to lead men in battle; and he harboured a fierce desire to cover himself with glory. He was a handsome, clean-cut, slight, but well-knit and athletic young man, standing five feet seven inches tall. His weak chin and jaw belied a resolute soldier. As he did not have, and could never expect to have, the money necessary to purchase advancement, he intended to succeed by seeking combat, by great daring and by constant study of his profession. His one fear, as he later confessed, was that he would die before he had made a name for himself.

On arrival at Calcutta, Wolseley, who 'longed to hear the whistle of a bullet fired in earnest', was eager to join his regiment, then in Burma fighting in the Second Burma War, but by the time he reached Rangoon, early in 1853, the war was winding down and he was dismayed to find that there was more drill on the parade ground than action against the recalcitrant Burmese. When a clever dacoit named Myat Toon began to cause trouble and a small expedition of 800 men was sent against him, Wolseley considered himself fortunate to be a part of it.

In spite of the melting heat and enervating humidity, Wolseley and the other officers wore tight shell jackets buttoned to the chin, forage caps with puggarees and white buckskin gloves. In this uniform he light-heartedly boarded a river steamer for a voyage up the Irrawaddy River. Floating down the river past them came rafts bearing grisly reminders of the fate of British prisoners. Men crowded the rail to stare in silence at the spread-eagle, mutilated and crucified corpses of British soldiers who had fought in earlier expeditions. On landing, the troops snaked for days along a narrow, winding path through dense jungle. It was a dreadful time. Myat Toon's snipers exacted a daily toll, and cholera struck the column, felling soldiers mysteriously and without warning.

Young Wolseley saw a man killed in action for the first time. 'I was not at the moment the least excited', he said, 'and it gave me a rather unpleasant sensation'. He was to see many more men die soon, for after a twelve-day march the column reached Myat Toon's fortified stronghold.

The first assault failed, and the general officer commanding called for volunteers. Wolseley and another young officer sprang forward to lead the forlorn hope. Collecting a party of soldiers, they led them cheering down a narrow ravine toward the enemy's stockade. Wolseley was ecstatic. This was the road to glory. Then he fell into a hole, a cleverly hidden mantrap, and was knocked unconscious. When he recovered, he found that his storming party had melted away, and there was nothing for him to do but bolt ignominiously to his own lines.

The general called for a second storming party, and again

Wolseley leading the storming party at Myat Toon's stronghold
(Photo: Mary Evans Picture Library)

Wolseley volunteered to lead it. Writing more than forty years later, he recollected his emotions:

> What a supremely delightful moment it was! No one in cold blood can imagine how intense is the pleasure of such a position who had not experienced it himself. . . . for the moment your whole existence, soul and body, seems to revel in a true sense of glory. . . . The blood seems to boil, the brain to be on fire. Oh! that I could again hope to experience such sensations! . . . in a long and varied military life. . . . I have never experienced the same unalloyed and elevating satisfaction, or known again the joy I then felt as I ran for the enemy's stockades at the head of a small mob of soldiers, most of them boys like myself.

This time the attack succeeded, but Wolseley was bowled over by a gingall bullet the size of a lemon that made a deep furrow through his left thigh. He tried to stop the bleeding by covering the wound with his hand, but the blood spurted through the fingers of his pipe-clayed gloves as he did his best to cheer his men on, shouting and flourishing his sword.

This first battle was Wolseley's last in Burma. He was taken downriver on a boat loaded with other wounded. The temperature soared above one hundred degrees Fahrenheit, and the debilitating humidity added to the horror of the journey. He had developed a fierce fever, and it was thought best to starve it, so throughout the days he watched as the doctors sat on deck drinking, eating, laughing, and talking while he lay hot, hungry and in pain. A deep, festering wound in a tropical climate was potentially fatal, and Wolseley was fortunate to have survived and not to have lost at least his leg. His gallantry in action earned him a mention in dispatches and promotion to lieutenant. He was shipped home and recovered just in time to take part in the Crimean War.

2

Wolseley transferred to the 90th Perthshire Light Infantry (later called the Cameronians), a regiment with which he always identified, and on 19 November 1854 he sailed from Kingstown, Ireland, for the Crimea. As he marched with his company past the Royal St George Yacht Club, he saw his mother sitting on a grassy bank watching him and crying. It was a sight that remained in his memory for ever.

He had missed the early battles of the Crimean campaign, and he was in agony en route to the seat of the war lest the fighting should end before he arrived. He need not have worried. Although there were no more set-piece battles such as the one at the Alma, and the army was bogged down in the seemingly endess siege of Sebastopol, there were still opportunities for action. As Royal Engineers seemed to lead the most dangerous existence, Wolseley volunteered to serve with them, and he so distinguished himself that he was again promoted. When it was discovered that he was only twenty-one, the promotion was withdrawn, an injustice Wolseley vehemently protested until the promotion was later confirmed. On 26 January 1855, after less than three years' service, he became a captain – a rare and spectacular rise for a young man in the infantry without wealth or great family connections.

Life in the Crimea was dangerous, unhealthy and uncomfortable, but Wolseley gloried in it. To his dowager aunt he rhapsodized, 'Man shooting is the finest sport of all; there is a certain amount of infatuation about it, that the more you kill the more you wish to kill'. He declared he could look upon the corpse of a comrade with whom he had dined the night before 'with as much indifference as if it were a dog [he] had killed at home' – a bit of bravado for a young man who throughout his life could never tolerate the sight of raw meat or bear to see a deer skinned or even steel himself to look into a butcher's shop.

One of the officers Wolseley met in the Crimea was Charles Gordon. They were almost the same age, and Wolseley was impressed with his 'indifference to danger of all sorts'. Gordon's high purpose and piety startled Wolseley and led him to remark, 'How inferior were all my aims in life to his'.

Wolseley was wounded once again, this time in the right thigh – a minor wound from which he quickly recovered. Shortly afterwards, however, he was severely wounded by a shell that killed two men standing beside him. A sergeant helped him back to a doctor. He was in dreadful shape: his left cheek flapped down to his collar; jagged bits of rock were embedded in his face; his right leg was cut by stones; a part of his shin was sheared off; one eye protruded grotesquely (he lost the sight in it for ever); a piece of his jawbone stuck out through his skin; and a large, sharp stone was embedded in his palate. The latter was extracted by a surgeon with forceps while another doctor held Wolseley's head between his knees. Chloroform was known then, but

it was not widely used, for pain was thought to be benefi-
cial. As J. J. Cole, an army surgeon during the Second Sikh
War, wrote:

> The practical surgeon views it [chloroform] in the hands of the
> military officer as a highly pernicious agent, which unques-
> tionably it is. . . . That it renders a poor patient unconscious
> cannot be doubted. But what is pain? It is one of the most pow-
> erful, one of the most salutary *stimulants* known. It often brings
> about reactions of the most natural kind. . . .

After some rough patching up, Wolseley was sent to a
monastery near Balaclava that had been converted into a
hospital, where he convalesced slowly. He had seen and
suffered enough to know the full horror of war, but he
remained an eager soldier. When he learned that a major
assault on Sebastopol was being prepared, he made a
determined effort to return to the front. Still nearly blind,
he groped his way to his horse and with a struggle managed to saddle it, but he was too weak to mount and, weep-
ing with frustration, was forced to give up.

When Sebastopol was finally taken, thanks mainly to the
assaults of the French, Wolseley's work in the trenches was
rewarded by a mention in dispatches, the French Legion of
Honour, and the Turkish Medjidie (Fifth Class). He was
recommended as well for promotion to major, but once again
his youth proved to be a stumbling block, although this
time the delay in confirming his promotion was a short one.
On 24 March 1858, when not yet twenty-five years old, he
became one of the youngest field officers in the British army,
and this without his purchasing a single step. It was a
remarkable achievement. His friend Chinese Gordon was
not promoted major until four years later, by which time
Wolseley had been a lieutenant-colonel for three years. Rapid
promotion continued; he was made a full colonel the day
after his thirty-second birthday and he was a major-general before he was thirty-five.

3

Instead of returning home to convalesce as he could have done after the occupation of Sebastopol, Wolseley took the post of DAQMG, and so was one of the last British soldiers to leave the Crimea. As he sailed away at last, he asked himself, 'Have I done well?'

He had done very well, but he was critical: 'I could have. . . . I ought to have done better'. There was some comfort in reflecting that perhaps God had spared him for some grander purpose and that there was still 'an opportunity of becoming at least known if not famous'. For Wolseley, fame was indeed the spur, and he lusted only for opportunities to distinguish himself. He was remarkably fortunate that many occasions to do so presented themselves.

After a few months of garrison duty at the newly established military station at Aldershot and a long home leave, he rejoined his regiment at Plymouth just as it was about to embark for China. The 90th Light Infantry, now up to full war strength of more than a thousand bayonets, was in fine physical condition, and the men were eager for a new campaign. They regarded the world, said Wolseley, as 'specially created for their own wild pleasures, of which . . . war with all its sudden dangers, and at times maddening excitement, was the greatest'. This was certainly the view the young Wolseley entertained, and it undoubtedly reflected the attitude of most other officers; how much it reflected the views of the other ranks is arguable, although in Britain's all-volunteer Victorian army there were doubtless many soldiers in the ranks who looked forward eagerly to the excitements of a campaign.

On 8 April 1857 Wolseley, with three companies of his regiment and some drafts for regiments already in China, boarded the troop-ship *Transit* (dubbed by the soldiers *Chance It*) and headed for Hong Kong. The *Transit* encountered a heavy storm in the Bay of Biscay and sprang a leak, forcing men to man the pumps constantly. In another storm the ship's mainmast was broken, and finally the *Transit* foundered on a rock in shark-infested waters off the coast of Malaya. The survivors lived on half rations of biscuits for several days until rescued and carried to Singapore. Captain (later General) Frederick Stephenson of the Scots Fusilier Guards described the voyage in letters to his mother and a nephew. 'I don't think I have ever been happier in my life than during the whole of the voyage here', Stephenson wrote. 'It has been one incessant flow of excitement the whole time'.

It was when the *Transit* had put in at Cape Town that the soldiers learned of the great mutiny in the Bengal army. The wreck of the transport so close to India enabled Wolseley and his men to be diverted from China to Bengal, where every British soldier was needed. And every British soldier was eager to avenge the atrocities that had been committed by the mutineers. Wolseley, reflecting not only his own fury but certainly that of the rest of the army, wrote to his brother Richard, 'My sword is thirsty for the blood of these cursed women-slayers'. Revenge was uppermost in the minds of all soldiers. Wolseley and his men, after landing in Calcutta, were hurried forward to join the army being assembled under the commander-in-chief, Sir Colin Campbell. On the way they captured a rebel sowar, and there was no trouble finding a hangman. At Cawnpore, where British women and children had been brutally massacred, Wolseley trembled with 'unchristian passions' at the thought that 'a native should have dared put his hands upon an Englishwoman'.

Wolseley took part in the final relief of Lucknow and was, in fact, the first man to reach the beleaguered defenders of the Residency. He hoped to be recommended for the Victoria Cross but instead found that he was the object of Sir Colin's wrath for having exceeded his orders in pushing his way into the Residency. He was not even mentioned in dispatches, although at the end of the Mutiny he was made a brevet lieutenant-colonel.

The young Garnet Wolseley *(Photo: ILN Pic. Lib.)*

It was nearly a year before the expedition actually reached China, and in the meantime life in India began to return to normal. Wolseley, the dashing young lieutenant-colonel, his chest ablaze with six medals, was regarded as a prize catch by young Englishwomen and their mothers, who were well aware of the rule of thumb that subalterns must not marry; captains may marry; majors should marry; and lieutenant-colonels must marry. But the elusive Wolseley contented himself with an 'Eastern Princess' who served 'all the purposes of a wife without giving any of the bother' and who at the same time improved his Hindustani – 'Buying a native dictionary' was the expression.

4

In February 1860 he boarded ship for China as deputy assistant quartermaster general on the staff of Sir Hope Grant, a brave and popular general who laboured under considerable difficulty, both in speaking and in writing his thoughts. 'Puzzle-headed', some called him, but he was an accomplished cello player, a likeable man, and Wolseley always expressed the highest regard for him.

In China, Wolseley took part in the storming of the Taku forts and he was present at the looting of the Summer Palace, where a small enamel figurine given to him by a soldier was his only loot.

When the war ended, Wolseley joined Sir Hope Grant in a pleasure cruise around Japan, after which he was dispatched on a mission to Nanking to gather information about the Taipings. He was well treated there and was left free to make notes and draw sketches of the fortifications, which reminded him of the primitive forts he had built as a schoolboy. He found the Taiping army equally unimpressive. There was some talk of offering Wolseley the command of the Ever Victorious Army, but it was probably fortunate that the appointment went to Gordon instead. Wolseley was best at commanding British regulars, and he had an undisguised disdain for all foreigners – Asians, Africans, Americans or Chinese.

Back in England, he was given eighteen months' leave. He spent a part of it in Paris studying art and most of the rest fox-hunting in Ireland. It was during this leave that he met Miss Louisa Erskine and fell 'most dreadfully in love'. There were, however, financial obstacles to the marriage, for Wolseley provided the sole financial support for his mother and his unwed sister. His brothers, too, were a burden: Dick became a surgeon and eventually earned his own way in the world, but Fred was an inventor whose inventions failed to earn money, and George, for whom Wolseley had purchased a commission and rank, was always in debt.*

The course of true love was also impeded by the threat of war with the United States. Wolseley was sent to Canada. A Union man-of-war had stopped a Royal Mail steamer, the *Trent*, on the high seas and had taken off two Confederate envoys who were on their way to Britain. The incident created a furore, and troops were at once dispatched to Canada. By the time Wolseley reached Nova Scotia, however, the incident was over: President Lincoln's government, unwilling to go to war with Britain while fighting to subdue the rebellious southern states, had apologized and released the captured Confederate envoys. Wolseley and his fellow officers were therefore able to board ship for Boston. Although warned that it would be prudent to be inconspicuous, they travelled peacefully to Montreal through the land they had been sent to attack, and were surprised by the friendliness and courtesy they met everywhere.

In spite of the lack of action, Wolseley enjoyed Canada, a paradise of soldiers', as he called it, with its fishing, hunting, ice skating, sleighing and beautiful, fresh-faced young women. A number of young officers quickly fell in love and had to be shipped home post-haste to prevent 'imprudent marriages to charming young women without fortunes'. The prudent Wolseley was content simply to admire the Cana-

---

* Although regarded as the family black sheep, and a drain on his elder brother's financial resources, George saw almost as much action as his famous brother, serving in the Indian Mutiny, the Second Afghan War, the Egyptian War of 1882, the Gordon Relief Expedition and campaigns in Burma in 1887 and 1889–91. He eventually became a general and was knighted for his services.

dian girls; it was the American Civil War raging to the south that he found irresistible. In 1862 he took a two months' leave to visit it.

Most of his time was spent with the confederates, with whom he sympathized. Near Winchester, Virginia, not long after the battle of Antietam, he was welcomed by General Robert E. Lee, who made a strong impression on him. Looking back on this meeting toward the end of his life, he wrote, 'I have met two men whom I prized as being above all the world I have ever known, and the greatest of the two was General Lee'. (The other was Chinese Gordon.) Wolseley was also taken by General Thomas ('Stonewall') Jackson, and referred to his 'fascinating smile' and 'impressive eyes'. Jackson did not want to speak of the war, but he talked much of a visit he had once made to England and of his memories of the seven lancet windows in York Minster.

Most European military observers of the American Civil War felt that there were no important lessons to be learned from these hastily enlisted, ill-trained civilians in uniform, but Wolseley was fascinated by all that he saw and heard, and he was impressed by the southern farm boys who made up the bulk of Lee's army. Late in life, after he had seen many armies and much of war, he wrote, 'This Southern army interested my beyond any army I ever saw before or since'.

When he returned to Montreal, he described his impressions in *Blackwood's Magazine* (January 1863), recommending that Britain enter the conflict on the side of the Confederacy and bring to an end a war in which 'the military despotism of one portion of the States under the dictatorship of an insignificant lawyer attempts to crush out the freedom of the rest'.

5

Interesting as his trip south had been, and pleasant as was life in Canada, Wolseley itched for action; he was often

depressed and spoke of 'these wasted years'. He even thought
of leaving the army and becoming a civil engineer, though
it is hard to believe he was serious. His ennui was relieved
when, in May 1866, Canada was invaded by 800 American
Fenians at Niagara. As many of the Irish-Americans were
experienced soldiers who had served in the Civil War, and
as the Canadian forces sent against them were ill-trained
militia units under incompetent officers, the Fenians at first
had some small success. Wolseley was sent to the scene,
but discovered on arrival that the American government
had already intervened and had captured and disarmed most
of the Fenians still on the American shore of Lake Ontario.
General George Meade was sent by the American army to
restore order on the American side of the border, and the
Fenian invasion fizzled out. Wolseley was put in charge of
a camp of instruction, and the Canadian volunteers were
drilled into semblances of soldiers, but it was soon evident
that the Fenians, deprived of the support of the United States
government, would not again invade.

Wolseley returned to Ireland on leave, and there his
enthusiasm for Miss Louisa Erskine was rekindled; he asked
for her hand and she gave it. She was a beautiful young
woman with a fair complexion, yellow hair and a figure
whose proportions, she was proud to admit, were identical
with those of the Venus de Milo.* Wolseley particularly
admired her ears and her feet, which he considered perfec-
tion (he had a plaster cast made of one foot). She was a
clever woman, well educated and fluent in French. She was
to prove helpful to him, not only socially but also in polish-
ing his spelling and grammar, teaching him the differences
between 'fir' and 'fur', and 'week' and 'weak'. Wolseley
entertained a low opinion of most men's intelligence, and
an even lower opinion of women's. (He once wrote that 'nine
men out of ten & ninety-nine women out of a hundred are
simply fools'.) Louisa was obviously an exception. She did

---

* That would be 37–26–38, though the Venus is six feet six inches tall.

not possess the highly desirable fortune, but her family did provide her with enough to give her financial independence so that she did not add to her husband's financial burdens.

The wedding was postponed when Wolseley was recalled to Canada in September 1867 to serve as deputy quartermaster general. In the following year he was able to take two months' leave to hurry home, marry Miss Erskine on his thirty-fifth birthday and then dash back to Canada, his bride following in October. In due course Louisa presented him with what was to be their only child, a daughter they named Frances.

It was at this time that the bright, bumptious young colonel put himself in the forefront of those advocating army reform by publishing in 1869 *The Soldier's Pocket-Book for Field Service*. It was packed with information about tactics, military law, surveying, scouting, the duty of staff officers and instructions for indenting stores, manoeuvring an army, caring for elephants, the management of spies and burial at sea. There were tables of weights and measures, recipes for Irish stew and rates of exchange for foreign currencies. Vaccination was advised for all officers going on active service, and homage was paid to athleticism:

> Being a good sportsman, a good cricketer, good at rackets or any other manly game, is no mean recommendation for staff employment. Such a man, without book lore, is preferable to the most deeply-read one of lethargic habits.

In addition to all this, there was a plethora of military opinions – Wolseley's. He freely criticized current policies, practices and military equipment, and he warned his readers against the 'Admiralty clique'. Soldiers, he advised, should be taught to 'despise those in civil life' and should not be 'brought into contact with the softening influences of old men and respectable women'. He plumped for temperance and warned officers to pay closer attention to the comfort and welfare of their men. He had hard words for newspaper correspondents, 'who eat the rations of fighting men and do no work at all'. But even this 'race of drones' could be turned to some advantage: a canny officer could, by feeding them misinformation, deceive the enemy. The book earned Wolseley both advocates and enemies; it went through numerous editions, for it was a readable adjunct to *The Queen's Regulations* and *Field Exercises*.

6

In 1869 the Canadian government took over large sections of western Canada from the Hudson's Bay Company, including the Red River area of Manitoba. There were those who objected to this, and Louis Riel, a métis (half-breed), led a revolt. Establishing the Republic of the North-West with headquarters at Fort Gary (today Winnipeg), he then 'executed' a minor Canadian official. A newly appointed lieutenant-governor was afraid to enter Riel's territory. The Canadian government organized a punitive expedition to move against Riel, and it appointed Wolseley to command what was to be the last British military expedition in North America. Of the 1,200 men in the Red River Expedition, most were Canadians, but there were 373 officers and other ranks of the elite 60th Rifles (later the King's Royal Rifle Corps), a battery of Royal Field Artillery, a detachment of Royal Engineers and assorted British staff officers.

Among Wolseley's officers were three who were to become famous as members of what came to be known as the Wolseley Ring, officers whom he found to be outstanding and whom he could trust. One of these was Lieutenant Redvers Buller of the 60th Rifles, a man of whom Wolseley later said, 'He was the only man with us of any rank who could carry a 100-pound barrel of pork over a portage on his back'. Another was Lieutenant Hugh McCalmont, who had taken leave from the 9th Lancers and, armed with a recommendation from General Sir Hope Grant, had come to Canada at his own expense to join the expedition. Wolseley at first refused to include him, but the young officer was so insistent, even insinuating that he would paddle his own canoe and go along anyway, that Wolseley finally relented and appointed him as an aide.

The third man was William Butler of the 69th Foot, an officer of little formal education who became one of the most literate soldiers of the Victorian era and who is credited with first suggesting the organization that became the North-West Mounted Police. He was in Ireland on leave when he learned that Wolseley, whom he had met two years earlier, was organizing the Red River Expedition. He telegraphed, 'Remember Butler 69th Regiment', and left for Canada without waiting for a reply. Later he wrote:

> Everybody wanted to go on this expedition, which, small as it was in numbers, had such an immense 'beyond' in it, a beyond into which steam power did not enter, where there were no roads, where there were still real live Indians and great silent lakes, vast woods and rushing rivers, and more than these, boats and canoes, in which brains would be at the helm, skill at the prow, and youth and muscle working at the oars.

Butler arrived to find that there was no place for him on the staff, but Wolseley sent him on a special mission to the Red River area to discover the exact state of affairs. Travelling mostly through the United States, where there were more roads and he could move faster, he reached Fort Gary, interviewed Riel and then doubled back to meet the expedition before it was half-way to its destination. He had carried out an arduous assignment with dash and courage, but what he had to report, the state of affairs at Fort Gary twelve days earlier, was of little use to Wolseley. However, he went into Wolseley's book as a good officer to remember.

The Red River Expedition was Wolseley's first independent command, and it, like all those that followed, was marked by careful planning from the start. Still, it was an

arduous journey, and to Louisa he spoke of 'the bubble reputation' that he sought 'not at the cannon's but the mos-
quito's mouth'. Butler later wrote the following description
of his chief:

> At this time Colonel Wolseley was in the prime of manhood,
> somewhat under middle height, of well-knit, well-propor-
> tioned figure; handsome, clean-cut features, a broad and lofty
> forehead over which brown chestnut hair closely curled;
> exceedingly sharp, penetrating blue eyes . . . the best and most
> brilliant brain I ever met in the army. He was possessed of a
> courage equal to his brain power. It could be neither daunted
> nor subdued. . . . I never knew him tired, no matter what might
> be the fatigue he underwent. I never knew his eye deceived, no
> matter how short might be the look he gave at a man or a plan.

The little army covered 1,200 miles by train, steamer,
canoe and overland marching, reaching Fort Gary, their
destination, with their uniforms in tatters but without the
loss of a single man and with not a single sick soldier. It
was an astonishing accomplishment, but when they arrived
and stormed the fort, they found it empty. Riel, fore-
warned, had fled to the United States to try again another
day. Wolseley wrote to Louisa, 'I cannot tell you how disappointed all are that we have not had a chance of ridding
the world of this cowardly murderer'.

Lieutenant Butler said ruefully that he was 'disgusted at
having come so far to hear the band play "God Save the
Queen" ', but Wolseley had told his men before they left
Toronto, 'Our mission is one of peace, and the sole object
of the expedition is to secure Her Majesty's sovereign
authority'. They had accomplished this mission ably and
had every reason to congratulate themselves. Wolseley
attributed the expedition's success to 'the fact that it was
planned and organized away from all War Office influence
and meddling'. It had cost the modest sum of £100,000.
Because no blood was shed, the government, in spite of the

arduousness of the campaign, did not see fit to issue a medal until thirty-nine years later.

7

Wolseley was a hero in Canada, but in Britain, where all eyes were focused on the Franco-Prussian War, scarcely a newspaper mentioned his feat. The government, however, recognized his services, and he was given a knighthood, but then for a time he was allowed to languish on half pay. He occupied his time writing on military subjects and became well known as a thinker and reformer in an army that distrusted thinkers and resented all attempts at reform.

It was fortunate for Wolseley that just at this time there happened to be a most remarkable secretary of state for war, the brilliant Edward (later Viscount) Cardwell. An interesting man, he had taken firsts in both classics and mathematics at Oxford; he was called to the Bar at the Inner Temple, and in 1842 he entered Parliament. In 1868 he became secretary of state for war, although he knew nothing about the army and loathed violence in any form. Still, he applied himself with a will to the problems of imperial defence and introduced the most radical reforms ever proposed for the British army. It was Cardwell who introduced short service, so deplored by Roberts, and it was he who first established a reserve. He also altered the regimental system and set about the abolition of the purchase of commissions in the infantry and cavalry.

To help him, he brought Wolseley into the War Office as assistant adjutant-general. He needed all the help he could get and was delighted to find a soldier ally. He could deal with Parliament, but his strongest adversaries were within the army. Army reform – or change of any sort – confronted a formidable obstacle: the Duke of Cambridge, cousin of the Queen and commander-in-chief of the army. To the Duke, Wolseley was 'that cocksure young bookworm' stuffed with 'new-fangled ideas'. To Wolseley the

Duke was 'too old to take in new ideas about a subject – war – of which he is most profoundly ignorant'.

The proposal to change the purchase system aroused the greatest controversy. It was fervidly discussed in the press, Parliament, drawing-rooms, clubs and regimental messes. Advocates of purchase feared that if it was abolished the army would no longer be officered by gentlemen; those who favoured abolition argued that the system held back good officers and promoted wealthy incompetents beyond their abilities. In the end, the government in effect purchased the army back from its officers – by royal warrant, not by acts of Parliament – but the public debate of the issue left a residue of bitterness, and much of the odium fell upon Wolseley. Still, his career did not suffer, and when a new colonial war appeared on the horizon, Wolseley was appointed a local major-general and sent off to fight it.

8

On the West Coast of Africa the most aggressive tribe was the Ashanti, led by King Koti Karikari (called King Coffee by the Tommies). Their warriors were well organized, bloodthirsty and ruthless. An inland tribe, the Ashanti harassed and often terrorized the more peaceful coastal people of the Gold Coast (today Ghana), who were under British protection. When it was decided that Ashanti depredations could no longer be tolerated, a military expedition under Wolseley was assembled to express Britain's displeasure to the savages.

To assist him in this enterprise, he consulted the list of exceptional officers he had been compiling for several years. He had a good eye for military talent, and the officers he selected became known first as the Ashanti Ring and then as the Wolseley Ring or the Wolseley Gang. For this little war in the African bush, it was said, he used 'the finest steel in our army to cut brushwood'. It is interesting to note that although Chinese Gordon was available, Wolseley, who

King Koti Karikari with his warriors *(Photo: ILN Pic. Lib.)*

always spoke of him in the highest terms, did not ask for him – not for this campaign or for any other.

In the past it had been the custom to select a general, give him soldiers and send him off to fight. Details of the enemy, the terrain and the military problems involved could be picked up at the seat of war. The Ashanti campaign was remarkable for the planning that preceded it. The British Intelligence Department was pitifully primitive, but it supplied Wolseley with all that it knew about the country, its people and its politics. And, for the first time in British history, the commander of a military expedition sat down and discussed arrangements with key men in the War Office, the Admiralty, the Colonial Office and the various departments that would supply him with the tools and stores for his work.

Whitehall was reluctant to expose British troops to the dreaded diseases of West Africa, 'the white man's grave', so it was hoped that the Ashantis could be smashed by the use of local manpower alone. If not – and Wolseley thought not – two battalions of regulars, the 2nd Welch Fusiliers and the 2nd Rifle Brigade, plus a battery of field artillery and a company of Royal Engineers, were placed on stand-by in Britain. All were equipped with tropical clothing, ready to embark on short notice. Having studied the meteorological conditions of the African West Coast, Wolseley wisely planned to land, swiftly march to the Ashanti capital of Kumasi, subdue the enemy and depart, all in the healthiest season of the year.

Wolseley and his staff recruited a small army of coastal Africans, but they proved almost worthless as fighters. Wolseley told Louisa, 'The negroes are like so many monkeys; they are a lazy good-for-nothing race'. The regulars in Britain were soon sent for. Wolseley also requested that a third battalion be alerted, and a battalion of the Black Watch was made ready and soon embarked for Africa.

Wolseley now prepared his plan of attack, carefully keeping it secret from all except those staff officers with a need to know. He lied to newspaper correspondents about the direction he intended to take, and supplied the Ashantis with misleading information about his intentions. He then scored a small victory at a place called Esaman. Shortly after the battle he fell ill with what the doctors diagnosed as 'ardent fever'. Delirious for days, he came close to death. Perhaps a thought that spurred him to recover was that Evelyn Wood, whose abilities he recognized but whom he characterized as 'that ambitious little red-headed colonel', might be scheming to take over his command.

Even while Wolseley lay sick aboard the hospital ship *Simoon*, the work ashore went on. The chief engineer, Major Robert Home, ploughed a road through the jungle toward Kumasi, building 237 bridges, corduroying a way through the swamps and stringing telegraph line. Stations were built at intervals of seven to twelve miles, and at each there were huts, provisions and a hospital.

9

Wolseley recovered but was still very weak when, on 27 December 1873, he seated himself in a light buggy drawn by six powerful Africans and set off from Cape Coast Castle for Ashantiland. Four days later the British troops disembarked and followed him along the road Major Home had constructed. They were dressed in special uniforms made to Wolseley's design and described as Norfolk grey. Thousands of coastal Africans, organized into a transport corps, carried stores and ammunition. On 5 January 1874 the vanguard of Wolseley's army crossed the Prah River and entered Ashantiland.

At forty Wolseley was young for a general in any army, but although he lacked charisma, he had command presence. When he gave an order, said William Butler, one had 'no more thought of questioning it than one would think of asking a bird why it flew, or a river why it flowed'. 'Wolseley', Butler added, 'was the only man I met in the army on whom command sat so easily and fitly that neither he nor the men he commanded had ever to think about it'.

On 31 January 1874 Wolseley fought and won the battle of Amoaful. It was a hard fight, but British casualties were light: 4 killed and 194 wounded. The Black Watch, with 2 killed and 113 wounded, suffered the most. The Ashantis carried off their casualties, so their losses were unknown. It was estimated that about 800 had been killed.

The Ashanti forces had been beaten, but they were not yet ready to stop fighting. Large marauding parties doubled back around Wolseley's main army to attack his lines of communication and supply. The coastal Africans in the transport corps, terrified of the fierce Ashantis, refused for several days to carry up supplies. Wolseley, now only sixteen miles from Kumasi, was forced to halt, and even to send back units to provide guards. He had only a four days' supply of full rations, and he estimated that it would take

Sir Garnet Wolseley and his forces entering Kumasi *(Photo: ILN Pic. Lib.)*

at least a week to restore his long line of communication, but he decided to plunge boldly on. A captured Ashanti town was converted into a fort, where all the heavy baggage and the sick and wounded were left. A flying column was formed, and, carrying only greatcoats, ammunition and food, it moved on the Ashanti capital.

Six miles short of Kumasi, at Ordahsu, the Ashantis made a futile, last stand; then, on 4 February, Wolseley, mounted on a mule, rode into Kumasi. Not a shot was fired. There was no resistance. King Coffee, his notables and the remains of the Ashanti army had fled, taking with them most of the gold and valuables the British had expected to find. Thirty carriers were loaded with the most valuable loot, and the rest was consumed in smoke and flames as gunpowder and fire destroyed the town. Soon afterwards, Kofi Karikari sent Wolseley 1,000 ounces of gold and agreed to sign a treaty by which he promised to pay an additional 50,000 ounces, abandon the rites of human sacrifice, recognize Britain as the paramount power in the area and open his country to trade.

On 4 March 1874, after a campaign that had lasted nearly six months, Wolseley embarked for home with the surviving members of his staff. Seven were dead and thirty-one were wounded or sick. Wolseley himself was remarkably fit, but it had been, as he later wrote, 'the most horrible war [he] ever took part in'. In all, there were 68 dead, 394 wounded and 1,018 invalided home.

In England, Wolseley was a national hero, and the efficiency with which the campaign had been conducted led to the creation of a new expression for anything done properly, with efficiency and style: 'All Sir Garnet'. The Queen granted him an audience and reviewed his troops at Windsor. He was invested with the Grand Cross of the Order of St Michael and St George and was made a Knight Commander of the Bath. He was given the thanks of both houses of Parliament, a grant of £25,000, promotion to the rank of major-general and honorary degrees from Oxford and Cambridge.

10

Wolseley now expected to be sent to India as adjutant-general, but instead he was appointed inspector of auxiliary forces and then soon afterwards, in February 1875, he was sent to South Africa as chief administrator of Natal. It was an uncongenial assignment: he was a soldier, not a diplomat or politician. Nevertheless, with his accustomed zeal he set about the task of reforming the government. On hand to help him were four members of the Wolseley Ring who had proved their worth in Ashantiland: George Pomeroy Colley, William Butler, Henry Brackenbury and the young Lord Gifford.

Wolseley's soldierly reaction to the political situation in Natal was to abolish the colony's democratic constitution and to rule by decree. Thwarted in this by the legislative council, he 'drowned the independence of the colony in sherry and champagne', as Sir John Robertson, a local judge, put it. At lavish parties, the young general turned on his charm; those he could not charm he browbeat. He amazed all with his energy and enormous capacity for work. Colley wrote of him to his sister, 'Work, play, difficulties, annoyances, all seem to be the same fun that a good run is to a hunting man'. In the end, the colonial legislators gave Wolseley pretty much what he wanted, at the expense of some of their own democratic ideals. To his brother Dick he boasted, 'No man in England could have got more out of the Council than I did'. He credited his success to the prestige of his name and to his 'admirable staff'.

Although never a politician in the conventional sense and with no desire to be one, Wolseley nonetheless saw many of South Africa's political problems in a clear light. He thought that Natal had too high a proportion of natives to Europeans and, fearing the powerful Zulus, whose lands bordered the colony, he advocated an immediate conquest of Zululand. He also advocated a confederation of the two British colonies (Natal and Cape Colony) and the two Boer republics (Orange Free State and the Transvaal). The Colonial Office rejected the suggested invasion of Zululand – that came two years later – and Wolseley did not stay long enough in South Africa to build up support for the amalgamation of the British colonies and the Boer republics, an event that did not occur until 1910, after two Boer wars.

At the end of August 1877 Wolseley and most of his staff boarded ship at Durban and returned to England. He resumed his old job at the War Office for a time and worked to make adequate provision for the army reserve, but Cardwell was no longer secretary of war, and his superiors evinced little enthusiasm. They did, however, find another outlet for his energies: they appointed him high commissioner and commander-in-chief of troops in Cyprus, which Disraeli had recently acquired for Britain from the Turks.

Wolseley landed at Larnaca on 22 July 1879. Like Napier on Cephalonia, he dreamed of converting the island into a model province. He announced that it was Her Majesty's intention (i.e. his own) to promote commerce and agriculture, and 'to afford to the people the blessings of freedom, justice and security'. But this was not easily done.

Disraeli and his colleagues had considered Cyprus a suitable base for naval and military operations in the eastern Mediterranean, a guard for the Suez Canal, and so had agreed to pay Turkey a 'tribute' of nearly £93,000 a year. It was thought that this sum could be acquired by taxing the inhabitants, but the population of the island was only 186,000 (two-thirds Greek and one-third Turk, in two mutually hostile communities), and they were mostly poor. After payment of the tribute, there was little left for roads, schools, agricultural improvements, railways, harbours and other public works – all of which were badly needed. In addition to the hostility between Greeks and Turks, antagonisms between farmers and shepherds made homicide a common feature of rural life. No one was enthusiastic about being ruled by the British, least of all the island's corrupt bureaucracy. Wolseley's reign failed to change the attitudes, curb the corrupt practices or improve the lot of his Cypriot subjects.

11

Roberts was fighting a campaign in Afghanistan, and Lord Chelmsford was fighting in Zululand. Wolseley, stuck in an uncongenial post, longed to be in a war. After the disastrous defeat of Chelmsford's forces at Isandhlwana, he put himself forward as the best general to beat the Zulus, and the government agreed. Over the objections of the Duke of Cambridge, he was sent to South Africa as high commissioner for South-East Africa and commander of the forces there with the local rank of general. It was an appointment that delighted Wolseley but displeased the Queen, who

thought Chelmsford was being ill-treated in favour of a
pushy radical. She would 'sanction the proposal', she said,
but 'she would *not approve* it'. Disraeli defended the choice
and did his best to reassure her: 'It is quite true that Wolseley is an egotist and a braggart. So was Nelson'. He
explained that men who achieve early success in life 'are
generally boastful and full of themselves'.

When Wolseley arrived in Durban, he learned that
Chelmsford had again invaded Zululand, this time with a
much larger force, and was now only seventeen miles from
Ulundi, the Zulu capital. He at once ordered Chelmsford to
concentrate his forces, not to negotiate with the enemy and
to send all reports through him. Chelmsford ignored him.
He won the final battle of the war at the gates of Ulundi;
opened communication with Cetewayo, the fleeing Zulu
chief; and continued to report directly to London. Like
Gough in the Second Sikh War, he managed to finish off
his enemies before he could be relieved of his command.
Although Cetewayo was not captured, the war was certainly over and Chelmsford went home. It was left for Wolseley to track down and capture the Zulu king and ship
him off to England, where he charmed everyone, from the
housemaids of Kensington to Queen Victoria. Among his
sequestered possessions was a necklace of lions' claws. This
Wolseley claimed; he had each claw mounted and engraved:
CETEWAYO 28 AUGUST 1879. These mementoes he presented to the wives of prominent politicians.

Although he did not have the opportunity to squash the
Zulus, and although the Boers in the Transvaal refused to
revolt when they were annexed, Wolseley did have the
chance to fight one small campaign. The Bapedi, a warlike
tribe related to the Basutos, occupied nearly 300 square
miles of sand, rocks and thorn bushes some 500 miles from
Durban, and they were not happy with their lot. Under their
chief, Sekukuni, they were a constant source of trouble to
both the Boers and the British colonists. Wolseley led a
punitive expedition against them, and, thanks to meticu-

Cetewayo, the Zulu king *(Photo: ILN Pic. Lib.)*

lous staff work by the Wolseley Ring, he was able to predict accurately that he would take tea in Sekukuni's hut on 28 November.

The small army organized for this expedition consisted of 1,400 British bayonets, 400 colonial horse and some 10,000 Africans, mostly Swazis. In spite of difficult logistical problems, Wolseley brought his force nearly intact to Sekukuni's mountain stronghold, the Gibraltar of the Transvaal, as it was called, and began a bombardment with shells and rockets. This little campaign was soon ended, and Seku-kuni, with a selection of his wives and children, was paraded through the streets of Pretoria in a mule wagon. Queen Victoria telegraphed her congratulations, and Disraeli expressed his approval.

12

Wolseley left South Africa in May 1880 and returned to England. He had not been decorated for his services in Cyprus or Natal, but he now hoped to be raised to the peerage, and in order to achieve that end he enlisted the support of his friends and relations. He was disappointed to receive instead the Grand Cross of the Order of the Bath – the same decoration, he noted disdainfully, which 'that failure Chelmsford' had been given. But if the government did not, in his opinion, properly reward him, the press and the public lauded him as a hero. He was called 'our only general' and hailed as a modern and scientific soldier. His popularity as supreme representative of the great, expanding British Empire soared. Gilbert and Sullivan made him 'the very model of a modern major-general' in *The Pirates of Penzance*, and George Grossmith, the actor who first played the part, was made up to resemble him, artfully aping his mannerisms on the stage. Wolseley, never known for his sense of humour, delighted in the caricature and even at times sang the major-general's song at the family piano.

Wolseley was a conservative in politics – 'an oligarchy is the only government to live under, except perhaps, an intelligent despotism' – and a firm believer in Britain's imperial destiny. He was, he confessed, 'a Jingo in the best acceptation of that sobriquet', yet most conservatives thought him a radical. It was his efforts to promote army reform that led soldiers and civilians alike to consider him a danger to the status quo. Before he left for Africa, he had learned he was to be appointed quartermaster general, a job that he professed not to care for but that enabled him to press vigorously for the reforms Cardwell had not been able to complete. Among these was the promotion of officers on the basis of merit: he thought it criminal to give the command of brave young soldiers to officers 'deplorably ignorant of their profession'. The Duke of Cambridge countered that promotion by selection was the curse of the republican French army and that the practice would turn officers into politically minded intriguers. Within the officer corps, the opinions of the Duke were more generally accepted. Wolseley himself admitted that the Duke was 'rooted alike in the confidence of the Sovereign and the affection of the Army'.

Promotion by merit was still too radical a concept, but there were other important changes that Wolseley helped to make in an army grown mossy with traditions. The regimental system was revamped, uniforms and equipment were made more efficient and flogging was eventually abolished. Food, housing and recreational facilities for the troops were improved. Wolseley proposed increases in pay and pensions, though Parliament refused to sanction them. Few generals ever evinced such concern for the soldiers in the ranks or did more to promote their welfare than Sir Garnet Wolseley. Sir Evelyn Wood said of him, 'Indomitable in action, undeterred by terrible wounds . . . with a most brilliant soldier's brain, he did more to improve the fighting efficiency of the Army than any soldier I have met'. Yet, although respected, he was generally unloved. His cool efficiency did not inspire; he won campaigns with his competence, not with his charisma. Ian Hamilton once compared him with Roberts: 'As for the Rank and File, to them Roberts was always "Bobs"; they had no nickname for Wolseley – even to think of it is ridiculous'.

The office of adjutant-general fell vacant in 1882, and Wolseley wanted it. Newspapers pressed for his appointment, and Hugh Childers, then secretary of state for war, put forward his name. The appointment was made despite the objections of the Duke of Cambridge and Queen Victoria herself, who took most of her military opinions from her cousin. But Wolseley did not remain long at his desk. He soon left it to fight yet another little war, this time in Egypt.

13

Technically the Khedive of Egypt owed allegiance to the Sultan of Turkey. In practice, the Khedive was virtually sovereign – that is, until the British arrived. Kedive Ismail had by his extravagance carried his country to the brink of bankruptcy. It was to assist him in his financial difficulties that Gordon had been summoned from the Sudan. But neither Gordon nor anyone else could find money and resources where none existed. Britain and France combined to have Ismail deposed in favour of his son Tewfik and to give the European Commissioners of the Debt control over Egypt's economy in order to secure the interest payments for European creditors. Among Egyptians of all classes there was much discontent. The army in particular was unhappy. There were cries of 'Egypt for the Egyptians', and all foreigners were bitterly resented. (Egypt's bureaucracies were filled with foreigners. There was even an American general, Charles P. Stone, serving as chief of staff of the army.)

Military coups were not then the commonplaces of African political life they have since become, and the army revolt in Egypt led by Colonel Ahmed Arabi in 1882 was the first in the modern style. However, in the Victorian era European powers did not hesitate to intervene in such matters, and Britain felt that her interests were at stake in the deteriorating political situation. When a naval bombardment of Alexandria failed to make Arabi recognize his mistake, Gladstone reluctantly decided that a military expedition was necessary and gave Wolseley the command. There was little objection this time. Even the Duke of Cambridge grudgingly agreed that Wolseley was 'decidedly as able a man for the field as we have got'.

Wolseley at once assembled members of his 'ring'. There was considerable resentment of this old-boy network, for every eager officer in the army wanted to take part in the Egyptian campaign, but Wolseley insisted on his choices and in general had his way, although he was pressured into taking a few he did not really want. The Duke of Cambridge privately asked that one of his illegitimate sons, a major in the 20th Hussars, be allowed to go, and, although Wolseley considered the man a 'horrid snob and . . . quite useless', he found a place for him on his staff. The Prince of Wales himself wanted to go but, to Wolseley's relief, the government and the Queen would not permit it. Nevertheless, the Queen's favourite son, Arthur, Duke of Connaught, after much pleading, was allowed to go.

The arrangements for the dispatch of 40,560 troops and 41,000 tons of supplies from Europe, Mediterranean bases and India in sixty-one steamers was handled with the extraordinary efficiency for which Wolseley was now famous. It was the largest single British expeditionary force ever launched at one time.

Just as Wolseley was about to set off with his staff for Egypt via an overland trip to Brindisi, he caught a cold and suffered an attack of erysipelas. His physician thought a sea voyage would improve his health and recommended that he make the entire trip by sea. It seemed to be the right prescription, for by the time his ship reached Malta he had recovered and went ashore to buy £50 worth of Spanish point lace for Louisa.

To deceive the Egyptians, elaborate preparations were made for an attack from the sea near Aboukir Bay in the Nile delta, and the swarm of newspaper correspondents was told in confidence that the invasion would take place there. Only a few naval and army officers were made privy to his real plan, which was to land his main force at Port Said, on the Suez Canal, by night. The landing was a complete success. The entire canal was soon in British hands with scarcely a shot fired and a 15-year-old midshipman led a landing party that seized the telegraph station before any information could be sent to Cairo.

The army moved west, and the first real battle was at Tel-el-Mahuta, where more British soldiers were felled by the sun than by Egyptian bullets. The Egyptian forces retreated along the line of the desert railway that connected the canal with the Nile. At Mahsama they made a stand but were driven out by the British, who captured seven Krupp guns and large quantities of stores. There followed a 12-day lull while the troops rested, supplies were brought up and all was made ready for the advance on the main Egyptian base at Tel-el-Kebir. The Egyptians, hoping to smash the British before they were ready for the next fight, made an attack on Kassassin, which the British had transformed into a strong base. They were repulsed with great loss and retreated in considerable confusion. Wolseley was criticized by some for not following up this success, pursuing the Egyptians to Tel-el-Kebir and capturing it, but he knew what he wanted to do and when he wanted to do it.

Arabi boasted that it would be impossible for the British to assault successfully the strong earthworks he had erected at Tel-el-Kebir. Wolseley, after a careful study of the fortifications, determined on a night march that would bring his forces into position for an attack upon the strongest section of the Egyptian line at dawn. A march by 11,000 infantry, 2,000 cavalry and sixty-one guns across an open, featureless desert at night against a well-entrenched superior force (20,000 Egyptian regulars and 6,000 Bedouin irregulars) was certainly a difficult and dangerous undertaking, and many of Wolseley's senior officers were doubtful that it could succeed. Nevertheless, on the night of 12 September 1882, the British left their camps with tents still pitched and camp-fires still burning, and, led by officers of the Royal Navy who navigated by the stars, they began their approach march in as much silence as a small army of marching men could manage. A drunken Highlander was chloroformed.

In spite of generally good march discipline, there was some confusion in the dark, and the army approached the Egyptian fortifications at an awkward angle. It fell to the Highlanders to attack first, near the centre of the Egyptian line, where the parapets were highest and the ditches deepest. Bugle calls, shouted commands and the roar of thousands of excited men broke the silence of the march as Cameronians, Gordons and Black Watch drove at the sleepy Egyptian soldiers stumbling to their posts. Wolseley watched anxiously as the Highlanders closed with the enemy in hand-to-hand combat. The fighting was long and hard, but the British prevailed and the Egyptians fled, leaving 2,000 of their comrades dead or dying on the desert floor. The sabres of British cavalry pursued the flying enemy and cut down those who fell behind.

This was the decisive battle. A few days later Wolseley telegraphed to the War Office from Cairo, 'The war in Egypt is over. Send no more men from England'. In Britain there was joy and immense pride in the British army. The Queen, the prime minister and even the Duke of Cambridge were delighted by Wolseley's success. The Duke wrote to the Queen, 'His great fault is that he has only a certain number of officers in whom he has any real confidence'. Along with many others, he objected to Wolseley's public presentation of his views; he 'advertised', it was said. 'If we could, on his return, only modify these two feelings', said the Duke hopefully, 'he would be twice the value he is to his country'.

14

It had been a tidy little war in Egypt, and Wolseley well deserved the honours now heaped upon him. Khedive Tewfik awarded him the Grand Cross of the Osmanieh; his own country presented him with £30,000, promoted him to the

Sir Garnet Wolseley being awarded the Grand Cross of the Osmanieh by Khedive Tewfik *(Photo: ILN Pic. Lib.)*

rank of full general and raised him to the peerage as a baron. He had long been embittered by the coldness of the Queen towards him, but this now changed. The Duke of Connaught, who had come home full of admiration for him, did not hesitate to tell his mother how wrong she was to distrust him, and in an interview with the Queen at Balmoral, Wolseley was careful to praise her favourite son, her favourite regiments and Disraeli, her favourite prime minister. Subsequently, the court was astonished to hear the Queen praise Wolseley.

While he was still basking briefly in his glory, events in the Sudan were creating still another excuse for a Wolseley campaign. Chinese Gordon was besieged at Khartoum, and after much foot-dragging by Gladstone and much urging by Wolseley and the press, it was belatedly agreed that an expedition should be sent to relieve him. On 5 August 1884 Parliament voted 174 to 4 to spend £300,000 to rescue Gordon should it become necessary.

The Gordon Relief Expedition was marked by controversy from beginning to end. The first source of disagreement came to be called the 'battle of the routes'. Wolseley argued for taking his army straight up the Nile Valley. General Sir Frederick Stephenson, in command of the army of occupation in Egypt, disagreed, as did most of the engineers and naval officers, who declared that boats could never negotiate the Nile's cataracts. It was argued that it would be better, rather than move troops the 1,650 miles from Cairo to Berber, to march across the desert from Suakin on the Red Sea, a distance of only 280 miles. In the event, it would seem that the Suakin–Berber route would indeed have been the better even after Berber fell to the Dervishes, but Wolseley had his way.

Again the Wolseley Ring was assembled – William Butler, Evelyn Wood, Baker Russell, Redvers Buller, Herbert Stewart and all the others Wolseley could lay his hands on. Butler was put in charge of the construction and delivery of the specially designed Nile boats, or whalers, that were to carry the army up the Nile. Each boat was to be thirty feet long and six and a half feet wide with a draught of two and a half feet, and each was to be fitted with twelve oars and two masts. Experts pronounced it 'an unfloatable flotilla' and called the project 'a wicked waste of money'. The Admiralty insisted that the boats could not be built in time to be put to use, but Butler contracted for 500 with forty-seven British factories and in just twenty-seven days, 100 were ready to be shipped. To man them, Wolseley recruited Kroomen from West Africa and voyageurs from Canada (few of whom, unfortunately, turned out to be true voyageurs).

Perhaps the greatest uproar in the army itself resulted from Wolseley's decision to make this a teetotal trip – no rum ration. Although Wolseley and most of his officers provided themselves with stocks of whisky, claret and champagne (for their health), the other ranks were to be treated to jam and marmalade, tons of it, in place of their treasured tot of rum. The War Office protested against such a departure from tradition, but Queen Victoria approved.

There appears to have been no objection to the 10,000 umbrellas Wolseley ordered. However, the Dervishes were spared the sight of a British army clutching umbrellas bearing down on them, for the order was not completed in time. What outraged the Duke of Cambridge was Wolseley's scheme to form a camel corps by skimming off 61 officers and 1,121 other ranks from the cavalry regiments, the Guards and the Rifle Brigade.

Wolseley's orders were to rescue Gordon and Colonel John Stewart and to bring out of the Sudan such civilians and Egyptian soldiers as wished to leave. On 13 September 1884, exactly two years after his victory at Tel-el-Kebir, Wolseley wrote to Louisa that if he was equally successful he 'ought to shake hands with Gordon near Khartoum about 31st of January next'.

Louisa wrote him encouraging letters, telling him what 'a wonderful and clever little general' he was. Wolseley treasured the letters from his 'Loo', his 'little Rumteefoozle' who sent him 'kisses on the back of your dear little head' and regaled him with all the latest gossip, which he loved to hear. Like her husband, Lady Wolseley was a snob, and she could also be caustic: an acquaintance had 'brokers' tastes' and a house that was a 'dirty, ill-arranged den'. She reported her household problems, and he responded with ready sympathy and indignation: 'It is not to be wondered at that those who keep servants should take little interest in them, for they are selfish, spoilt, and ungenerous, an ungrateful lot'.

Wolseley and his staff left Cairo by train and at Assiut boarded one of the Khedive's yachts, the *Ferooz*. At the last minute he gave permission to an artist from the *Graphic* to join them and then discovered to his annoyance that his party now numbered thirteen. Wolseley was superstitious: he was afraid of the number thirteen and all enterprises that began on a Friday. On the *Ferooz* he invited the Egyptian captain to dine with them every day. The captain could hardly have been a boon companion, for he spoke no language but his own; still, his presence avoided the disaster of thirteen at table.

Wadi Halfa marked the southernmost limit of Egypt and the beginning of the Sudan. As it was about half-way to Khartoum, British soldiers called it Bloody Half-way. From a nondescript collection of mud huts it had been transformed into a large military depot, containing, along with much else, more than a million and a half tins of bully beef from Chicago, more than a million pounds of ship's biscuits, a ton of pickles, and 1,003 pints of champagne – for medicinal and restorative purposes. On reaching Wadi Halfa, Wolseley learned of the murder of Colonel Stewart and the other Europeans whom Gordon had sent away from Khartoum on 10 September.

Patrols and spies operated south of Wadi Halfa, and Major Horatio Herbert Kitchener, who was running spies and secret messengers, was the link between Gordon and the relief expedition. Gordon cursed him for a fool in his journal, and Wolseley thought most of his reports unreliable, but he did the best he could under difficult circumstances at daily risk of his life.

Working the Nile boats, hauling tons of supplies and

thousands of men up the river and through the treacherous cataracts under a burning sun, was a task that tried the patience of officers and other ranks alike. So, too, did the task of turning Guardsmen, Riflemen and a company of Royal Marines into a camel corps. The neophyte riders tried the patience of their mounts as well. One soldier told his officer, 'Very clever camel, mine, sir. Why, he's been playing cup and ball with me for an hour and a half and he's only missed me twice'. Wolseley himself detested the beasts, even the magnificent riding camel given him by the Khedive; it gurgled disgustingly and reminded him, he told his wife, of Henry Brackenbury (the ugliest member of the Wolseley Ring, whom Louisa found repulsive).

Acutely conscious that time was running out, Wolseley pushed his camel corps across the desert to Korti, just below the fourth cataract, a short cut that avoided a great bend in the river. This division of his forces into a desert column and a river column would, he hoped, save time. He still felt certain of success and told Louisa, 'I never was more confident about any operation I had entrusted to me'. Others were not so sure.

Members of the Wolseley Ring did not always work harmoniously together. Redvers Buller, the expedition's chief of staff, even questioned the value of the mission, saying that Gordon was not worth the camels. Wolseley wrote about his officers to his wife, saying, 'They torture themselves with jealousy one of the other, and sometimes even with me are inclined to kick over the traces. It is often difficult to keep them in their places. . . . a number of them together form a team very difficult to drive'. Nevertheless, he defended his practice of seeking out and using the best officers he could find: 'The fact is, there are very few really able men in the world, and a small proportion only of that clever lot join the army'.

Eager to push on, Wolseley again sent his camel corps across the desert to cut off another large bend in the river. This time their goal was Metemma, deep in the Sudan, only about a hundred miles from Khartoum. Like the old war-horse he was, Wolseley wanted to go with his desert column, but he realized that in this complex operation his place was to command at Korti. He told Buller, 'This is the first time in my life that I have been chained to the rear in a campaign, and I hope it may be the last. To lead a storming party a day would be child's play to the anxieties of this position'. Herbert Stewart was in command of the desert column. He was a great favourite, a man in whom Wolseley had the greatest confidence, but Wolseley could not help worrying. To Louisa he wrote, 'I am nervous about Stewart, for his loss – even being wounded – would really, at this moment, be a national calamity'. His hair began to turn grey; he gave up cigars and tea; he even considered giving up claret with his supper. In his journal he wrote, 'This suspense, this longing for news, drives the blood from my heart: Oh God have mercy on me'.

At an oasis called Abu Klea the desert column was attacked, and it fought a battle that Winston Churchill described as 'the most savage and bloody action ever fought in the Sudan by British troops'. It was here that the Dervishes broke a British square, though all who penetrated it were killed in a savage mêlée. When the battle was over, more than a thousand Dervishes lay dead in the sand. The British, too, had suffered grievous losses, and the next day, while they were preparing to continue their march on Metemma, a sniper's bullet struck Stewart in the groin, a wound that proved mortal. Colonel Fred Burnaby, the second-in-command, had been killed at Abu Klea, so command of the column fell upon Colonel Sir Charles Wilson, RE, a scholar, a linguist, a Fellow of the Royal Society and a good staff officer, but an inexperienced and uncertain commander. Wolseley described him as 'one of those nervous, weak, unlucky creatures that [he hated] to have near [him] on active service'.

Wilson took the desert column on to the Nile, where the last of Gordon's steamers found him, but there he tarried for three precious days. He was worried about the reduced size of his force and the care of his wounded; his confidence was not restored by a vain attempt to take a nearby Dervish town. The delay was fatal for Gordon. It was not until 24 January, after cautious reconnaissances of the river, that Wilson loaded troops onto two of Gordon's steamers and made his way up the river to Khartoum. He was less than forty-eight hours too late.

15

Wolseley received the news on 4 February, a day he later described as the saddest in his life. The report from Wilson left him 'utterly knocked out'. For the first time as a commander, he had encountered failure. 'He has won', he wrote of the Mahdi, 'and we all look very foolish'. After all the detailed planning, the exertions of thousands and the deaths of many brave men, it was hard indeed to find that lives, energy and treasure had been wasted. Weeks later he wrote to Louisa, 'My mind keeps thinking of how near a brilliant success I was, and how narrowly I missed achieving it'.

Wilson was blamed by his colleagues for his failure, but in truth he had been placed by cruel circumstances in a position of command for which he had neither aptitude nor desire. Wolseley, too, was blamed, for it was thought by some that he could have moved faster; but he had not been given his marching orders soon enough. Later, he told a friend, 'The sun of my luck set when Stewart was wounded'. Indeed, it was so. He was never again given another command in the field. Gladstone, who was most to blame for the disaster, was booed by *hoi polloi* and chastised by the Queen, who, she said, was made ill by the news. But although soon turned out of office, Gladstone was a political survivor and rose again to occupy high office.

At first the British people thirsted for vengeance, and Wolseley was ordered to prepare to 'smash the Mahdi' and turn his rescue mission into a punitive expedition. However, an advance had to be delayed until cooler weather; the troops now had to be moved into summer quarters. Wolseley was ordered to Cairo, where he was joined by Louisa and Frances. He grumbled about being separated from his army, but in truth he needed the rest. He was fifty-two years old; his one good eye pained him from the desert sun and the sand; he suffered from diarrhoea, overwork and, most of all, from the unaccustomed pain of failure.

The cries for vengeance soon subsided. A campaign whose only purpose was revenge and whose cost would be enormous quickly lost its popularity. When the Russians occupied the obscure village of Pendjeh on the northern border of Afghanistan, Gladstone screamed that the Russians were planning to invade Afghanistan and threaten India. Every soldier would be needed to fight them. It was excuse enough for withdrawing the British army from the Sudanese frontier and sending Wolseley back to his desk at the War Office.

Wolseley was made a Knight of St Patrick and raised in the peerage to a viscountcy; as he had no sons, it was decreed that the title could pass to his daughter, Frances. The failure of his mission in the Sudan did nothing to diminish his pugnacity, and he was soon in the midst of an uproar created by his outspoken complaints about the poor quality of the weapons and equipment with which he had been supplied. He attacked the army's seniority system and renewed his struggles with the Duke of Cambridge. As if he had not aroused enough controversy, he also launched an attack upon the reputation of General Ulysses S. Grant.

There were, at the same time, solid accomplishments. The Intelligence Department was expanded, the use of automatic weapons was encouraged, a realistic mobilization programme was proposed and supply and transport arrangements were reorganized. Then, in 1890, he turned over the adjutant-general's office to his protégé Sir Redvers Buller. He refused the post of commander-in-chief in India, hoping still that he would in the near future take the place of the Duke of Cambridge as commander-in-chief at

THE LAST SALUTE!

Tommy Atkins (to Commander-in-Chief H.R.H. The Dook of C-mbr-dge) "SORRY TO LOSE YOU, SIR! YOU HAVE ALWAYS BEEN A VERY GOOD FRIEND TO US!"

"In this, his first Army Order, Lord WOLSELEY wishes, in the name of the Army, to assure His Royal Highness of the affectionate regard of all who have served under him during his long period of office."—*London Gazette*, November 1, 1895.

The resignation of the Duke of Cambridge – a *Punch* cartoon *(Photo: Mary Evans Picture Library)* the Horse Guards, but he did accept the command of the forces in Ireland, closer to home.

Wolseley disliked the Irish and had once called them 'a howling, begging lot of savages'. In Dublin he liked them no better: 'What an amusing, provoking, inconsequent people these Irish are: untidy and unpunctual beyond measure', he wrote. Still, he enjoyed himself. There was hunting, shooting, a rich social life and time to work on a biography of Marlborough. In 1894 he was made a field marshal, and he took secret delight in the fact that Lord Roberts, his rival for glory, was still only a general. The following year the 76-year-old Duke of Cambridge was finally persuaded to resign, and Wolseley assumed that he would at last be appointed to the post. There was, however, a move afoot to give the post to the younger Buller, or perhaps even to Roberts, and the Queen hoped that her favourite son, Arthur, Duke of Connaught, would be chosen.

When at last the decision was made to give Wolseley the appointment, he was vastly relieved, and to Louisa, on holiday in Germany, he wrote, 'I feel as a man condemmed to die must feel when suddenly reprieved'. The Queen was displeased, but Roberts seemed content to accept Wolseley's former post in Ireland, and Buller was actually relieved not to be pushed ahead of his superior and mentor. However, Wolseley's pleasure turned sour when he learned that with the retirement of the Duke the power that was attached to the office of commander-in-chief was to be considerably reduced while the authority of the secretary of state for war was to be increased. Soon he was to feel that he was merely 'the fifth wheel on the coach'.

16

Wolseley's career, which had followed a constant upward path until the death of Gordon, now proceeded steadily downward. While he sat in the glittering, nearly powerless seat of commander-in-chief, Roberts was to win new laurels in South Africa. His star was fast fading. He was ignored when he warned that the Boers would prove difficult to subdue and urged that proper preparations be made. He was not even consulted when, the war going badly, it was decided to replace General Buller with Lord Roberts. He was deeply hurt.

In spite of the fact that he had served in South Africa and that he knew the British army, as opposed to the Indian army, far better than Roberts, he was not even considered for the command. He was told that he was needed at the Horse Guards and that there were fears for his health. He had indeed suffered a severe attack of influenza, and he was plagued with indigestion, but the truth was that this most intellectual of generals was losing his memory in what would appear to have been the beginning of Alzheimer's disease. His memory of the recent past went first. Though he could still remember the entire list of Roman emperors from his first Latin book, he would write a report one day, then forget it or deny he had written it the next. As he grew worse, he sometimes failed to recognize his own secretary or treasured old comrades. At the same time this once energetic man, formerly bursting with ideas and plans, now wrote to Louisa, 'I have lost all interest in my work'.

In November 1900 he retired. He was replaced by Roberts, that 'cute, little, jobbing showman'. He received no honours for his labours at the War Office. Instead, Lansdowne launched a vicious personal attack on him in the House of Lords, casting aspersions on his competence, sneering at his achievements and insinuating that he had wilfully neglected his duties.

It was a bitter end for a brave and once brilliant soldier. There were twelve more years to be lived, and he lived them quietly, his face and name all but forgotten. He had often expressed his dread of 'dying in bed, like an old woman', and he frequently spoke of wanting to die with his 'colours flying and the band playing "God Save the Queen", and the cheers of victory ringing in [his] ears'. But it was not to be.

He died quietly in bed on 26 March 1913 while on a visit to France.

Wolseley was a master of the small war. Perhaps he would also have been a great general in a large war; perhaps he would have been the military commander Britain so badly needed in 1914–18 had he not been born thirty years too soon. But he was.

6

Evelyn Wood
(1838–1919)

From Midshipman to Field Marshal

1

Like many Victorian army officers, Henry Evelyn Wood was the son of a clergyman. He was born in a vicarage near Braintree, Essex, on 9 February 1838, the youngest of the three living sons of the Reverend John Page Wood. Although his mother had produced six children in rapid succession before his birth and was to bear six more, only nine of her children survived infancy. They came from a distinguished lineage: their paternal grandfather was twice Lord Mayor of London, and their maternal grandfather had been an admiral in the Portuguese navy. One of their mother's brothers rose to be an admiral in the Royal Navy, and another became surveyor general of Cape Colony in South Africa.

Emma Wood, or Lady Wood, as she became when her husband inherited a baronetcy in 1843, was a woman of exceptional vitality and determination, a strong character who had a greater influence on the lives of her children than did her husband. In 1866, when Sir John Wood died, Lady Wood, then sixty-six years old, was left in reduced circumstances. She was helped by a rich sister,* but she worked prodigiously to help herself, taking up her pen and writing fourteen three-volume novels, editing a book of poems, and translating Victor Hugo's *L'Homme qui rit* under the English title *By Order of the King*.

Late in life Field Marshal Sir Evelyn Wood (he was never called Henry) wrote a two-volume autobiography and a book of memoirs. In none does he do more than mention his siblings. Yet, the Wood women were remarkable. At least two of his sisters were well known, and all were interesting personalities. His sister Anna was a popular novelist who wrote under her married name of Steele, having married a Lieutenant-Colonel Thomas Steele in 1858. Her active married life was short, however. She fled home a week after the ceremony, still a virgin, it was said, after discovering that her husband expected to have sex with her. She never returned to him in spite of his repeated attempts to reclaim her. Evelyn once struck Steele while defending her from his advances, an action for which he was sued for assault.

Another sister, Emma, who had married well and had no need for money, wrote popular songs and poetry as a diversion. Maria Wood married an army officer named John Chambers and went with him to India. During the Mutiny she managed single-handedly to convey her children to safety, travelling a great distance through mutineer-controlled country, carrying phials of poison for each child in case of capture. A fourth sister, seven years younger than Evelyn, is remembered to this day as the Kitty O'Shea who, while married to Captain O'Shea, became the mistress of Charles Stewart Parnell, the famous Irish nationalist.

---

* Anna Maria Michell Wood, an eccentric, childless woman, known to her nieces and nephews as Aunt Ben. She had married the Reverend John Wood's brother.

In his youth Wood saw little of his sisters. He grew up to be a small but firmly built young man with reddish hair. He entered Marlborough at nine and received only five years of formal schooling before he was given an appointment as a naval cadet, thanks to the influence of his uncle Frederick Michell, then a post captain, under whom young Wood was soon serving on board HMS *Queen*. Two years later, in 1854, he was a 16-year-old midshipman and part of the 1,400-man naval brigade under Captain William Peel that landed in the Crimea. Captain Michell sent him, he said, because he wanted the family to be represented.

2

The mission of the naval brigade was to man batteries of 68-pounder and 32-pounder guns positioned on a ridge facing Sebastopol. It was dangerous work, and young Wood later confessed that he felt 'nervous' when he came under fire for the first time, but after a week he 'was conscious of a decided feeling of exultation in the presence of danger, such as men feel when they do well in manly sports, or women feel when they realise they are pre-eminent among their compeers'.

After the war he was recommended for the Victoria Cross, a newly instituted medal, but was not then awarded it. He had many narrow escapes in the course of the siege, and while taking part in the assault on the Redan* he was severely wounded by case-shot, a 5½-ounce ball striking his left arm just below the elbow. He lay unconscious on the field until an Irish corporal bent over him and shook him by his wounded arm, saying, 'Matey, if you are going in, you had better go it at once or you'll get bagoneted'. Jolted to life by the intense pain, Wood answered with a string of oaths. His benefactor sprang erect. 'I beg your pardon, sir. I didn't know you was an officer', he said.

* A redan is a fortification with two faces that form a salient.

Back in his own lines an Irish doctor he knew greeted him cheerily: 'Sit down, my dear boy, an' I'll have your arm off before you know where you are'. Wood fled from this kind soul and was eventually carried to a hospital by four bluejackets. The doctors there also favoured amputation, but he managed to persuade them to try to save it. Not long afterwards, he received a kind message from Lord Raglan, the commander-in-chief, putting his carriage at the young midshipman's disposal to carry him to the port where he could be transferred into HMS *Queen* as soon as he could be moved. A few days later he was back on board his uncle's ship.

Captain Michell wrote a thank-you note to Lord Raglan for his kindness to his nephew. Raglan replied five days before his own death, mentioning that young Wood's 'distinguished career [could not] fail to elicit everybody in his favour'. This was to be a useful letter.

The splintered bones in Wood's arm caused problems, and the wound refused to heal. He was sent back to England, and at his father's house in Essex he slowly recovered – after he himself pulled eight splinters of bone from his arm. For some unstated reason – perhaps because he was a passionate hunter – Wood decided that he wanted to become a cavalry officer. He resigned from the navy and, thanks to the letter of Lord Raglan and to a mention in dispatches for his services in the Crimea, he was gazetted a cornet in the 13th Light Dragoons.

With his arm still in a sling, he reported to his regimental depot at Dorchester and was soon made painfully aware of the cost of living in a fine cavalry regiment in England. Although he did not gamble, smoke or drink (not even wine at this stage of his life), he had to pay his full share of the mess costs, including the wine bill. Most of his colleagues had at least £400 a year of private income; Wood's family could spare him only £250. He was soon in debt, as he was to be for most of his life, though a shortage of money rarely interfered with his pleasures. He began hunting while still able to use only one arm, and he twice reopened his wound, once by falling down the barracks steps. He was already on his way to becoming the most accident- and illness-prone officer ever to serve in the British army.

It was at the depot in Dorchester that Wood made friends with a young man who was soon to become Viscount Southwell. He possessed 'a cultivated, refined, artistic temperament', which, said Wood, made him a poor cavalryman; twelve years later Wood married his sister.

3

At the end of 1855 Wood received orders to proceed to the Crimea. He arrived at Scutari in Turkey on 22 January 1856, and one month later he was in hospital with pneumonia and typhoid fever. The doctors despaired of his life and telegraphed the sad news to his parents. Although he was attended by a soldier servant and two female nurses, his treatment at times was brutal. He had become so emaciated that the bones of both hips had come through the skin, and one of Miss Nightingale's nurses, instead of wetting the lint before changing it, simply ripped it off, tearing away flesh and drawing blood. Lady Wood rescued her son. She arrived at Scutari on 20 March and went immediately to his bedside. When she saw a nurse strike him, she flew at her in a fury and insisted on removing him immediately and carrying him back to England. His doctors predicted he would not live to reach the ship, but Lady Wood was adamant. She had him carried aboard the *Great Western*, and under her care he not only survived but by the end of the voyage had begun to mend.

An uncle paid for Wood's advancement to lieutenant, and at the end of 1856 he had recovered sufficiently to rejoin his regiment, then in Ireland. He was, however, still weak and was suffering from a badly ingrown toenail, which had to be removed. In the following year the Indian Mutiny broke out, and Wood, wild for action, transferred to the 17th

Sir Evelyn Wood *(Photo: Mary Evans Picture Library)*

Lancers in order to get to India.

 Delhi had already been taken when he reached Bombay on 21 December 1858, but there was fighting yet to be done, and after he had recovered from sunstroke and a severe attack of low fever, accompanied by facial neuralgia, he still had a chance to take part. While with the force pursuing Tantia Topi, the last of the rebel leaders who offered a serious threat, Wood suffered considerably from 'indigestion and face-ache'. His aches and pains did not keep him out of action, however, and in fighting near Sindhara he killed several mutineers with his sword in hand-to-hand fighting. He was again recommended for the Victoria Cross, but again was not awarded it. As there was then no lesser medal for valour, he was rewarded only by a mention in dispatches.

Leisure also had its perils. When out hunting he was attacked by a wounded tiger and was saved only by the quick action of a companion. Visiting the menagerie of a nawab, he accepted a fellow officer's wager that he could not ride a giraffe. He managed to mount and to stay on long enough to win his bet, but the beast threw him and then brought its hind foot down on his face, cutting a hole in each cheek and 'making a mash' of his nose. Nevertheless, he was soon back on his feet and resumed his duties.

He suffered for months from intestinal complaints and indigestion. Medicine that he put in his mouth to ease a toothache burned a hole in his cheek. At Poona, where he went to take an examination in Hindustani, he awoke one morning with a severe pain in his ears and became almost deaf for a week, a condition he attributed to his overtaxing himself with study. He was suffering from 'face ache' when in December 1859 he at last won the Victoria Cross by successfully leading a small party in an attack in a Sironj jungle on a large band of robbers; in the process he rescued a rich landowner who had been kidnapped and was being held for ransom.

Except for breaking his collar bone when he galloped his pony into a tree, Wood enjoyed for a time what was, for him, a period of good health. Tiger hunts and pigsticking provided recreation until he was put in charge of a regiment of irregulars and had to contend with an incipient mutiny, straighten out regimental accounts that had been allowed to fall into a chaotic state, handle an outbreak of cholera and mop up bands of mutineers who had become dacoits. When he was again laid low by fever, ear problems and sunstroke, doctors ordered him home. He reached his father's house on 28 December 1860, after an absence of more than three years.

4

In April 1861 Wood became a captain, paying £1,000 to the government and £1,500 'over regulation' to the officer who retired in his favour. Sixteen months later he became a brevet major, as a reward for his services in Central India. In the meantime, he paid a visit to his friend Viscount Southwell, met Southwell's four sisters and instantly fell in love with one of them, the Honourable Mary Paulina Anne (called Paulina). As a man of honor, he did not declare himself, for he was in no financial position to marry.

After a stay at a crammer to prepare for the Staff College entrance examinations, he entered the College in January 1863. He applied himself with a will, but he still managed to hunt regularly five days a fortnight during the two-year course and to take boxing lessons from several pugilists. In one heavy fall while hunting, he landed on the crown of his head with such force that his neck swelled 'till it protruded beyond the cheek-bones, giving the appearance of a large double goiter'.

On graduation from Staff College in 1864 he went to Ireland as aide-de-camp to Colonel William Napier (son of George Napier, who had married a cousin, Emily, one of Sir Charles Napier's daughters). Ireland's climate did not agree with Wood. Every time he got thoroughly wet, which was often, he suffered from 'recurring attacks of fever, which affected [his] ears, accompanied with neuralgia and swollen face'. He went to London to consult dentists, all of whom agreed that the eight stumps of teeth in the back of his mouth should be extracted. When he found a dentist willing to give him chloroform, he submitted.

In the autumn of 1865 Wood's regiment, then the 73rd (Perthshire) Regiment, was ordered to Hong Kong. Brevet Major Wood would have gone with it, had it not been that its commanding officer, Lieutenant-Colonel Hugh Jones, whom Wood liked, decided to retire and that his place was taken by Lieutenant-Colonel Somerset Molyneaux Wiseman-Clarke, whom Wood for some reason detested so heartily that he paid £500 to exchange into the 17th (Leicestershire) Regiment and remain in Britain. Not long afterwards, he was offered an appointment as military secretary to a general whom he had known in India, but he refused it, 'feeling sure that we would not find each other's society congenial'.

After a brief tour as deputy assistant quartermaster general, he became brigade major of the North Camp at Aldershot, but throughout 1865–66 he suffered from 'neuralgia of the nerves of the stomach'. In addition, while on a hunt he got completely soaked and was in bed for a fortnight with double penumonia.

When at last Viscount Southwell, the head of his family, learned that Wood was in love with Paulina, he forbade a marriage, for although he greatly admired and liked Wood, his family was Catholic, and he had strong objections to any of his sisters marrying a Protestant. For the next four years Wood seldom saw Paulina and wrote not a line to her until 1867, when he proposed by letter, confessing that he had no money and warning that his proposal was made 'on the distinct understanding that she would never by a word, or even a look, check [his] volunteering for War Service'. He waited impatiently for ten days for her answer. Then he read in the *Irish Times* that an expedition under General Napier was to be sent to Abyssinia, and he at once packed his bags and set off for London, telegraphing to Miss Southwell to delay her reply until he returned from the war. Once in London, however, he learned that the expedition was not to be under his old chief, William Napier, but under Robert Napier of the Indian army, whom he did not know. Most of Napier's staff would be selected from officers in the Indian army, and Wood knew that he had no chance of being included.

It was marriage instead of war. Paulina Southwell, overriding her brother's objections, accepted Wood's proposal and its conditions. They were married a fortnight later, and the first of their six children was born the following year.

The recently widowed Lady Wood was unable to give her favourite son more than a small allowance. Aunt Ben, who had bestowed £5,000 (then a most healthy sum) on each of his siblings when they married, refused to give him a shilling, because he had married a Catholic. She subsequently relented to the extent of providing him with an allowance, but soon revoked it after a dispute. Luckily his sister Emma's husband, Sir Thomas Barrett Lennard, generously advanced him £5,000 and arranged to pay him a salary for supervising his estates in Ireland. How Wood was to do this when he was so frequently required to serve abroad is not known, but he was grateful and always spoke of his brother-in-law in glowing terms – as well he might. Thanks to Sir Thomas, he was able to keep several horses, grooms, servants and a pack of hounds. At this time Wood also made the curious decision to study law in the Middle Temple and to qualify for the Bar, which he eventually did, becoming a barrister in 1874.

In the summer of 1871, shortly before the purchase system was abolished, Wood paid £2,000 to exchange into the 90th Light Infantry. Soon afterwards, he broke his ankle when his horse failed to clear a gate. No sooner had it mended than his two children fell ill with diphtheria; he sent his pregnant wife away and nursed the children back to health himself. He then began to suffer from insomnia. To help him sleep, a doctor gave him morphia – in an overdose that nearly killed him.

5

On 1 January 1873 Wood was promoted brevet lieutenant-colonel and not long afterwards was selected by Wolseley to be on his staff for the Ashanti campaign. His batman begged to go with him, but his request was denied by the War Office on the grounds that the climate was 'particularly fatal to the constitutions of Europeans'. Young Lieutenant Arthur Eyre of the 90th Light Infantry also applied to go. The only son of a widow whose husband had been a distinguished soldier, he was in many ways typical of young officers of the era: he possessed charming manners, wore a monocle and was a master of horses who loved to ride a charger at a five-barred gate. Wood endorsed his application to go with the short comment 'The son of a good soldier, his mother is a lady'. Eyre was selected and found death in Africa: a bullet passed through his bladder, and he died after two hours of intense agony.

On the Gold Coast, Wood took a prominent part in the battle of Esaman, the first successful bush fight in West Africa. A few days later he was ordered to recruit a regiment from among the coastal African tribes, and this he did, though the whole exercise was of doubtful value. Of the Fantis, Wood said that 'it would be difficult to imagine a more cowardly, useless lot of men'; nevertheless, he tried, with only partial success, to prevent their exasperated British officers from using physical abuse to stir them into action.

Wood was, of course, soon wounded. A piece of a nail fired from an Ashanti musket at close range hit him in the chest and lodged just above his heart. After a day lying on a stretcher, he struggled to his feet and was soon leading the advance. On the fall of Kumasi, he was ordered to take charge of the sick and wounded and escort them back to the coast. In pain from his chest wound, he was also afflicted with his old intestinal complaint and was kept on his feet only by frequent doses of laudanum and chlorodyne.

It was in this campaign that Wood wrote his first published works. He sent back eight articles to a London newspaper and, to his surprise, was paid £100. It was also in this campaign that an evening newspaper reported that he had been wounded, taken prisoner and probably flayed alive. When this news was cried through the streets of London, one of his female relatives was heard to complain, 'These tiresome newsboys shouting such horrid things, spoiling my night's rest, as if it wouldn't be quite time enough to read it in *The Times* tomorrow morning'.

After several staff postings in England, Wood went to South Africa with his regiment in 1878. There, under Lieutenant-General Frederick Thesiger (who that year became Lord Chelmsford), he took part in a small campaign against the Gaika tribe. He was still suffering from severe abdominal pains, for which he swallowed large doses of chloral and bismuth. An aide complained that it was necessary to 'carry a chemist shop' to treat his many ailments. By the end of the campaign he was seriously ill with a new set of symptoms: 'For a fortnight the glands in my groin, armpits, and neck had swollen; my skin peeled off like a mummy, and chilblain-like openings appeared on my hands'. Doctors attributed his symptoms to 'overwork, want of sleep and of nutritious food', and prescribed milk and eggs every four hours.

When it was finally decided to invade Zululand with four columns, Wood was put in command of one consisting of about 3,000 men. Fortunately, this was not the column scuppered at Isandhlwana, but on 29 March 1879 at Kampala he was attacked by a strong force of Zulus, said to number 28,000. They were beaten off with heavy losses, the British burying 785 who fell close to their camp. Wood himself shot three at 250 yards with a soldier's Swinburne-Henri carbine. British losses totalled about 200.

In July he took part in the successful capture of Ulundi, the Zulu capital, while suffering from pains in his eyes and stomach. He was now so deaf that one officer on his staff followed him whenever he went out at night to inspect outposts, fearing that he would not hear a sentry's challenge.

When Wood returned to England, he was disappointed that he was not promoted to the rank of major-general, but he was given a knighthood, (KCB), the county of Essex presented him with a sword of honour and a service of plate and he was entertained by the Queen at Balmoral.

6

In the course of the Zulu War the 25-year-old Prince Imperial of France, only heir to a toppled throne, was permitted to go to South Africa as an observer, but he was eager for action and, in spite of the efforts of senior officers to protect him, he was killed by Zulus. His death caused considerable excitement in Europe, and in Britain more newspaper space was devoted to this incident than to any of the victories or disasters in the war. The Prince's mother, the Empress Eugénie, wished to see the spot where her son had fallen, and a trip to South Africa was arranged for her. Wood was given the honour of escorting her and making arrangements. Paulina went with him, and he took two aides-de-camp, a full complement of servants – and a doctor. The trip occupied six months; although he was in the service of the Queen, the War Office, much to his chagrin, denied him even half pay for this period.

Not long after his return, the First Boer War erupted, and Major-General George Colley, one of the stars of the Wolseley Ring, who had succeeded Sir Garnet as high commissioner, suffered several military reverses at the hands of the Boers in Natal. Early in January, Wood agreed to return to South Africa as a brigadier-general and Colley's second-in-command. He was in Natal only a few weeks when, on the night of 26/27 February 1881, Colley was killed and the British forces were dealt a resounding defeat at Majuba Hill.

Wood, now in command of the British forces operating in south-east Africa, proposed to renew the fight and to relieve the towns then under siege. On 5 March, Wood telegraphed Lord Kimberley, the colonial secretary, that he expected to engage the enemy within a fortnight, and he confidently predicted victory. There was to be no more fighting, however. Wood was instructed first to make an armistice and subsequently to conclude a peace that many Britons considered disgraceful; eighteen months later, when the Boers again took up arms, they were quick to see the treaty as the source of the renewed conflict. To his wife, Wood wrote on 23 March 1881, 'I shall sign a peace tomorrow which will cause me to be the best abused man in England for a time'. Indeed it was so. Wolseley referred to the treaty as 'infamous' and 'ignominious'; he thought Wood ought to have resigned his commission rather than be a party to such a document. Many other officers agreed.

Back in London, however, Her Majesty's government was pleased with Wood, praising his 'skill and judgement' in dealing with the Boers. Lord Kimberley wanted him to go to Pretoria, capital of the Transvaal, to explain Britain's position, so on 3 April he set off, riding in a 'spider' pulled by two artillery horses. Along the way, the horses bolted, the spider struck an anthill and the impact threw Wood out. He landed on his spine on the off horse's head. This, he claimed, caused his feet to swell to an enormous size, and he was, as a result, in pain for many days.

Wood was offered the governorship of Natal, but he declined the appointment and returned to England in February 1882. He was honoured by being invested with the Grand Cross of St Michael and St George, and he and Lady Wood were commanded to Windsor, where the Queen, he said, treated him 'with a condescension for the memory of which [he would] be ever grateful'.

He was once again short of cash, and he appealed to his rich Aunt Ben, writing a piteous letter describing how humiliating it was when Paulina, while riding with the

Peace negotiations between General Sir Evelyn Wood and General Joubert *(Photo: ILN Pic. Lib.)*

Queen, was forced to wear a threadbare waterproof and to raise an umbrella that was riddled with holes. Even as a general officer, Wood seemed incapable of living within his income. He had neither the knack of acquiring money nor the prudence to economize.

7

Wood did not remain at home for long. In early August he left for Egypt to command a brigade in the campaign against Arabi Pasha. He saw little action, for he was left behind in Alexandria when Wolseley made his brilliant attack on the Suez Canal and achieved his stunning victory at Tel-el-Kebir. He returned to England in early November, but was back in Egypt before Christmas as sirdar (commander-in-chief) of the new Egyptian army.

The old Egyptian army, which Arabi had commanded, was riddled with disaffected officers and demoralized men.

After Britain had in effect annexed Egypt, she set about creating an Egyptian army based upon her own, using twenty-five seconded officers and a handful of non-commissioned officers.* (Kipling wrote of the miracle that could be achieved by a British sergeant: 'He's a charm for making riflemen from mud'.) This service was made attractive to British officers seconded to the Egyptian service by giving them higher pay and Egyptian ranks that were one or two grades above their ranks in the British army. Many of these officers later rose to high rank in their own service, including Reginald Wingate, Hallam Parr, Archibald Hunter, Leslie Rundle, Hector Macdonald, Horace Smith-Dorrien and Horatio Kitchener. Some of the officers in the British army of occupation under Lieutenant-General Frederick Stephenson grumbled at the higher pay Wood's officers were given, and there was some friction, perhaps unavoidable, between Wood and Stephenson. In June 1884, to Wood's chagrin, Stephenson was confirmed as the supreme commander in Egypt.

Wood adapted the Queen's Regulations, with little change, to the Egyptian army. He managed (almost) to abolish bribery and corruption in the army; the soldiers, to their astonishment and delight, were paid regularly and were allowed to go home on furloughs. The army drilled for five days a week with two free days: Friday (the Muslim holy day) and Sunday, for, as Wood wrote, 'it is an error to allow any soldier to believe that their [sic] officers are without religion'. He was soon rewarded by eight battalions of soldiers willing to learn their trade. The trust of the Egyptian soldiers in their British officers was considerably strengthened during the great cholera epidemic of 1883, when Egyptian officers refused to go near the army hospitals and

---

* The American officers in the Egyptian army had now resigned, including Charles Stone Pasha, the former chief of staff, who returned to the United States and built the pedestal for the Statue of Liberty in New York harbour.

British officers nursed the soldiers, 'performing every menial service'.

When Gordon was cut off at Khartoum and Wolseley mounted his relief expedition, Wood, although suffering at the time from 'neuralgia in the head', was put in command of the line of communication, 'a most difficult, arduous and responsible task', Wolseley told him. In the battle of the routes, Wood was the only member of the Wolseley Ring who opposed the Nile route and the only officer in the army who had opposed Wolseley's choice who was given an important command. After Herbert Stewart's mortal wound at Abu Klea, Sir Redvers Buller, who had been chief of staff, was sent to take command of the desert column; Wood took his place for a time, although he was then in considerable pain, having sat down on a folding chair with his finger between the joints, 'crushing the top so that it was in a jelly-like condition'. Doctors finally pulled the nail. He was now so deaf that Wolseley complained of being hoarse from roaring at him.

A part of the friction that developed between members of the Wolseley Ring sprang from a quarrel between Wood and Redvers Buller. The two men were friends; it was Wood who had recommended Buller for the Victoria Cross after the Zulu War. The cause of the quarrel was the limitation on the transport available for moving men and supplies up the river. Buller was eager to push men forward as fast as possible to meet the Dervishes. Wood insisted that it was silly and wasteful to send soldiers up the Nile until rations and other supplies could be stockpiled at Wadi Halfa. To send the men first would increase the time needed to build up the depots, for the troops would eat the rations as they were sent up. William Butler, too, became angry with Wood when he discovered that none of the 120 whalers for which he was responsible and which he had managed with such difficulty to work as far as Wadi Halfa had been passed up the second cataract.

Others also grumbled. The army doctors complained because Wood insisted on employing nursing sisters as well as soldier orderlies in the large hospital at Aswan. (Throughout his career Wood advocated more female nurses, against the almost universal advice of army doctors.) An officer at one Nile station noted, 'General Wood's baggage passed through today. Besides tents, camp furniture, etc., he had 96 cases with stores, about 40 being wine of different sorts. He evidently intends being comfortable'. Many of these boxes probably contained medications for Wood's multifarious illnesses.

Although Wood was a member of the Wolseley Ring, Wolseley never cared much for him as a person and, although he always employed him, denigrated his abilities. Of Wood's performance on the line of communication, he said, 'He has done worse than I expected'. Just before leaving London for Egypt he described him in his journal as

> the vainest but by no means the ablest of men. He is as cunning as a first-class female diplomatist and he himself, and his family who flatter him in a manner that is enough to turn most men's heads, mistakes this sharp cunning that he possesses to a remarkable degree, for real sound judgement and native inborn genius. . . . he has a depth of cunning that I could not have believed it possible for any brave man – such as he most undoubtedly is – to possess. . . . his vanity must be flattered in many little ways by the commander, but his intrigues with Newspaper correspondents & his popularity-hunting propensities must be kept in check. . . . Newspaper correspondents are easily taken in by a man of his temper & disposition especially as he lays himself out to please and curry favour with them. . . . Well to wind up my opinion of him, he has not the brains or the disposition or the coolness or the firmness of purpose to enable him to take command in any war. . . . I know he will fail to do anything great. . . . he will not be able to take in posterity by whom he will be found out and rated as a very second-rate general and an unpatriotic & selfish public servant, whose two most remarkable traits were extreme vanity & unbounded self-seeking.

In a letter to his wife during the Egyptian campaign, Wolseley wrote:

> He is a very puzzle-headed fellow, who drives all his staff wild from want of method. During the few days he was my Chief-of-Staff . . . he nearly drove me mad. His vanity offends his equals, and all the set of his own age will never forget the unworthy Convention of Majuba Hill. The army think it was his bounden duty to have resigned sooner than put his name to such a paper. The Queen is very fond of Wood, so you must deal tenderly with the subject.

Queen Victoria never cared for Wolseley, much to his dismay, but she did like Wood, who became one of her favourite generals. After the Zulu War she had referred to Wood and Buller as 'our two most distinguished men'. She once wrote to Disraeli, urging him to talk to Wood:

> Sir E. Wood is a remarkable man; not only an admirable General with plenty of *dash* as well as prudence, but a man of what is called *Imperial* views, loyal and devoted to Sovereign and country, and who takes in *all* the *difficulties* of the position. He is most agreeable as well as amusing, very lively yet *very discreet*.

Disraeli did meet Wood, and he reported to the Queen that in his opinion Sir Evelyn had 'a mind rich with practical conclusions, which [would] be ever ready to assist him in the continued conduct of affairs and the management of men'. Wood was also admired by Gladstone, proving that he possessed those political qualities useful to soldiers who aspire to become field marshals.

The end of the Egyptian campaign found Wood suffering from a bad case of diarrhoea. He had lost much weight, and the general state of his health was bad. Wolseley, who saw him in Cairo in early June, wrote to his wife, 'Evelyn Wood has returned here today, aged and very much pulled down. He could not stand for more than a few minutes. I am grieved to see him looking so ill'. Wood turned over his command of the Egyptian army to Sir Francis Grenfell and boarded ship for England.

8

Although Wolseley officially praised his work in his final dispatch from Egypt, Wood was disappointed that no honours were awarded him in the gazette for the Nile expedition. However, he was now given three years in Britain as commanding general of the Eastern District with headquarters at Colchester. His health slowly improved and he found the work interesting. Then, in January 1889, he was given one of the finest appointments available to a general in England in peacetime: command of the army's main training centre at Aldershot. There he worked to introduce more realistic training, not always with success. When he sent cavalry to practice night patrols, the Duke of Cambridge expressed his strong disapproval. He himself had never carried out night marches, he said, and he especially disapproved of horses being employed at night as it interfered with their rest.

In introducing reforms that improved the welfare and efficiency of his troops, Wood was more successful. He put a stop to the unsatisfactory practice of feeding hospital patients meals carried in tins from their battalions and arranged for food to be prepared for them at the hospital; he eliminated unnecessary sentry posts, improved musketry training and established a 'School of Cookery'. He tried 'to make the soldier when off duty as free as a civilian' and to do away with night roll-calls, but he encountered considerable resistance to such heresy. He experimented with training infantrymen to ride bicycles and persuaded the directors of several railway companies to offer reduced rates to soldiers proceeding on furlough.

In his memoirs there is not a hint of the national uproar in 1890 when it was discovered that the tall, handsome

Stewart Parnell, the Catholic leader of the Irish Home Rule
lobby in the House of Commons, the man who, if Home
Rule became a reality, seemed destined to become the first
prime minister of a semi-autonomous Ireland, was living
with and had sired children by his Protestant mistress,
Katherine (the newspapers called her Kitty) O'Shea, the
wife of Captain William O'Shea and the youngest sister of
Lieutenant-General Evelyn Wood, commanding at Aldershot. It was the most notorious love affair of the Victorian
era.

In March 1887 *The Times* had launched an attack on Parnell, who had not at first been disturbed, even though there
was a reference to his mistress. Indeed, as he fully expected,
he might have ridden out the storm if there had not been
turmoil within the Wood family.

Aunt Ben, to whom all her nieces and nephews turned
when in need of funds, lived in solitary splendour in a large
house on a vast estate. She appears to have been a woman
of taste and intelligence, her peculiarities well within the
bounds allowed the eccentrics of her day. As she grew older
– and she lived to a great age – she turned more frequently
for comfort and companionship to Katherine, whose itin-
erant and improvident husband was seldom seen in the
house Aunt Ben provided. As she saw little of her other nieces
and nephews, she not unnaturally altered her will several
times in favour of the one relative who responded to her
needs.

When Sir Evelyn, his brother Charles and his sister Anna
united in hectoring her to leave her fortune in equal por-
tions to all of the surviving Woods, she grew angry and
defiantly changed her will one last time on 8 March 1888,
leaving everything (£150,000 plus considerable lands) to
Katherine and cutting the others off without a penny.
Informed of their disinheritance, Evelyn, Charles and Anna
did not scruple to claim that Aunt Ben was insane. Katherine flew to the defence of her aunt – and of her own interests. Sir Andrew Clark, president of the Royal College of

THE O'SHEA – PARNELL

MR CHARLES STUART PARNELL M.P.   SERVANTS WATCHING MRS

The O'Shea – Parnell Divorce Case *(Photo: Hulton Picture Library)*

Physicians and Gladstone's personal physician, was persuaded to look into the matter; he found Aunt Ben not only sane but also charming. On his testimony the Woods' petition was dismissed.

On 19 May 1889, Aunt Ben died and Sir Evelyn and others of the family contested the will, claiming that Katherine had exercised undue influence on their aged aunt. At this point the egregious William O'Shea reappeared as another contestant on the grounds that the will contravened his marriage agreement. In a side action he began divorce proceedings. Whether Sir Evelyn and the other contestants urged him to seek a divorce has never been proved, but it is certain that they benefited from the blackening of their sister's name in the action. The ruin of Parnell was a side-effect in which they took little interest – although the enigmatic Anna may have had her private

emotions, for she was accused, with some reason, of having herself had sexual relations with Parnell.

Newspapers covered every detail of the case, and the House of Commons passed a special act of Parliament to inquire into *The Times*'s allegations. Moral outrage was the note of the day. Although Parnell married his Katherine when the divorce was final, his career, once so brilliant, was ruined. He might have salvaged it if he had followed the sensible advice cabled to him by Cecil Rhodes, 'Resign. Marry. Return', but he refused to resign.

The family brawl that involved the nation ended in 1892 in an out-of-court settlement that gave the Woods contestants fifty per cent of the estate. Sir Evelyn must have received about £20,000. (Anna used her share to live as a recluse surrounded by pets, including a favourite monkey she regaled with anchovy paste sandwiches.)

In the midst of the difficulties involved in trying to break Aunt Ben's will, tragedy struck Sir Evelyn's family when on 11 May 1891 Paulina died, ending a 24-year marriage that Wood described as 'uninterrupted happiness'. There were, though, those, his sister Anna among them, who considered he had been henpecked. In Anna's novel *Clove Pink*, when a character remarkably like Wood is told 'You are a V.C. man, why don't you insist on your wishes being carried out?' he replies, 'You ought to know how helpless the boldest man is in his own house'. Whatever the nature of the relationship, Wood felt the loss of his wife deeply, describing her as 'the most loving and tender of women, endowed with the highest principles of morality'. He added, 'She was to me not only an affectionate wife but also advisor and confidential secretary'. She had accepted his love of his profession and the many and long separations it had entailed. In one seven-year period, employment on foreign service had allowed him less than fifteen months in Britain. She had borne him three sons (all of whom became soldiers) and three daughters.

Wood was moved by the letters of condolence he received, particularly from forty-six non-commissioned officers and privates living in various parts of Scotland who had served under him in South Africa, and by 'the gracious solicitude of Her Majesty the Queen'. Work was a solace, and the day after his wife's funeral he supervised the training of an infantry brigade.

The scandal surrounding his sister Katherine appears not to have hindered his career. On 9 October 1893 he was appointed quartermaster general to the forces; two years later he was promoted full general; and four years later he became adjutant-general. During these years he also managed to write three books by rising before daylight and writing for an hour or more before leaving for his office: in 1895 a book on the Crimean War; in the following year a book on the cavalry at Waterloo; and in the next year *Achievements of Cavalry*. Then, in 1906, at the age of sixty-eight, he published his autobiography.

Somehow time was always found for hunting, and, indeed, he hunted almost to the day of his death in 1919, at the age of eighty-one. Of the sixty days' leave each year allowed to staff officers, he usually hunted on an average of forty-six. He was convinced that hunting was of great value in the training of officers and that it was a means of acquiring, when leading troops, 'the habit of quick decision combined with judgment in critical situations'. He could recite instances from his own experience and from history of 'brilliant brain power being handicapped by want of horsemanship". In June 1894 he became prime warden of the Fishmongers' Company, which he had joined as a liveryman twenty years earlier, and when, as prime warden, he was allowed to select guests for an annual dinner, he chose thirty-five masters of hounds, headed by the Duke of Beaufort, and more than 200 sportsmen, including one who had hunted with the Blencathra hounds for sixty-six years.

It was during his years in London that the bicycle craze hit England and Wood learned to ride. He was then in his fifties, and the learning was not without pain. Once, on the Edgeware Road, he collided with a hansom cab horse, which retaliated by biting him viciously on the arm. On another occasion he hit the horse drawing an omnibus in front of the Mansion House. And near Hyde Park Corner, the off-wheel of a fast-moving four-wheeled cab carried his bicycle seventy yards down the road.

9

On Wood's first day in office as adjutant-general he submitted a memorandum to the commander-in-chief in which he pointed out the inadequacies of the military forces. He noted that while the British Empire continued to expand, there had been no increase in the size of the army. He advocated 9,000 more men. Wolseley agreed in principle but thought there should be 13,000 more men. Although this was almost exactly two years before the outbreak of the great Boer War, which would in the end require nearly half a million troops, no action was taken.

When in 1899 war broke out in South Africa, Wood was eager to go, but Wolseley warned him that he would never be sent, because he had signed the peace treaty in 1881. When Sir Redvers Buller was selected to be the commander-in-chief in South Africa, Wood volunteered to serve under him, even though Buller was his junior in age and in years of service. His request was rejected. It was understandable that a younger general was required, but Wood was hurt anew when the unsuccessful Buller was superseded by Lord Roberts, six years Wood's senior. However, all three of his sons – Evelyn, Charles and Arthur – were sent out, and so Wood found some consolation for his disappointment in not being sent to South Africa, where, in his own words, he had 'suffered as a Soldier for [his] loyal obedience to orders'.

The long hours of work the war demanded and the strain told on his health. His old trouble, 'neuralgia of the nerves of the stomach', returned to plague him. In 1900, when riding an impetuous horse to hounds, he had a heavy fall that drove a crucifix he was wearing, which had belonged to his wife, into his ribs.

On 1 October 1901 Wood received his last appointment as a general officer when he took command of the Second Army Corps (later the Southern Command), and on 8 April 1903 he became a field marshal. He selected as his home for the final three years of his active career a house near Sherborne because it had stabling for his horses and was in Blackmoor Vale Hunt country.

He continued to the last to improve the lot of the men in the ranks. With difficulty he persuaded the government to supply soldiers with three shirts instead of two but he failed to obtain 'sleeping suits' for them. He inspected kitchens, latrines and barracks, upbraiding commanding officers who had not inspected them themselves. He abolished unnec-

essary guard posts, his favourite reform; he ordered can-
teens to be cleaned and made sanitary; and he took an
intense interest in the personal hygiene of his soldiers. At
Tidworth he even considered installing showers, noting,
'While we are doubting as to the desirability of having
shower baths, I think it is because the name deters us'. He
thought that 'rain-bath' would be a more correct term.

Perhaps as a result of Wood's many accidents and illnesses, he took a far greater interest in the Army Medical
Corps, military hygiene and sanitary measures than most
combatant officers of his day. He wrote articles pleading
for more-sensible clothing for the soldiers on active service
and urged that closer attention be paid to sanitary
arrangements, pointing out that more concern was expressed
for the ventilation of stables than for fresh air in the barracks.

Like Gordon, Wood was an admirer of Isaiah. He once
said that he believed in 'the absolute accuracy of Isaiah's
teaching' and that 'the morality of ordinary life is the real
proof of a true religion'. Although the son of a Church of
England clergyman, he was, by Victorian standards,
remarkably liberal in his religious views and in his toler-
ance of the beliefs of others. For a time he made contributions to a Baptist chapel, and he made certain that Baptist
services were as well advertised in the barracks as those of
other denominations. He married a Catholic, and he tried
to reduce Protestant–Catholic friction in the army. In Irish
regiments, almost all the officers were Protestant, even the
chaplains, and when new colours were consecrated, devout
Irish Catholic soldiers were offended by the Protestant service until Wood, with the help of some high-ranking Catholic friends, worked out an ecumenical rite that satisfied
all. It was a noteworthy achievement in an age not noted
for its ecumenicalism.

Although field marshals never officially retire, at the end
of December 1904 Field Marshal Sir Evelyn Wood ceased
actively to serve his sovereign and country. In a career

spanning half a century, he had earned six campaign medals. He lived on for fifteen years more, during which time he published a book of popular military history, *Our Fighting Services* (1916), and also *Winnowed Memories* (1917), a book stuffed with adulatory letters he had received, extracts of speeches he had given and anecdotes in which his wisdom or cleverness figured. His last book was dedicated to 'A.C.S.', his eccentric sister Anna. He continued to ride to hounds, although suffering from deafness, ill health and the injuries resulting from his many accidents until, at the age of eighty-one, he died peacefully in bed in his native Essex. At St Paul's they erected a plaque to him in a crypt:

INTREPID IN ACTION, UNTIRING IN DUTY
FOR QUEEN AND COUNTRY.

CHAPTER

7

Hector Archibald Macdonald (1853–1903)

'Fighting Mac'

1

As class-ridden as Victorian society was from top to bottom, the higher ranks were never completely closed to men of ability, energy and ambition. It was even possible for a soldier in the ranks to become a major-general. It was difficult and it was rarely achieved, but it was possible. In 1854 Luke O'Connor, a sergeant in the 23rd Foot, won a commission and the Victoria Cross during the Crimean War. He went on to fight in the Indian Mutiny and the Ashanti War, and after thirty-three years as an officer he was promoted major-general in 1887. William Robertson (1860–1933) rose from the rank of private to that of field marshal, the only British soldier ever to do so, and during the First World War he was chief of the Imperial General Staff. But perhaps the most famous ranker ever to rise to general officer's rank in the British army was Hector Archibald Macdonald.

He was the youngest son of a poor Scottish crofter who supported a wife and raised five sons as a subsistence farmer and a builder of dry stone walls. Hector was born on 4 March 1853 on the family croft at Rootfield, near Dingwall in Ross-shire. By the age of twelve he was helping his father and brothers and was known as a strong and willing worker. He was able to acquire some elementary education at a local school, where his favourite subjects, it was said, were history and mathematics.

At fifteen he was taken on as a probationary apprentice by a draper, William Mackay, who owned the Clan Tartan Warehouse in Inverness. He was quick to learn and was well liked by his fellow workers, including the shop-girls, one of whom later gave a newspaper reporter a description of him:

> A braw loon. . . . And the great broad shoulders o' 'im! He was mair like a smith than a draper. But mind ye, there was nae-thing surly about Hector. . . . He was terrible obliegin'; aye, offerin' to lift up or doon for us lassies.

A fellow apprentice remembered that he was 'Dooricht mad on volunteering' and spent his spare time poring over drill books.

As soon as he could, Hector joined the Iverness-shire Highland Rifle Volunteers. On 11 June 1870, although he had passed his five-month probationary period with Mackay and was engaged for a five-year apprenticeship, he enlisted in the 92nd Highlanders, lying about his age (giving his birthday as 13 April 1852) and without bothering to tell his master or perhaps even his parents. (When William Robertson enlisted, his mother cried that she would rather see him dead than in a red coat.) When Mackay learned that he had lost an apprentice, he predicted sadly that the young man would regret his decision for the rest of his life. Ten years later, Macdonald wrote to him from Afghanistan, begging his forgiveness for having broken his apprenticeship agreement, and saying, 'I regret the duplicity I exhibited then, and my want of confidence in you, who were always indulgent – I fear, too indulgent – always kind, and ever a cheerful and gentle master'.

The rough treatment of recruits common in most armies, particularly during the nineteenth century, was, in general, not the custom in Highland regiments. Macdonald himself once described his reception at the regimental depot in Aberdeen:

> I was met by a non-commissioned officer of the 92nd, and conducted to Castle Hill Barracks. And I must say, from the commanding officer to the smallest drummer boy, I was treated exactly as if I had been a member, or rather as if I had been with my own family. Everything possible was done. I was shown what I had to do and how to do it. . . .

George Stuart, who enlisted at about the same time as Macdonald and became a pipe major, later described him as being about five feet eight and a half inches tall with broad shoulders, dark hair, a moustache and a 'full chest'. As a recruit Macdonald was quiet and persevering: 'He was not much at the canteen, being, indeed, a man not very fond of the pewter or the pipe'. He was soon given his first stripe as an unpaid acting lance-corporal, and he kept his stripe when in January 1871 he was shipped off with a draft of eighty-six NCOs and men to join the Highlanders' active service battalion in India. In an exceptionally rapid advancement, only two years after his enlisting, he was made a full corporal, and on 20 December 1873 he was promoted sergeant, his commanding officer telling him, 'Remember that a sergeant in the 92nd Highlanders is at least equal to a Member of Parliament, and I expect you to behave accordingly'.

In India, Macdonald studied Hindustani, Urdu and Pashto.

'Study, study, study, was the keynote of his life, and promotion ever in his head', wrote a soldier who knew him then. (When he was commissioned, his language skills enabled him to pass the interpreters examinations and thus earn extra pay.) He was selected to be a sergeant in the guard on the royal tent during the visit of the Prince of Wales in 1876–77, and he was present at the great durbar held in Delhi on 1 January 1877, when Queen Victoria was proclaimed Empress of India. By 1879, when the 92nd Highlanders were made part of the field force commanded by Major-General Frederick Roberts, Macdonald was a colour sergeant.

2

In his very first engagement Macdonald was able to distinguish himself. Near a place called Karatiga, Roberts's advance towards Kabul was held up by 2,000 hostile tribesmen, who barred his way by occupying a vital pass known as the Hazar Derakht. Roberts described what happened:

> ... presently large numbers of the enemy were seen retreating before a small detachment of the 92nd Highlanders and the 3rd Sikhs, which had been sent out from Karatiga, and which were with excellent judgment and boldness led up a steep spur commanding the defile.
>
> The energy and skill with which this party was handled reflected the highest credit on Colour-Sergeant Hector Macdonald, 92nd Highlanders, and Jemadar Sher Mahomed, 3rd Sikhs. But for their excellent service on this occasion it might probably have been impossible to carry out the programme of our march.

Back in camp that evening one of Macdonald's men prophetically called out, 'We'll mak' ye an officer for this day's work, sergeant!' and another added, 'Aye, and a general too!'

Soon afterwards, at the battle of Charasia, about twelve

miles from Kabul, Macdonald was again the leader of an attack on the Afghans, who were pouring in a hot fire from behind rocks on a ridge, and again he came under the eye of the column commander. Roberts wrote, 'This service was performed in a very daring manner by a few of the 92nd, under Lieutenant [John] Grant and Colour-Sergeant Hector Macdonald, the same n.c. officer who had a few days before so distinguished himself in the Hazard-darakht defile'.

Legend has it that Roberts offered Macdonald his choice of a Victoria Cross or a commission and that he chose the latter, saying that he would win the VC later. But there is no evidence to support this tale, which seems most unlikely. However, he was recommended for a commission in his own regiment, and on 7 January 1880 he was duly gazetted, at the age of twenty-seven, after nine years in the ranks. The men cheered and carried him on their shoulders while a piper led the way to the officers' mess. The sergeants of the regiment gave him a dirk; his brother officers presented him with a claymore.

Although regimental quartermasters and, in cavalry regiments, riding-masters were frequently men promoted from the ranks, it was rare indeed for a soldier in the ranks to become a combatant officer. Such promotions were generally frowned upon. As late as 1893 General Sir Redvers Buller, then adjutant-general of the army, wrote:

> I am strongly opposed to any scheme which would tend to increase the number of candidates for commissions from the ranks.... To deliberately descend to debased articles when we can usually expect to get the pure ones would be a grave mistake.

Macdonald, however, appears to have been liked and respected by all ranks. He took part in the fighting at Sherpur, in the famous Kabul-to-Kandahar march and in the final battle that ended the war. Now, with two mentions in dispatches, the Afghan medal with three clasps, the Roberts Star and a commission, he must have been eager to return to Scotland and display his success. His battalion was scheduled to return, but suddenly, on 6 January 1881, it received orders to embark for South Africa. The 92nd had recently amalgamated with the 75th Highlanders and was now officially the Second Battalion of the Gordon Highlanders. They arrived in Natal in time for the First Boer War and to take part in one of the most humiliating defeats ever suffered by a British army.

3

The Boers in the Transvaal, hating British rule, rose in revolt and besieged a number of British garrisons. The British high commissioner, Major-General Sir George Colley – one of the Wolseley Ring – set out to defeat them and to relieve the besieged garrisons. He did neither. While trying to march a small force of about 1,000 and six 9-pounders over the Drakensberg Range through the pass at Laing's Nek, he encountered a strong force of about 3,000 well-armed Boers led by Commandant-General Piet Joubert.

After losing three battles in quick succession, Colley hit upon a brilliant plan. On the night of 26 February 1881 he led a mixed force of about 650 soldiers and sailors, including 180 Gordon Highlanders, to the crest of a steep hill called Majuba, which dominated the Boers' right flank. At dawn the next day the British could look down and see the consternation they had created in the Boer laagers below. Colley sent a triumphant heliograph to his headquarters below: 'All very comfortable. Boers wasting ammunition. One man wounded in foot'. He was so confident that he was in an impregnable position that he did not even order his men to entrench or construct sangars, but the Boers put together a scratch force of men and boys and began a careful climb, taking care to use all available cover. They massed under the cover of a slope and then stormed the crest.

According to Major Thomas Fraser, a survivor, the Boers

British forces in the Drakensberg *(Photo: ILN Pic. Lib.)*

were 'firing so rapidly we could only see their rifles through the smoke as they crept up'. Their fire was not only fast but also accurate. The British retreat began just before noon and quickly became a rout. Fraser noted, however, the bravery of Lieutenant Macdonald, who 'behaved with the greatest coolness and courage, and to the last made every effort to turn the course of events'. But Colley was dead, and most of his men either were killed or wounded or had fled for their lives. Macdonald, commanding twenty men on a small knoll on the west face of Majuba, was one of the few British soldiers to distinguish himself in this battle. Eight of his men were killed; only Macdonald and a lance-corporal were completely unscathed. By two o'clock in the afternoon it was all over; Macdonald was taken prisoner, and his pistol and accoutrements and the claymore presented to him by his fellow officers were all taken from him at gunpoint. The Gordons alone lost 44 dead and 52 wounded out of 180 officers and other ranks. The Boers lost only one man killed in this fight.

Macdonald was taken to Colley's corpse and asked to identify it. After giving his parole, he was permitted to give such help as he could to the wounded. Later he was taken to Newcastle in Natal, where Piet Joubert personally returned his claymore; not long afterwards he was freed. Macdonald was present when Wood signed the armistice and then the peace with the Boer leaders. In his dispatch Wood said that he had 'heard much of the conspicuous gallantry displayed by . . . Second Lieutenant Mac Donald [sic], 92nd Highlanders'.

In January 1882 the 2nd Gordons returned to Britain and were sent to Edinburgh. For the first time in twelve years, Macdonald was back in Scotland.

4

The two and a half years Macdonald spent in Great Britain at this time were as eventful for him in their way as his years in Afghanistan and South Africa had been. In the spring of 1882 one of his brothers introduced him to a friend called Duncan, a shipowner living at 40 Frederick Street in Edinburgh, and it was there that he became acquainted with Duncan's only child, Christina McDonald Duncan, then a 15-year-old schoolgirl.

During a tour of temporary duty in Ireland, where he served on a committee appointed to revise the drill regulations, Macdonald began a correspondence with the Duncan family, never failing to inquire in his letters about Christina. For Christina's sixteenth birthday in July, he sent her a brooch with the Macdonald crest. When in March 1883 he returned to his battalion, he stayed for a few days with the Duncans until his quarters at Edinburgh Castle were ready. Thereafter he was a frequent visitor, and it became obvious to all that he had fallen in love with the blossoming Duncan girl, and she with him.

With the permission of her father, Macdonald began an intimate correspondence with Christina, whom he affectionately called Missie Baba. He soon professed his love for her and, in the words of court papers later, 'succeeded in entirely gaining her affections'. They wanted to marry, but there were obstacles: her parents thought their daughter too young (although sixteen was the age of consent in Scotland), and, more importantly, the 30-year-old lieutenant could not possibly support a wife.

Very few junior officers, unless they enjoyed a substantial private income, could afford to marry. Indeed, many found it impossible even to support themselves on their pay. By practising the most careful economy and taking every opportunity to increase their income by learning languages and seeking staff appointments, subalterns could with difficulty live on their pay in India or elsewhere abroad. Some officers who managed to live comfortably on their pay, plus a small private income while in India, were forced to resign when their battalion was transferred to Britain.

Back in Britain an officer needed respectable civilian

clothes. Macdonald acquired some, but he did not appear at his best in them. T. P. O'Connor, a newspaper correspondent, once commented on his 'mufti':

> He was one of those men who ought never to have appeared out of uniform. He gave you the idea of strength and splendid manliness and bulldog power, but there was nothing of distinction in his air, in his manner, or in his dress. He looked a Tommy in his Sunday clothes, which is not Tommy at his best.

Unless Mr Duncan could provide an income for his daughter's continued support, Macdonald could not afford to marry. Nevertheless, he explained that he was soon to take his examination for promotion to captain and that he hoped to obtain an appointment to the Commissariat Department, thereby increasing his income. Reluctantly, the Duncans agreed to a marriage when Christina had turned seventeen.

When Macdonald learned that his battalion was to be transferred to the south of England, he begged Christina to consent to a secret marriage, and she finally agreed. The Duncans had recently moved to a new home at 2 Kew Terrace, and there, standing in Mr. Duncan's study, the young couple on 16 June 1884 furtively recited their vows, promising to be faithful as husband and wife. After they both kissed a small Bible that Christina held, Macdonald solemnly pronounced that they were legally married, as indeed they were.

In Scotland, prior to 1 July 1940, a couple could, without witnesses or a marriage licence, marry by a 'declaration *de praesenti*'. They needed only solemnly and deliberately to give consent. Although such a marriage was legal, it was sometimes found necessary to ensure the rights of the parties or their children by having the marriage recognized in a court of law. In this case, Macdonald begged his bride to keep their marriage secret until he could return in a few months, promising that they would then have a public marriage. To contract a *de praesenti* marriage was, of course, highly unusual for an officer in a famous regiment.

Although it was not legally necessary that the marriage be consummated, Macdonald, after two weeks of pleading, convinced Christina that it was. On June 29 and again on the following day, she went to his quarters in Edinburgh Castle, and there they had intercourse. Shortly afterwards Macdonald left for Plymouth.

He was soon in deep financial trouble. In August 1884 he wrote a pleading letter to his brother William, begging him to try to borrow thirty pounds for him so that he could pay off the most pressing of his debts. He hoped to repay the loan when he received his appointment on the commissariat staff. This was not the sort of appointment that would further the career of a combatant officer, but it paid more and would give him a respite from his creditors. He had not told William that he had married or even that he intended to marry.

On October 15 Macdonald took leave and returned to Edinburgh, where he stayed with the Duncans for nearly a month, often creeping into Christina's bedroom during the night. It was during this stay that arrangements were made for a public wedding on 13 July 1885, Christina's eighteenth birthday. Yet marriage may already have begun to lose its appeal, or perhaps he at last came to realize that he faced financial ruin and the loss of his career. The coveted commissariat appointment did not materialize, and, without telling Christina, he exchanged into the First Battalion of his regiment, then in Egypt taking part in Wolseley's vain attempt to rescue Gordon in Khartoum.

On 13 November, Macdonald left Edinburgh to visit friends in northern Scotland, or so he told Christina. Perhaps he went to try to borrow money. While he was absent from Edinburgh, word came through that he had been exchanged, and in a few weeks he left for Egypt. He told Christina that he expected to return within six months. He was gone for nearly three years.

5

The Gordons formed part of the river column and, except for one company under Ian Hamilton, saw no action. No opportunity for distinction presented itself. After the campaign collapsed, Macdonald was for a time garrison adjutant at Assiout, but before the battalion embarked for Malta in September 1885, he left the regiment, never to return. Probably for the increased pay, perhaps to avoid the promised public wedding, he volunteered to join the Egyptian Constabulary, a semi-military gendarmerie that the British had instituted. It was officered by British soldiers except for its commander, Valentine Baker (1827–1887), younger brother of Sir Samuel Baker, the African explorer.

For thirteen years Valentine Baker had commanded the aristocratic 10th Hussars; he had written on military subjects and became AQMG at Aldershot; he seemed to have a promising career until, in 1875, he was convicted of having assaulted a young lady in a railway carriage. He was dismissed from the army, fined and imprisoned. When he was free, he left England for Turkey, where he commanded a division during the Russo-Turkish War (1877–78). At Tashkessan he was said to have fought one of the most brilliant rearguard actions on record. In 1882 he was delighted to be offered the command of the new Egyptian army that the British were raising and training. By the time he reached Cairo, however, the authorities had changed their minds, for it was thought that British officers would object to serving under a man so disgraced. Evelyn Wood was given command of the army, and Baker was offered the constabulary.

In February 1884 Baker led a force composed of his constabulary and some Egyptian regulars in an attempt to relieve the besieged town of Tokar in the eastern Sudan. He suffered a humiliating defeat at El Teb at the hands of a Dervish force only a third as large as his own. The Egyptians, terrified by the ferocity of the Dervishes, simply threw down their arms and begged for mercy from their merciless enemies. Some Dervishes merely picked up the Egyptians' rifles and used them to beat the soldiers to death. It was this demoralized constabulary that Macdonald joined in 1885, and he remained with it until 1888.

He returned to Edinburgh on leave in May and June 1887 but told Christina that they could not be publicly married until he obtained his captaincy. She agreed to continue to keep their marriage secret, and he promised faithfully that as soon as he was promoted he would come home and marry her or send for her to join him in Egypt. On 18 January the anticipated promotion came, but he neither returned nor sent for her. By this time their marriage could no longer be kept a secret, for Christina was pregnant and on 16 March 1888 gave birth to a son, Hector.

We can only guess at the embarrassment, the stammered explanations and the difficulties of Christina. No one knows the reaction of her parents, but four years later she was no longer living with them, having moved to 7 Coats Place. The following year Macdonald returned to Edinburgh for a brief visit and presumably saw his son for the first time. Once again he postponed the public marriage; there were now, he told Christina mysteriously, 'obstacles which he could not disclose'.

On 6 July 1891 Macdonald was promoted major in the British army (not in the Gordons but in the Royal Fusiliers), and he was serving as a lieutenant-colonel in the Egyptian service. With these advancements and the higher pay, he was, or ought to have been, free of financial worries and able to marry. He had also been able to gain some professional kudos, for he saw action in the eastern Sudan that earned him a mention in dispatches, and in 1889, at the battle of Toski, when a Dervish army under Wad el Nejumi attempted to invade Egypt, he was given not only a mention in dispatches but also the Distinguished Service Order, a new award instituted in 1886 to rank just below the Victoria Cross.

It must finally have become evident to Christina that Macdonald would never consent to a public wedding or willingly acknowledge publicly their *de praesenti* marriage, for in the summer of 1892 she applied to the Court of Session (the central civil court in Scotland) asking that it be found either that she was legally married to Hector Archibald Macdonald or that he should pay her at least £5,000 in damages. There was no bitterness evident in Christina's deposition; she declared that since the birth of young Hector the father had sent her money for his support: 'He has behaved very nicely', she said.

The messager-at-arms (process server) found Macdonald at the Junior Travelers Club at 8 St James on the afternoon of 6 July and gave him a copy of the summons. Two years later, on 7 July 1894, Macdonald signed a paper in which he admitted that he had married Christina by declaration *de praesenti* and that she was his legal wife. Ten days later in the Court of Sessions, Lord Stormouth Darling granted a decree of marriage. There was now no doubt as to young Hector's legitimacy, for Scottish laws, unlike English, declare all children born before a legally declared marriage to be legitimate.

Curiously, although the marriage decree was a matter of public record and was publicized in the *Scotsman*, no one in the army or in London seems to have noticed, and when, only four years later, Macdonald became famous, no one remembered. Christina never lived with him as his wife.

In Egypt, Macdonald had learned Arabic, and his primary duty was the command of the 11th Sudanese Battalion, composed of Blacks from the southern Sudan who had been brought north as slaves – or their parents or grandparents had – and whom he transformed into some of the finest soldiers in the Egyptian army. Macdonald introduced his troops to British discipline, Highland drill and bagpipes.

In 1896 the British decided to invade Dongola Province in the northern Sudan under the curious assumption that this would be of some aid to the Italian forces who were being pressed by the Dervishes near Kassala in the south-eastern part of the country, some 600 desert miles away. Macdonald was ordered to march south to a place called Akasha and establish a fortified base there, which he did. He then commanded a brigade in an attack on Firket and in the advance on the town of Dongola, occupying it on 23 September. For his services he was rewarded with a brevet lieutenant-colonelcy. The province of Dongola was thus 'reclaimed from barbarism' at a cost of 411 lives, of whom 364 died of diseases, mostly cholera.

Encouraged by this first step back into the Sudan, the British began to think of bolder measures. The Egyptian army under its sirdar, Horatio Herbert Kitchener, was ready and willing to reconquer the entire Sudan, but the British government displayed what Lord Cromer described as 'financial timidity and . . . the reluctance always felt by British ministers to decide on anything but the issues of the moment'. So during 1897 Kitchener devoted himself to amassing supplies, improving his transport arrangements and pushing a desert railway in the the Sudan toward Dongola.

By July 1887 the railway was approaching Abu Hamed, which, although designated as the terminus, was still in Dervish hands. Kitchener therefore sent Major-General Archibald Hunter with a flying column of 2,700 men, 1,300 camels, six Krupp 12-pounders and four Maxim machine-guns up the north bank of the Nile just below the fourth cataract to capture the town. One of Hunter's brigades was commanded by Macdonald and consisted of the 9th, 10th and 11th Sudanese and the 3rd Egyptians. Hunter arrived just before dawn on 7 August, and they attacked at 6:30 a.m. An hour later Abu Hamed was occupied and the Dervish commander made prisoner. Anglo-Egyptian losses were two British officers and twenty-five native other ranks killed. Macdonald's brigade took part in the occupation of Berber, which was entered unopposed.

Kitchener was at last unleashed, and with his Egyptian army reinforced by British troops, he began his march south. His first major engagement was near the confluence of the Atbara and Nile rivers, where the Dervishes had built a zariba (a fortified camp protected by thorn bushes). On 8 April 1898, before a gallery of newspaper correspondents on a nearby hill, the Dervish zariba was assaulted and Kitchener was victorious.

Macdonald's performances in these operations stirred the British press to take an interest in this brigadier who had risen from the ranks and earned a reputation as a first-rate battlefield commander. Newspaper correspondents began to call him Fighting Mac. He was praised in extravagant terms by G. W. Steevens, a well-known war correspondent, and by Bennett Burleigh of the *Daily Telegraph*, one of the most famous war correspondents of his day, who commented particularly on his pride in his men.

6

After the battle of the Atbara, Kitchener began his buildup for the final drive on Omdurman, the Dervish capital across the river from Khartoum, which was now largely in ruins. By 1 September 1898 he had assembled an Anglo-Egyptian army of 22,000 men on the Upper Nile only seven miles north of Omdurman. It was equipped with the latest weapons, including Maxim machine-guns and breech-loading howitzers that fired, for the first time in action, the new lyddite explosive shells whose active ingredient was picric acid. The Anglo-Egyptian camp formed an arc, its back to the river, in which were anchored several armed steamers. Between the arc of men and the river were supplies, hospital tents and tons of ammunition. Macdonald's brigade, reinforced by eighteen guns and eight machine-guns, was posted to the right of centre of the arc. Behind a barricade of thorn bushes stood the infantry in a double rank. About thirty yards behind them stood a line of reinforcements to fill in the gaps as men in the forward line fell. The battle of Omdurman was about to be fought: soldiers and Dervishes were on hand to fight it, and plenty of newspaper correspondents were present to record it.

It was feared that the Dervishes, who had a clear view of the camp from the surrounding hills, would launch a night attack. The outcome might well have been different had they done so, for they enjoyed a clear superiority in numbers. The troops slept on their arms, and at first light the next morning they saw the Dervishes advancing in masses, their banners flying, their upraised swords and spears flashing and the roar of battle in their throats. When they were still 2,000 yards away, Kitchener gave the order to commence firing. Not a single Dervish got nearer than 200 yards. G. W. Steevens described their attack:

> It was the last day of Mahdism, and the greatest. They could never get near, and yet they refused to hold back. By now the ground before us was all white with dead men's drapery. Rifles grew red hot; the soldiers seized them by the slings and dragged them back for cool ones. It was not a battle but an execution.

By eight o'clock it seemed to Kitchener that the battle was over, and he ordered the cease-fire to be sounded. Half an hour later most of the brigades and batteries had swung into marching columns and were echeloned across the plain, moving towards Omdurman. Kitchener thought the Dervish army had been destroyed. He was wrong.

Macdonald's brigade was to bring up the rear of the army, and he had not yet put his four battalions into marching order when a screaming mass of 15,000 men of the Khalifa Abdullahi bin Said Mohammed's bodyguard, hand-picked fanatics, emerged from a series of rolling sand-hills. Only Macdonald's brigade stood between them and the marching columns. While Kitchener, in a white heat, flew about, trying to reverse his army and put it back into fighting formations, Macdonald coolly steadied his men and beat off the attack. No sooner was this accomplished than another, even larger force of Dervishes appeared from a new direction. Macdonald moved his troops with parade-ground precision to meet this new threat. It was a difficult manoeuvre carried out in the presence of an aggressive enemy that outnumbered his brigade by more than seven to one. Some 120 of his Egyptian and Sudanese soldiers fell within twenty minutes. According to Winston Churchill,

> Amid the roar of the firing and the dust, smoke and confusion of the change of front, the general [Macdonald] found time to summon the officers of the IX Sudanese around him, rebuked them for having wheeled into line in anticipation of his order, and requested them to drill more steadily in brigade.

By this time, however, the other brigades had come up on either side, and now, at last, the battle was truly won, the Dervish survivors fleeing westwards into the desert. Nevertheless, as the Duke of Wellington said of Waterloo, it had been a 'near run thing'.

Macdonald had clearly saved the day and was the hero of the hour. The correspondents fell over themselves in praising him. One reported that Macdonald had received an order to retreat but had said, 'I'll no do it. I'll see them damned first. We maun just fight!' Bennett Burleigh told readers of the *Daily Telegraph*:

> Beyond all else the double honours of the day have been won by Colonel Macdonald and his Khedival brigade, and that without any help that need be weighed against the glory of the single-handed triumph. He achieved the victory entirely off his own back. . . . The army has a hero and a thorough soldier in Macdonald, and if the public want either, they need seek no further.

The most famous account was that of G. W. Steevens in the *Daily Mail*, which described Fighting Mac and his brilliant handling of his brigade:

Sir Hector Macdonald *(Photo: BBC Hulton Picture Library)*

Beneath the strong, square-hewn face you can tell that the brain is working as if packed in ice. He sat solid on his horse, and bent his black brows towards the green flag and the Remingtons. . . . He saw everything; knew what to do; knew how to do it; did it . . . all saw him, and knew that they were being nursed to triumph.

Kitchener also praised Macdonald in his dispatch, but gave him no more credit than the other brigade commanders in Hunter's division. All had done well, he said, and were 'fully qualified as commanders of troops in the field'; Macdonald's extraordinary performance was not emphasized. Kitchener was elevated to the peerage, and Parliament gave him £30,000. Macdonald was promoted colonel, given the thanks of Parliament and made an aide-de-camp to the Queen, although, as a Scottish journalist pointed out, this was an honour that brought no cash and only the expense of another uniform. When the honours list appeared, there was a general feeling, particularly in Scotland, that Macdonald had not been given proper recognition by the government. The *Northern Weekly* said that Macdonald 'ought to be singled out and recommended for special distinction'. The *North Star* pointedly asked if Britain wanted no more Highland recruits.

7

When Macdonald returned to Britain in April 1899, he was not altogether comfortable, for he was canny enough to know that Kitchener did not relish sharing his glory. Macdonald is said to have remarked, 'Little do my friends know the harm they are doing me with my superiors in thus making so much of me'. Also, of course, there were aspects of his life that he was not anxious to have made public. He must have winced if he read the *Weekly News* when it declared, 'Colonel Macdonald's life-story can bear any test. . . . There is no blemish in his career'.

Macdonald was treated to a round of banquets, which began with one sponsored by the United Highland Societies of London at the Hotel Cecil on 6 May attended by more than 500 distinguished guests. The Duke of Atholl presided, and he was supported by General Sir Evelyn Wood, who drank Macdonald's health and pronounced that 'as long as Scotland sent the army men like Colonel Macdonald, they would never complain'. Accompanied by cheers, the Duke presented the hero of the hour with a splendid sword of honour. Kitchener did not attend this banquet for his subordinate, and it probably did Macdonald no good when newspapers reported that the sword he was given was superior in design to that which had been presented to Kitchener.

Three days later the *Glasgow Herald* said of him, 'He remains modest and manly, a trifle self-deprecatory . . . an admirable specimen of the modern soldier who "do not advertise". Some English friends are annoyed at the Macdonald "boom". . . .' He moved through Britain as if on a triumphal progress; at every station there were guards of honour, pipers, local dignitaries and crowds of admirers. There were receptions and dinners in his honour; he was given more swords, freedoms of cities and other gifts; and he listened to speeches that linked his name with Wolseley, Roberts and, of course, Kitchener.

He was a curiosity: a brave, capable senior officer and a proven hero who had risen from the ranks in perhaps the most class-conscious army in the world. Newspapers gleefully reported on a dinner where he was presented to the Prince of Wales, who said to him courteously, 'I think, Colonel, this is the first time I have had the pleasure of meeting you', to which Macdonald replied, 'No, your Royal Highness, we have met before, for I was sergeant of your guard of honour when you were in India'.

On 11 May he arrived in Inverness from Glasgow. He did not stay long, but went to visit his home town of Dingwall (to which he presented some Dervish relics), then back to

Aberdeen and again, briefly, to Inverness. He was the guest of many notables as he moved about, and in June he was commanded to Windsor to meet the Queen. Whether he saw his wife and son during this period is not known, but it is certain they were not at his side when he received his honours and acclaim, even though by this time Christina Macdonald had legalized their marriage.

After such a long absence, his wife and son would have been strangers to him. Indeed, after nearly thirty years spent in India, Afghanistan, South Africa, Egypt and the Sudan, even Britain doubtless seemed somewhat strange. His sudden rise from obscurity to fame must have been nearly overwhelming. He soon grew tired of dinners and receptions and was eager enough to get back into the saddle when he was ordered to India to command the Sirhind District in the Punjab with headquarters at Ambala. He spent less than six months in India, however, for the Second Boer War began in October 1899, and on 23 January 1900 Macdonald arrived in Cape Town to take part in it with the local and temporary rank of major-general.

8

The Highland Brigade in South Africa consisted of proud battalions of the Black Watch, Seaforths, Gordons, Argylls and Highland Light Infantry. It was part of the army commanded by Lieutenant-General Lord Methuen, which had set off to relieve the diamond-mining town of Kimberley, besieged by Boer forces under Piet Cronjé. On 10 December 1899, at the battle of Magersfontein, the entire brigade had been badly mauled when it tried to attack entrenched Boer positions. A soldier in the Black Watch later said, 'We were led into a butcher's shop and bloody well left there'. Total British casualties were 971, of which 23 officers and 182 other ranks were killed. The brigade lost more than a quarter of its officers, including Major-General Andrew Wauchope, its popular commander. The Black Watch was the most severely mauled battalion, losing 17 of its 22 officers and 338 out of 943 other ranks killed, wounded or missing. Magersfontein was a bitter blow for the army in South Africa; it was a demoralizing shock to the Highlanders, and there was public as well as private mourning in Scotland.

It was this brigade, now weakened by casualties and sitting idle with the rest of Methuen's army on the banks of the Modder River, that Macdonald reached on 23 January. Taking command, he was appalled by the brigade's demoralized state. Three days later, going over the head of Methuen, he wrote directly to Kitchener, who had arrived with Roberts in Cape Town less than two weeks earlier:

> The feeling here, although not openly expressed, is one of profound helplessness. I am actually afraid to put pen to paper in fear of what I say falling into hands other than yours. Could you come here yourself for a few days? You would see and hear what I dare not write.

Both Roberts and Kitchener were soon on the scene, and Roberts took direct command. Macdonald was ordered to make a distracting demonstration by seizing Koodesberg. He almost achieved a splendid little victory, but unfortunately he was thwarted by a lack of cooperation from Major-General J. M. Babington (who was subsequently relieved of his command). Meanwhile, Roberts began his Great Flank March around the Boer positions that stood between Methuen and Kimberley. His cavalry, under Major-General John D. P. French (who in 1914 was to command the British Expeditionary Force in France), raced to relieve Kimberley while Roberts with the bulk of the army hastened to cut off the Boer forces under Cronjé, now trying to fall back on Bloemfontein.

Cronjé was caught at Paardeberg Drift on the banks of the Modder River at a time when Roberts was in bed with a fever at Jacobsdal, several miles away. Kitchener took charge and launched an all-out attack on the Boer laager.

Macdonald, who led his men in a gallant but futile assault, was wounded, 'the bullet going right through his foot and the left ankle. It went in the outside and came out the inside. He was at once carried away to hospital'.* Although he never left his command, it was several months before he was able to walk, and he rode about in a pony trap. Queen Victoria sent him a solicitous telegram.

Great things were expected of Macdonald in South Africa, and the press were eager to report brave or brilliant acts, but he did not add to his laurels. An officer in the Argyll and Sutherland Highlanders said after the war, 'What we really required was a leader who would instil confidence into the troops and buck them up. This I do not consider Hector Macdonald ever did, fine soldier that he was'. This was one man's opinion. It is difficult to pinpoint any fault in his handling of the brigade. That he did not add to his reputation was not entirely his fault, perhaps not his fault at all.

Opportunities to distinguish himself seldom occurred. In part this was because the brigade was still demoralized when he took command, and in part because it was in the division commanded by General Henry Edward Colvile, who did not enjoy Lord Roberts's confidence – and rightly so, for he was one of the least competent of generals and one of the least endearing of men. Nevertheless, Macdonald and his brigade did see some action. On the advance from Lindley to Heilbron in May 1900, the Highland Brigade took part in several hotly contested engagements, and Macdonald was active in the operations in Brandwater Basin that resulted in the capture of General Marthinus Prinsloo. After Roberts returned home and Kitchener was left to direct the operations against the Boer guerrillas, Macdonald directed columns in the south-eastern part of the Orange Free State with his headquarters at Aliwal North (named by Sir Harry

---

* From an unpublished diary of George Henry Kirter of the 1st Argyll and Sutherland Highlanders.

Smith for his victory at Aliwal, India, in the First Sikh War).

It was while Macdonald was at Aliwal North that the first nasty sexual rumours surfaced. His Highlanders were standing guard at the British concentration camp there, and it was whispered that Macdonald had had a homosexual relationship with a Boer working in the camp or with a Boer prisoner. There were never any charges, nothing official; there were only rumours.

Later his command was broken up and distributed among several towns as garrison troops. There was no glory to be found in this dull work, and Macdonald was unhappy. He complained of the arrangement, and when no changes were made, he sulked. Finally, in July 1900, he asked to be reassigned.

In April 1901 Roberts, now commander-in-chief at the Horse Guards, wrote to Kitchener, 'Macdonald can return to India whenever you like'. Kitchener wanted him gone and sent him packing. His reasoning is unknown. It has been suggested that perhaps he feared that Macdonald would again steal some of his glory, but this seems unlikely. Macdonald was an almost constant complainer, and Kitchener may simply have wished to be spared his grumbling.

9

Macdonald certainly appears to have been disgruntled when he left South Africa. He was scheduled to go to India, but first he was ordered to London. There he dined with Lord Roberts, but did not visit relatives or friends in his short stay. He met the new King, Edward VII, and was knighted (KCB) on 13 May, but he complained that he wanted a promotion (which paid) rather than a knighthood (which did not). He was only a colonel in Britain, and he wanted to be a substantive major-general, but Roberts wrote, 'I doubt his being qualified for higher rank than he now holds'. In a revealing letter to Kitchener, Roberts said:

Hector Macdonald sent me a piteous letter begging to be given command elsewhere than in India. He asked for Ceylon and this is about to become vacant. I have told [Sir Arthur Power] Palmer to offer it to him. It carries the local rank of Major-General, and I suspect this is the real reason why Macdonald asked for it, for he frets over not being made a Major-General in South Africa. . . . Macdonald begged if he could not be given Ceylon to be sent back to South Africa, but I know you do not want to have him.

Perhaps all the publicity had engendered inflated expectations in Macdonald. In any case, he left England on 15 May 1901 for southern India, where he assumed command of the Belgaum District.

He remained dissatisfied with his Indian appointment. There had been talk, or at least some comments in the press, that he ought to have been made commander-in-chief in Australia. As the post paid £3,000 a year, Macdonald, too, thought he might like it. So after only a few months in India, he took a long leave to pay a visit to Australia and New Zealand, where he was given a hero's welcome, his private visit becoming a triumphal tour, much like the one he had enjoyed on his return to Britain after the Sudan campaign. In Auckland his carriage was pulled through the streets by exuberant Scottish expatriates. In his talks, he spoke of the glories of the British Empire, the valour of Scotsmen and the need for universal conscription. The Australia–New Zealand trip was his last taste of popular acclaim. He was given not the Australia command but Ceylon, as he had requested before his trip.

The social climate in Ceylon (today, Sri Lanka) was different from that of Britain or Australia. Neither the British colonials nor the natives were particularly impressed by Fighting Mac. The colony was peaceful, and there were no wars to be fought. The Times of Ceylon spoke briefly of Macdonald's prowess as a soldier and then added:

Socially the one drawback is that the Major-General is a bachelor, and consequently, the hospitality which the wife of retir-
ing Major-General F. T. Hobson dispensed will be missed
together, with the many special indications of interest in Ceylon affairs which Mrs Hobson evinced.

Macdonald, who had never mentioned his wife in Scotland, certainly had no intention of bringing her to Ceylon.
Dr Lester Clements, who made a recent study of Macdonald, excuses his failure ever to bring his wife and son with
him by arguing that he could not afford to do so; that he
was accustomed to camp life and his family would have
complicated his normal routine; and that perhaps Lady
Macdonald, as she could now style herself, did not wish to
leave Scotland. Perhaps so, but the evidence seems to indicate that he regretted his youthful indiscretion and wanted
to forget his family, or if he could not forget them, then to
ignore them.

Although far from any fighting, Macdonald seemed happy
enough to work at his administrative and social duties. He
attended meetings of the Legislative Council, where the
island's governor, Sir Joseph West Ridgeway, presided; he
attended dances, dinners and horse races; he presented colours to the Boy's Brigade, served as a patron of the cricket
club, handed out awards at schools and inspected the volunteers.

It has been said of Ceylonese society at that time that it
was caste-ridden and its elite was 'gossip-mongering'. This
appears to have been true. On 20 May 1902, just after his
arrival, an extraordinary letter appeared in the *Times of
Ceylon:*

Dearest Mab, Do you really mean to say that, besides yourself,
three ladies (all up-country ones, too) were the only ones who
went to see our new general arrive? . . . Then, dear, you know
we heard a whispered rumour that he does not like ladies, and
possibly may have been pleasantly surprised to find he had

dropped on a spicy little island where ladies were few and far between.

What is to be made of this? It seems obvious that rumours concerning Macdonald's sexual preferences were circulating about the world and had preceded him to Ceylon.

The Victorian view of homosexuality is difficult to assess. Modern notions of Victorian morals to the contrary, a generally permissive and uninquiring view was taken of strong emotional friendships between males. In England the Criminal Law Amendment Act of 1884 introduced eleven new penalities for various kinds of homosexual behaviour, but prosecution was rare. Unless there was a specific complaint, the police did not seek to control homosexual activity. Participation in homosexual acts usually had to be quite flagrant or had to involve socially prominent men before anyone was brought to court. In 1889 a son of the Duke of Beaufort was swept up in a police raid on a notorious house in Tottenham Court Road that specialized in providing young boys. The Marquess of Queensberry's eldest son committed suicide when accused of having an affair with the Earl of Rosebery, while another son, Lord Alfred Douglas, had a notorious relationship with Oscar Wilde that, largely through his own foolishness, eventually landed Wilde in Reading Gaol.

Although it is quite clear that neither Kitchener nor Gordon was ever sexually attracted to women and that Gordon enjoyed the company of boys and Kitchener that of young men, neither was ever convincingly accused of an overt homosexual act, and it seems doubtful that either was a practising homosexual. The polite terms, still used and perhaps justified, is that they were 'natural celibates'. Whatever tendencies or temptations they may have had were probably suppressed and certainly concealed. There is, of course, nothing inconsistent in a good soldier, even a general, being a homosexual, and 'gallant homosexual', while scarcely a common expression, is not an oxymoron. Good soldiers and intelligent, courageous men can indulge in sexual perversions – witness Lawrence of Arabia who paid to be whipped to orgasm.

Unlike England, Ceylon had no laws against homosexual acts. Nevertheless, on 15 and 16 February 1903 a clergyman and several schoolmasters registered a complaint with Governor Ridgeway that General Hector Macdonald misbehaved 'habitually' with a number of English schoolboys, aged twelve and upward. The exact nature of the alleged offence is unknown and now probably unknowable, for many documents relating to Macdonald are no longer to be found in government files. (The records of the judge advocate for Ceylon for 1903, for example, are missing from the Public Record Office.)

There has been much speculation since the alleged incidents occurred, but hard facts are scarce. Lord Tollemache, Ridgeway's grandson, remembers his mother saying something about Macdonald's being discovered doing something with four native boys in a railway carriage. There was also something about indecent exposure, again in a railway carriage, but not a single provable incident is known today.

Governor Ridgeway appears to have been more concerned with avoiding scandal than in seeking justice. In his report to London he stated, 'There are seven or eight alleged cases but probably more will follow if secrecy is not observed'. He summoned Macdonald to his summer residence in the Ceylonese hill country and confronted him with the allegations, which Macdonald stoutly denied. Ridgeway's foremost thought seemed to be to get Macdonald out of the way, for he counselled him to return at once to England and seek advice from his superiors. On 19 February 1903 he telegraphed St John Broderick, the secretary for war, telling him, 'General Macdonald leaves today on six months leave with my full approval. His immediate departure is essential to save grave public scandal, which I cannot explain by telegraph. I take full responsibility for this unusual step. . . .'

10

It is debatable whether it was wise of Macdonald to leave Ceylon so precipitately. Lord Roberts telegraphed that he would not approve the six months' leave, because he did not, he said, want to remove him from the ordinary process of law, but his telegram arrived too late: Macdonald was already at sea.

Meanwhile, back in Ceylon, Ridgeway tried to keep the lid on the affair by bullying the complainants, telling them that Macdonald had denied the accusations and warning them against 'spreading vile charges on the authority of schoolboys'. Also, expressing his own fears, he told them that a 'scandal of a public and probably inconclusive enquiry' would be 'politically inexpedient'. He reported to London that the clergyman and teachers had agreed to remain silent but that they reserved the right to take action if Macdonald returned. Having got rid of Macdonald, and having succeeded in temporarily muzzling his accusers, Ridgeway did not want him back in Ceylon, and by telegraph he warned that his return 'would cause deplorable scandal which may now be stopped here and in India'. Not long afterwards he sent another telegraph: 'There are many new rumours prevalent of other cases but no new charge has been made and of course I do not seek evidence. Silence of press and those who originally complained is ensured until Macdonald's future is settled'.

In Britain the news that Macdonald had left Ceylon to attend to 'urgent private affairs' created much speculation. It seemed even more puzzling when the War Office professed ignorance of his leave. On arriving in London, he talked with no one outside the War Office and stayed for only a couple of days. He spoke with an unsympathetic

Roberts, who wrote to Kitchener (19 March), now commander-in-chief in India:

> Hector Macdonald goes back to Ceylon to be tried by court martial. He sees his mistake in leaving his command without clearing his character, and I had to tell him that he could not remain in the army while such terrible accusations went unrefuted. . . . He protests his innocence, but if he is innocent, why on earth did he not insist upon having the matter cleared? I am sending Kelly to be President of the Court Martial, and you will be asked to provide the required number of members.

Newspapers later reported that Macdonald had begged to be spared a court martial and that when this was denied him, he burst into tears. Macdonald may at this time have paid a quick visit to his wife and son, who were living in Dulwich, where young Hector was at school, but this seems doubtful. If he did so, it would have had to be a quick trip indeed, for he arrived in Paris on 22 March.

It appears that he intended to return to Ceylon, for he had booked passage on the SS *Britannia,* due to sail from Marseilles at the end of the month. Reuters reported that he was on his way back to resume his duties there. At the meeting of the Ceylonese Legislative Council on 24 March, a Mr Stanley Bois asked Sir Joseph if this was true. Ridgeway said that it was, adding, 'It is known to all here that grave, very grave charges have been made against Sir Hector Macdonald'. Questioned further, he revealed that the general was to be tried by court martial. Ridgeway later defended himself by telling the Colonial Office that had he not made these statements 'there would have been an outbreak of indignation and revelations regarding Macdonald's acts and antecedents most prejudicial to him and demoralizing to the colony'. Sir Joseph displayed his own belief in Macdonald's guilt when he referred to his schoolboy accusers as 'his victims'.

11

The telegraph carried Ridgeway's remarks to Europe, and the next morning they appeared in the English-language newspapers, including the Paris edition of the *New York Herald*, which featured them on its front page. Macdonald was staying at the Regina Hotel in the Rue du Rivoli, and he saw the story when he picked up several newspapers in a small room off the hotel's foyer. He walked with them up the stairs and down the hall to his room, number 105, at the back of the hotel. The room was tidy. There were two unopened letters on a table, but his mind was on other things. He took off his coat and hung it carefully in the *armoire;* he pulled off his shoes and placed them under his bed; he emptied his pockets onto the table next to the unopened letters. Then he took an eight-millimetre revolver from his valise and shot himself behind the right ear. The bullet exited at the left temple, destroying in its path the brains and all life.

Courage can take many forms. Fighting Mac had coolly faced the fury of Afghans, Dervishes and Boers, but he quailed at the thought of a trial and the probable public exposure of his sexual preferences. From Paris he had written to Lord Roberts, saying he could never face a court martial. Roberts 'felt sure he would disappear' and hoped 'he might go to some out of the way part of the world'. Had he done so, he might, like Valentine Baker, have earned fresh fame commanding foreign armies, but Macdonald had no money and no place to hide.

To Kitchener in India, Roberts wrote:

> Ridgeway writes that there is great indignation in Ceylon about him having been sent there, as it is reported that there were similar scandals about him in South Africa and in India.
>
> I have been told since that there were grave suspicions about him when he was commanding at Aliwal North in South Africa, and I have been wondering whether his anxiety to leave Belgaum was due to the same thing.

However, Kitchener replied that he had 'never heard any rumours of this kind about Macdonald'.

Britain was shocked by the news that one of the army's heroes, when threatened with a court martial, had shot himself. The military correspondent for the *Westminister Gazette* wrote, 'I do not know any story more grievous and more pitifully sad than the end of that brave soldier and loyal comrade, Sir Hector Macdonald'. There were songs and poems about him, including a poem by Robert Service. Some believed he was the victim of the spite and envy of the Establishment because he was a ranker. Many believed him innocent of the largely unknown charges – as do many Scotsmen today.

It was immediately after his death that the widow and her son surfaced. The War Office had not known of their existence, for William Macdonald was listed as Colonel Macdonald's next of kin. Perhaps William and other members of the family were also surprised to learn of the wife and son. Certainly William, who left a sick-bed to go to Paris, was astonished when he arrived to claim the corpse and found that young Hector Macdonald and a solicitor had already taken it.

In spite of protests from friends of the dead man and from Scottish clans and organizations, Lady Macdonald refused all offers of assistance from the War Office and had the body taken to Edinburgh, where it was privately buried without military honours at Dean Cemetery at the unusual hour of six o'clock in the morning. On the weekend following, more than 30,000 people came to visit the grave of Scotland's hero, and forty constables were on hand to keep order. The *Scotsman* reported (5 April 1903) that 'the crowds at the cemetery were so dense that one might have imagined some great football match was about to take place'. The crowds kept coming, and so did the flowers and wreaths. Lady Macdonald was subjected to a vast amount of abuse for denying Scotland a chance to honour its hero, and she even successfully sued a Glasgow politician who in a pamphlet

The burial of Sir Hector Macdonald *(Photo: Mary Evans Picture Library)*

had described her as a 'revengeful woman' and suggested that her husband had fallen in love with Governor Ridgeway's daughter, Violet Aline.

Macdonald was scarcely buried when the rumours began. D. P. Menzies, a Glasgow businessman, was the first to suggest – to the Clan Macdonald Society – that perhaps Hector Macdonald had not committed suicide. Menzies thought he was probably murdered, and this story seemed attractive to some for several years. Macdonald was reported to have been seen alive and well in the uniform of a Japanese officer during the Russo-Japanese War, and then he was said to have been seen in Russia, but the most widely believed and most persistent rumour, however improbable, was that Macdonald had joined the German army and that Field Marshal August von Mackensen (1849–1945), the 'conqueror of the Balkans' and one of the most successful of German generals in the First World War, was really Hector Macdonald. Von Mackensen was almost the age Macdonald would have been, he had similar facial features and, of course, the names were similar; the story circulated that he fought in the Balkans because he refused to fight against his own countrymen on the Western Front. Though the life of the aristocratic von Mackensen is well documented, the tale persists because there are still those people, mostly Scots, who wish to believe it.

A monument with a bust stands beside the grave of Macdonald in Dean Cemetery in Edinburgh. Lady Macdonald was also buried there when she died in 1911, and their son, who died in 1951, is buried beside his parents. There is another memorial to Macdonald, standing one hundred feet high, at Dingwall, and a more modest one near his birthplace at Rootfield.

Admirers of Macdonald in Scotland put together a sizeable fund for the education of young Hector, who was left about £4,000 by his frugal father. He grew up to be an engineer and worked in North Shields, a coal-mining town in Tynemouth. He seems to have been regarded as a dour, taciturn, unsociable man and, in later life, a recluse. He never married.

Horatio Herbert Kitchener (1850–1916)

They Called Him K of K

1

Unlike Macdonald, Horatio Herbert Kitchener came of typical Victorian officers' parentage. His father, Henry Horatio Kitchener, had been a soldier who reached the rank of lieutenant-colonel before he sold his commission in 1849 and settled in Ireland. His mother, Frances Ann (née Chevallier), was the daughter of a clergyman and twenty years younger than her husband. Horatio Herbert – always called Herbert by his family – was their third child and second son. He was born on 24 June 1850 at a shooting-lodge called Gunsborough Villa, about three and a half miles from Listowel in County Kerry, Ireland. (Two other sons, Arthur and Frederick Walter, were born in 1852 and 1858.) A governess who joined the Kitchener household when Herbert was eight years old remembered him as a fair and pretty boy with golden hair, pearly teeth, blue eyes and an angelic smile: a portrait that contrasts strangely with the stern, unsmiling Lord Kitchener that emerged in his maturity.

His mother fretted about him, for he seemed too sensitive (he cried over dead birds) and, unlike her other sons, showed little interest in what were regarded as manly pursuits. Colonel Kitchener, who detested schools, had his children tutored, but Herbert's tutors seemed to make little headway. A university-educated cousin, Francis Elliot Kitchener (1837–1915), tested the boys from time to time, and he once declared that he had never known a boy more totally devoid of educational basics than Herbert.

In 1864 the estates in Ireland were sold, and the family moved to Switzerland in the vain hope that the air would improve Mrs Kitchener's diseased lungs. She died at Montreux soon afterwards. Two years later, Colonel Kitchener married his daughter Millie's music teacher, Mary Green, and moved out to New Zealand where another daughter, Kawara, was born. Herbert and his two younger brothers were left at a school in Switzerland, where they became fluent in French and acquired some German. It would appear that Herbert's educational deficiencies were repaired, though not without the humiliation accompanying the discovery of his ignorance by schoolmates and masters, an experience that seems to have left deep emotional scars.

Colonel Kitchener wanted his sons to be cavalrymen – he himself had begun his military career in the 13th Light Dragoons – but Herbert preferred Woolwich to Sandhurst and, coached by his cousin, Francis, and by the Reverend George Frost, a professional crammer in London, he worked hard to qualify for the entrance examinations. It was at Frost's establishment that he formed the first (as far as is known) of a series of lifetime intense emotional friendships.

Claude Reignier Conder was two years older than Herbert and had spent much of his youth in Italy. The two young men became close friends, and their careers were intertwined for many years. In January 1868 they both entered Woolwich. Their European education set them apart from their fellows, most of whom had attended English public schools. Unlike his fellow cadets, young Kitchener had no interest in games and, probably following the lead of Conder (who was to become a noted Altaic scholar), spent much of his time studying Hebrew.

On 15 July the Franco-Prussian conflict broke out, and Colonel Kitchener, now living in Brittany, urged his son to come see the war. Young Kitchener obediently crossed to France and attached himself as a volunteer to a field ambulance unit of the French Second Army of the Loire. Near Le Mans in January 1871 this army was badly mauled in a bloody three-day battle. The young volunteer did indeed see the war. Le Mans introduced him to it in its full horror, but he no longer cried over dead birds, and if he was moved by the sights of dying and maimed men, he did not reveal it. He had already learned to conceal his feelings. Years later, Lord Edward Cecil noted that Kitchener 'preferred to be misunderstood rather than be suspected of human feeling'.

Not long after the battle he eagerly accepted a French officer's invitation to be a passenger in a balloon ascent and, thinly clad, caught a chill, which turned into pneumonia and pleurisy. His father came to collect him, and as soon as he was well enough to travel, he returned to England.

Curiously, Kitchener had been gazetted into the Royal Engineers on 4 January 1871 while he was still in France, so he was summoned by the Duke of Cambridge, who lectured him sternly on the impropriety of a serving British officer taking part in a foreign war. Doubtless the reprimand was laced with the profanity for which the Duke was noted, but it ended on a different note, as he added, 'I'm bound to say, boy, that in your place I should have done exactly the same'. (Forty-three years later France awarded Kitchener a decoration for his services to her army.)

When his health was recovered, Kitchener joined Conder

at the School of Military Engineering, Chatham, where he was sometimes badgered for his ardent High Church beliefs and his meticulous attention to minor fasts, vigils and festivals. It was here that he developed an intense interest in porcelains. He remained interested in *objects d'art* all his life.

In 1873 he was graduated from the School of Military Engineering, took part in the summer manoeuvres of the Austrian army and was then assigned for a short time to a troop of mounted Royal Engineers at Aldershot, where he was rated 'a most zealous and promising officer'. This was his only experience with British troops until he became a general and his only experience as a company officer. He hated it. Claude Conder was on special service with the Palestine Exploration Fund (a well-funded organization with which the army cooperated, established to carry out scientific research in the Holy Land, then a part of the Ottoman Empire). At Conder's urging Kitchener applied to join the fund and was accepted. On 19 November 1874 the two friends were united at Conder's camp on the Plain of Philistia. The current project was the survey of the west bank of the Jordan in order to produce a 26-sheet map on a scale of one inch to a mile. About twenty sheets had been completed when Kitchener arrived as a replacement for Charles Tyrwhitt-Drake, who had died of a fever.

2

The young officers interested themselves in archaeology. They made copies of inscriptions, took photographs, made notes and sketches of ancient ruins and collected a vast quantity of information on the country, which, as the secretary of the fund pointed out in his report for 1875, was proof of 'their zeal and ability'. They also studied Turkish and Arabic together.

Kitchener, tall (6'2"), slim and healthy (after an initial bout of dysentery), thoroughly enjoyed himself in Palestine, and the work itself went well until the afternoon of 10 July 1875. He and Conder were camped in an olive grove in the hills north-west of the Sea of Galilee, when they were set upon by Arab fanatics. In his report of the incident Conder stated, 'I must inevitably have been murdered but for the cool and prompt assistance of Lieutenant Kitchener. . . .'It was mostly a fight with stones and clubs: Kitchener was badly bruised on the left thigh and arm; Conder was more seriously injured by a blow to his neck.

Operations were suspended for a time. Then both officers fell sick with fever and finally had to return to England, where they spent two years working on a narrative to accompany their map. When the time came to return to Palestine, Conder's health was considered too precarious, and Kitchener was appointed to replace him. (Left behind, Conder married the daughter of a lieutenant-general.) By February 1877 Kitchener had resumed the survey of Galilee.

When war broke out between Turkey and Russia, the Arab provinces of the Ottoman Empire grew restive, but Kitchener carried on, and by the end of October the survey was completed. In November he sailed for Constantinople and then paid a visit to the front, where Valentine Baker Pasha, who was then commanding one of the Sultan's divisions in the Balkans, entertained him. Reports of the Turkish atrocities had horrified the British, but Kitchener observed Bulgarians dangling from lampposts and trees with equanimity, and in an article he contributed to *Blackwood's Magazine* he referred to them as 'a most despicable race'.

In January 1878 Kitchener returned to England. He helped complete the Jordan map, was warmly congratulated by the directors of the fund and gave a talk on the survey to the British Association for the Advancement of Science. At home he tried without success to mediate a dispute between his father and stepmother (which finally led to a judicial separation). His stay in England ended when the Foreign Office gave him an assignment similar to the work he had done in Palestine, this time in newly acquired Cyprus.

Kitchener was delighted with his posting to Cyprus, and he looked forward to producing within three years a map to which he could put his own name and that would be a model of its kind and a delight to geographers, administrators and archaeologists. Sir Garnet Wolseley, the new high commissioner, had other ideas. He disapproved of army officers working for the Foreign Office, and the kind of map he required was not at all what Kitchener had in mind. He had no intention of waiting three years for a beautiful, detailed map of the island that would be of use to scholars. He needed as soon as possible a rough survey giving enough information to enable a map to be made for use in taxing the country, and one that would show him all uncultivated lands that had at some time in the past yielded revenue, for he intended to settle Maltese peasants on them.

When Kitchener continued to press his ideas, Wolseley curtly reminded him of their relative positions in life. Kitchener then angered Wolseley still further by writing directly to the Foreign Office for advice. Wolseley wrote to Lord Salisbury, who had succeeded Lord Derby as foreign secretary, explaining why he wanted Kitchener and his party to work full time on the revenue survey: 'The scientific work he is employed upon may safely be postponed. It is of no immediate practical value to us'. To Kitchener's chagrin, Salisbury agreed.

Before Wolseley departed for South Africa in April 1879, Kitchener wrote to Colonel Charles Wilson, RE, who had praised his work in Palestine and who was now serving as consul-general in Anatolia. He told the tale of his discontent and begged for employment in Turkey. Wilson was able to arrange for him to be sent to northern Anatolia as military vice-consul, but Kitchener stayed only eight months. When Major-General Sir Robert Biddulph, who had succeeded Wolseley in Cyprus, offered him a higher status, a doubled salary and a free hand to make the kind of map he wanted, Kitchener returned to the island in March 1880.

He was generally content during his second tour in Cyprus, although he was vexed by Biddulph's refusal to release him to lead an archaeological expedition to Mesopotamia, to be sponsored by the British Museum. He shared a house with a pet bear he had brought from Anatolia and with Lord John Kennedy, a rakish young subaltern in the Scots Guards. It was during this period that Kitchener cultivated the thick bristling moustache that was to become so famous.

When Arabi's rebellion broke out in Egypt and British and French warships were anchored off Alexandria, Kitchener asked for a week's sick-leave, took a ship to Alexandria and there contacted Lieutenant-Colonel Alexander Bruce Tulloch, military liaison officer with Admiral Sir Beauchamp Seymour, who commanded the Mediterranean Fleet. He persuaded Tulloch that they should make a secret reconnaissance, and, disguised as two Levantines, they were rowed ashore at night. They inspected the Egyptian defences and the disposition of Arabi's troops; they drew sketches, made notes and then reported their findings to the admiral, who, well pleased with their enterprise, warmly congratulated them both.

Tulloch persuaded the admiral to ask General Biddulph for an extension of Kitchener's leave, but Biddulph refused. Kitchener defiantly remained there anyway and witnessed the all-day bombardment of Alexandria by British and French warships on 11 July 1882. It was fortunate that Biddulph, although thoroughly angered by Kitchener's insubordination, did not, as well he might, insist on a court martial; Kitchener wrote him a contrite letter.

When Sir Evelyn Wood became sirdar of the Egyptian army, Kitchener was one of the twenty-six officers selected to help him reconstitute and train it. Unfortunately, there was another year's work to be done on the Cyprus scientific survey that he had so badly wanted to make and that Biddulph had given him the chance to complete. The Egyptian appointment, which carried the rank of *bimbashi*, or major,

Lord Kitchener *(Photo: Mary Evans Picture Library)*

was tempting in every way. Still, he realized that he could
not again offend Biddulph, who had been more than kind
to him. With the connivance of Wood's aide-de-camp,
Kitchener solved his dilemma by engaging in a bit of
duplicity. He telegraphed Wood, 'Very sorry – present work
will not permit me to leave Cyprus for one year'. Biddulph
was apparently touched by this example of Kitchener's
loyalty; when, as arranged, a second telegram arrived saying that he was wanted as second-in-command of the cavalry, Biddulph, feeling it would be selfish to keep an officer

from accepting such a promising post, urged him to accept. He left at once for Egypt, where promotion, fame and eventually a peerage awaited him.

3

Up to this point in his career Kitchener appears to have been accepted as a somewhat eccentric, though not unpopular, officer. In Egypt this changed. Ambition overwhelmed him, revealing a streak of ruthlessness, glaringly evident to his fellows but not, it seems, to his superiors. As second-in-command of the cavalry, Kitchener earned high praise from his commanding officer for his 'general professional acquirements", which he enhanced by taking his leaves in the East instead of returning to England. He was also praised for his 'judgement and tact' and his 'unfailing self-reliance'. Sir Evelyn Wood added, 'This is an excellent officer in every respect – a good Arab linguist – a fine horseman – great determination and courage'.

In 1883 Kitchener was excused from his cavalry duties in order to assist Professor Edward Hull in making a survey of the Arabah Valley from the Dead Sea to Aqaba. Walter Besant, on behalf of the Palestine Exploration Fund, asked Claude Conder to help Kitchener link the work of Hull's expedition with that of the Palestine survey, but Conder refused. His relations with his former friend had cooled considerably since his marriage, and he told Besant:

> In 1877 I worked very hard to equip the expedition which Kitchener took out. My reward then, and in 1879, was that he appropriated my discoveries and gave out a great deal of my work as his own; that he told people he had 'slipped into my shoes', and made my brother officers believe that he was the explorer of the greater part of Palestine.
> He may now help himself.

The Arabah Valley expedition was aborted when General Wood sent news to Kitchener and Hull on Christmas Eve 1883 of the defeat of an Egyptian army under an English officer, William Hicks Pasha, at the hands of the Dervishes in the western Sudan; Wood feared for their safety should this news excite the Arabs in the Arabah Valley to mischief. Professor Hull was fearful and wanted to return to the coast by way of Gaza, a safe route, but Kitchener, who had taken a dislike to Hull, scornfully rejected this roundabout route and, taking only four Arabs with him, set out to cross 200 miles of desert straight to Ismailia. He made it through, but sandstorms and the desert's glare permanently impaired his eyesight, and he now began to suffer severe headaches. He was soon back with the Egyptian army, grumbling that he had been neither paid nor praised for his work with Hull.

In March 1884, when the Mahdi's Dervishes began to invest Khartoum, Kitchener volunteered to open communications with Gordon. It was agreed that he was to go to Berber and establish a system for sending and receiving messages. He was to obey any instructions Gordon sent out and to assess and report daily on the attitude of the surrounding tribes. He was to be Wood's – as he later became Wolseley's – eyes and ears in the Sudan. Kitchener and his assistant, Major (later General) Leslie Rundle, were unable to reach Berber, for the Dervishes captured the town on 20 May, but in early June they established themselves in Korosko, forty miles north-east of Wadi Halfa. In July, Kitchener was ordered to make a reconnaissance to Amara, 170 miles to the south-east, in order to obtain information, try and persuade the Kababish tribe to rescue Gordon, and discover the political leanings of the mudir (local governor) of Dongola.

Kitchener donned Arab dress and with twenty Ababda tribesmen reached Dongola on 2 August. He found the Kababish uncooperative and, after conferring with the mudir, reported that he was a lying intriguer who should not be trusted or supported. Wolseley, however, recommended that the man be given the KCMG, and on 4 November 1884 he personally fastened the decoration around his neck.

Not all of Kitchener's messages to Gordon got through, and some of those that did reach Khartoum infuriated him. In a message addressed to Colonel Stewart, Kitchener asked obtusely, 'Can I do anything for you or General Gordon? I shall be awfully glad if you will let me know'. Shortly afterwards he requested Gordon to tell him *exactly* when he expected problems 'as to provisions and ammunition'. In his journal Gordon commented:

> It is as if a man on the bank, having seen his friend in the river already bobbed down two or three times, hails 'I say, old fellow, let me know when we are to throw you a life buoy; I know you have bobbed down two or three times, but it is a pity to throw you a life buoy until you are really *in extremis*, and I want to know exactly, for I am a man brought up in a school of exactitude. . . .'

Whatever Gordon's opinion, Kitchener's direct superiors were pleased with his work, and General Stephenson wrote to the Duke of Cambridge:

> I consider the services performed by Major Kitchener . . . – performed single-handed, as it were, and far removed from the possibility of support – as of the greatest value to the security of Egypt, and to Her Majesty's forces now protecting it.
>
> These services have been carried out in an adventurous spirit, and with great intelligence and a high sense of duty. . . .

Even Wolseley seemed almost prepared to forget the unfavourable impression Kitchener had made on him in Cyprus.

Shortly after Kitchener had been seconded as a major to the Egyptian army he was gazetted major in the British army. However, he had already awarded himself the local, unpaid rank of lieutenant-colonel, and he explained this extraordinary step to General Wood by insisting that without this higher rank all his influence with the tribesmen would have been destroyed.

Kitchener's clandestine activities in the Sudan expanded into organizing irregular forces and moving about in Arab guise as a spy – though it is difficult to imagine the tall Kitchener, with his wide-set blue eyes and military moustaches, passing for an Arab. After watching the tortures inflicted on one captured spy, he furnished himself with poison to take if he was caught. All his heroics were in vain, of course. On 7 April 1885, after the fall of Khartoum, he wrote to Charles Wilson of his disappointment and frustration: 'Since Gordon's death, I personally have very little interest in the Sudan and its future'. However, ambition was to revive interest.

4

It was while Kitchener was in Egypt and the Sudan that there is supposed to have occurred the only heterosexual romance even to be hinted at in his life. Kitchener was friendly with both Sir Samuel Baker, the explorer, and his brother, the once disgraced Valentine Baker. In 1883 Valentine Baker's eldest daughter, Hermione, then only sixteen, fell madly in love with the handsome, dashing 33-year-old Major Kitchener. Although family legend has it that her love was reciprocated and that Kitchener intended to marry her, there is not a shred of evidence to support this and it seems most unlikely. In any case, Valentine Baker, his wife and Hermione all died in Egypt within four years.

On 3 June 1885 Kitchener returned to England for a well-deserved rest and to assess – if possible, to improve – his opportunities for further advancement. He spent most of his leave in a rented flat near Buckingham Palace, but he was often invited to stay in country houses, where he assiduously cultivated the friendship of influential people.

When Kitchener learned that he was to be given a routine assignment in Ireland, he used all of his influence to have it changed to a more interesting posting, and on 6 November he was appointed as Britain's representative on the Zanzibar Boundary Commission, the purpose of which was to determine how much, if any, of the Sultan of Zanzibar's ill-defined territories on the African mainland he should be allowed to keep, in view of French, German and British interests in that area. Kitchener was ideally suited for the position, for he was fluent in French and German, the mother tongues of his colleagues on the commission, as well as Arabic. None of the governments concerned fully accepted the recommendations of this joint commission, but Kitchener was awarded a CMG for his efforts.

His next assignment was as governor of the Eastern Sudan and the Red Sea Littoral. It was a lovely title, but the reality was less grand: he ruled only the dusty town of Suakin and a narrow strip of coastline; the Dervishes held the rest. The British government wanted no more to do with the Sudan after the failure of Wolseley's expedition to relieve Gordon, but Kitchener hungered for glory. He was specifically ordered not to use the regular Egyptian troops stationed at Suakin for offensive operations, but he put together a force of irregulars (which, indeed, included some of his regular troops costumed as irregulars), and on 17 January 1888 he led them in an attack on a position held by Beja tribesmen (Kipling's 'fuzzy-wuzzies') under Osman Digna, one of the best of the Dervish leaders.

This was the first battle in which Kitchener commanded, and it was a fiasco. He was severely wounded in the lower right jaw, but he continued to command and fought his force back to Suakin. He was transferred to a hospital in Cairo, and his sister, Millie Parker, came out from England to nurse him.

In spite of its lack of success, this first real fight with the Dervishes since the withdrawal of Wolseley's army titillated those at home. The press in general praised his initiative, as did other soldiers. The Duke of Cambridge sent him a congratulatory telegram, and he was promoted colonel; the Queen frequently inquired about his wound and made him one of her aides-de-camp.

5

In June 1888 Kitchener returned to England and stayed for a time with the prime minister, Lord Salisbury, at Hatfield. In September he was back in Egypt as adjutant-general. Before taking up his new duties, he was sent back to Suakin to organize its defences, and on 20 December 1889 he enjoyed a small victory over some of Osman Digna's Dervishes just outside the town. Returning to Cairo, he set to work, diligently as always, on his tasks as adjutant-general. Sir Evelyn Wood reported on him to Lord Salisbury: 'Kitchener possesses many excellent qualities, but he is headstrong and wanting in judgement'. He remained unpopular with officers of his own or lower rank, but he continued carefully to cultivate the good opinion of his military and civilian superiors, and all others who might be of advantage to him.

Staff and command functions were not sharply defined, and when Wad el Nejumi launched his invasion of southern Egypt with some 13,000 warriors, Kitchener commanded the cavalry at the decisive battle of Toski, where Sir Francis Grenfell, the sirdar, ended for ever the expansionist dreams of the Dervishes. Kitchener earned a CB and the praises of Grenfell, but the sirdar, like others who had seen him perform, commented on his lack of tact, his brusque manner and his unpopularity with his colleagues, one of whom said simply, 'We hated the sight of him'. As for the men in the ranks, Kitchener had no interest in them. He never spoke to a private or a non-commissioned officer except in the line of duty, and as he moved up the hierarchical army ladder, he had less and less need to do so.

In 1891 he took on the additional role of inspector-general of police, and when Sir Francis Grenfell accepted a post in England, Kitchener asked for his place. Lord Salisbury, the Duke of Cambridge and Sir Evelyn Baring all agreed that he was the best man, and so, on 13 April 1892, at the age of only forty-one, and to the disgust and dismay of his military colleagues, he was made a local major-general in the British army and sirdar of the Egyptian army.

One of the chief reasons for Kitchener's appointment was that he had impressed upon Baring that he was a soldier who understood economy, and he proved himself ruthless in his pursuit of it; Baring thought him 'a good man of business'. He refused to use British cloth for uniforms because it was more expensive than Egyptian cloth; when pay, allowances, even hospital amenities, could be reduced, he reduced them. All British officers who wanted to be considered for secondment to the Egyptian army were personally interviewed by Kitchener at the Junior United Services Club in London during his annual leave in England. No married officer and no officer engaged to be married need apply. Marriage, he said, divided a man's loyalty and interfered with his work. He justified his hiring of bachelors to Baring (who became Lord Cromer in June 1892) by telling him that it was ridiculous to pay marriage allowances when it was unnecessary to employ married officers.

There was one important person whom Kitchener failed to enlist in the ranks of his admirer: Abbas Hilmi II, the twenty-year-old Khedive, who in January 1892 succeeded his father, Tewfik. The young Khedive, feeling the British pressure as applied by Lord Cromer and resenting it, set out to prove that he was still a power in the land. In January 1894, accompanied by Kitchener, he set out on a formal inspection of the British-trained Egyptian army. As he moved up the Nile from post to post in his yacht, he became increasingly critical, particularly of the British officers and their work. After a march past at Wadi Halfa he exclaimed, 'To tell you the truth, Kitchener Pasha, I consider that it is disgraceful for Egypt to be served by such an army'. Kitchener, who since the inspection began had found it increasingly difficult to control his temper, at once announced his resignation. The Khedive, realizing he had gone too far, begged him to reconsider, but Kitchener would not be mollified.

The upshot of this small tempest was that, after a flurry of telegrams between Cairo and London, Kitchener did not resign, an anti-British Egyptian army, was forced to resign and the Khedive was required to write a letter for publication in which the army, and particularly its British officers, were highly praised. Furthermore, the government in London, to show its faith in Kitchener, awarded him a knighthood (KCMG) for his services. Khedive Abbas Hilmi never forgave Kitchener or the British government.

6

In March 1896 the British deliberately provoked the Dervishes by invading the northern Sudan in order to relieve pressure on the Italians and, as Salisbury told Cromer, 'to plant the foot of Egypt rather further up the Nile'. Cromer urged Salisbury to keep Kitchener in command: 'He is cool and sensible, knows his subject thoroughly, and is not at all inclined to be rash'. Others, however, felt that Wolseley or some other senior officer should take command in the field. Cromer tried to assure those at home that Kitchener was reliable and could be controlled. He told Salisbury, 'So long as I have him at the end of a telegraph wire, I feel pretty confident that I can keep him and the Egyptians generally in hand'.

The Dongola campaign in the northern Sudan was a 'Foreign Office war'. The War Office, Wolseley and the Horse Guards had nothing to do with it. Under the direction of Lord Cromer, it was carried out by Egyptian troops with Egyptian funds under Kitchener, the Egyptian sirdar. Among Kitchener's first acts was to send for his younger brother, Frederick Walter (always, like his older brother, called by his middle name), who was then a major in the

Prince of Wales Own (West Yorkshire) Regiment in India, and to put him in charge of the camel transport. In Cairo, Walter had a look at his brother grown grand. Herbert was, he said, 'a real aristocrat – he does just as he pleases'. This was not quite true, but such was the impression he created, and certainly he had a free hand with the Egyptian army.

Walter was also exposed to another side of his brother's character. The austere man who could live like an Arab, endure great hardships and make himself hard, physically and emotionally; the man who could cut medical services to save money and see no need to repent of the suffering he caused; and the man who resorted to the hated corvée and the lash of the hippopotamus-hide whip on the backs of peasants rather than pay for Egyptian boatmen – this same man had a taste for luxury, works of art and life on the grand scale. His house in Cairo was a mansion stuffed with statues, carved screens, expensive draperies, magnificent tiles and fine furniture. His interest in porcelain had grown and his enthusiasms expanded. That tenderness which most men reserve for women was, by Kitchener, lavished on *objets d'art*. But for glory and the wherewithal to acquire more, Kitchener was willing to leave civilized Cairo and his treasures for the wild and primitive Sudan.

The first battle of the Dongola campaign was at Firket, on the right bank of the Nile, on 6 June. The Dervish commander and more than 800 of his warriors were slain; another 1,100, mostly wounded, were taken prisoner. Anglo-Egyptian losses were 20 killed and 83 wounded. The Dervishes fought valiantly, but, as Kitchener reported to Cromer, they 'were like rats in a trap, and most that escaped did so by swimming the river, naked and without arms'.

After Firket, Kitchener might have pushed on to Dongola, but he preferred a cautious, more certain campaign. He brought up supplies and built up his strength. With the aid of experts, he had designed gunboats to be used on the Nile, but they were still being built in England; his railway was pushing its way through the desert toward Dongola, but it was not yet complete. Patience would be rewarded with victory.

In spite of two calamities – a severe outbreak of cholera among his troops and an unprecedented series of unseasonable torrential rainstorms – Kitchener managed, early in September 1896, to concentrate 15,000 men and five gunboats for a march on Dongola, which after a short battle at Hafir, thirty-five miles downriver from the town, he occupied unopposed on 23 September. For this little campaign he received a KCB and was promoted to be a substantive major-general in the British army.

7

On 9 November, Kitchener arrived in London full of plans for a further advance into the Sudan. All he needed was money: he wanted British taxpayers to provide £500,000 for a railway, gunboats, arms, stores and other military necessities. To get his way he pulled every string he could and convinced Queen Victoria, the Duke of Cambridge and finally the all-important government ministers, including Sir Michael Hicks-Beach, the tight-fisted chancellor of the exchequer.

Back in the Sudan with the backing he needed, he abandoned the railway that paralleled the Nile from Wadi Halfa almost to Dongola; instead, on 1 January 1897, against the advice of almost all the experts, he began to build a new desert railway from Wadi Halfa to Abu Hamed, cutting off the great bend in the Nile and the second, third and fourth cataracts.

Much of the success of the Sudan Military Railway, as it became known, was due to a remarkable 29-year-old French-Canadian officer, Lieutenant Percy Girouard, who quickly became a favourite of Kitchener. Girouard was the son of a Canadian judge and a graduate of the Royal Military College, Kingston, who had had some experience on the Canadian Pacific Railway. He was handsome, high-spirited and brave, having won the DSO in the Dongola campaign. Like Gordon's boys, Kitchener's favourites (his 'cubs', as he called them) were granted liberties denied to others; they could say and do things that others would never dare.

Kitchener insisted on a three foot six inch gauge railway track with the notion that one day it would connect with the north–south railway in South Africa. The Cape-to-Cairo railway was Cecil Rhodes's dream, and he diverted to the Sudan several locomotives intended for Cape Colony and Natal. Fortunately, wells dug in the desert along the route produced enough water for locomotives as well as construction crews. Work progressed at the rate of one and a half miles per day.

On 7 August, Abu Hamed was taken, and three weeks later it was reported that the Dervish commander at Berber had panicked and abandoned the town. When a reconnaissance confirmed this, Kitchener moved swiftly to occupy it. He then reopened the Suakin–Berber route, connecting the Nile with the Red Sea, and sent his gunboats to bombard Metemma. Next, he opened a political campaign designed to convince the British government that he should be allowed to complete the conquest of the Sudan. For this he needed British troops and more money. He felt a sense of urgency, for he feared that with delay, even if a decision to reconquer was made, some senior general would be given the command and reap the glory that he felt was rightly his. Doubtless he remembered how Wood, when sirdar, had been pushed aside by Wolseley for the Gordon Relief Expedition. His anxieties were not lessened when, in July 1897, Sir Francis Grenfell returned to Egypt to command the British army of occupation.

Cromer did nothing to relieve Kitchener's anxieties, and he refused funds for various projects that he interpreted as preparing for a further advance. The relations between Cromer and Kitchener, which had been excellent until now, became so strained that on 18 October Kitchener, in a fit of frustration and indignation, telegraphed his resignation. Cromer, coolly reporting this to Salisbury four days later, said:

> The difficulties here ... are materially increased by Sir Herbert Kitchener's frame of mind. A few days ago he formally resigned, but as I have heard no more of this I fancy he will not carry out his intention. He complains of the strain, and, generally, leaves on my mind the impression that, for the moment, his nerve is gone. This is very awkward. ...

In a letter to Salisbury, Cromer said that Kitchener seemed 'a changed man', whose telegrams 'were diffuse and altogether wanting in the businesslike ring to which I was formerly accustomed'. Cromer enclosed a letter Kitchener had sent to his friend Clinton Dawkins (then under-secretary for finance in Egypt and later a partner of J.P. Morgan). In it Kitchener spoke of his 'continual anxiety, worry and strain', adding, 'I do not think I can stand much more, and I feel so completely done up that I can hardly go on and wish I were dead'. Cromer characterized this letter as 'the production of a sick man'. However, he thought that the sirdar's condition would improve: 'Those who know Kitchener best tell me that he is liable to fits of extreme depression from which, however, he rapidly recovers'. Matters did not improve, and Cromer found him increasingly difficult to control. In December Cromer complained, 'It is sometimes difficult to extract the whole truth from him. He is inclined to keep back facts which he does not wish to be known'.

Here, too, Kitchener was unpopular with those who worked for him, except for his 'cubs', his 'happy family of boys'. He possessed an extraordinary memory, but he was a poor administrator and refused to delegate. Lieutenant-Colonel Henry Rawlinson, when appointed to his staff in Egypt, wrote:

I was told that he was a queer customer. . . . He is a curious and very strong character. . . . He is a long-headed, clear-minded man of business, with a wonderful memory. . . .

He keeps all information regarding the details of railways, transport, steamers, supply and intelligence in his own hands, and shows wonderful skill in working the various strings. Everything works smoothly and well, as long as he is at the head of affairs, but he does too much.

Later, in a letter home, Rawlinson wrote:

K. is a rum 'un, and a ripper. He is hard as nails and as cool as a cucumber. . . . He is full of brains. . . . Here he is an absolute autocrat, does exactly what he pleases, and won't pay any attention to red-tape regulations and to keeping records of telegrams and letters. . . . There is very little correspondence except by wire and in the field almost every order is given verbally.

As Kitchener preferred to act as his own chief of staff, no one else knew where to find anything and his office was chaotic. His appointed chief of staff was kept idle at Wadi Halfa while he himself managed everything from Berber. He bullied his subordinates unmercifully, except for his 'cubs', and neither sickness nor acts of God excused an underling from executing his orders to the letter. Between 1896 and 1898 he was, in the words of his biographer Philip Magnus, 'brusque, dour and uncouth'.

8

The debate as to whether to complete the conquest of the Sudan ended when, in December 1897, it was reliably reported that the Khalifa was about to send a huge army to attack and recapture Berber. Kitchener advised Cromer that British troops would be needed; Cromer alerted Salisbury; and all Kitchener's anxieties and frustrations were put to rest when the Cabinet agreed to send him whatever was required and he was specifically given command of all troops, British and Egyptian, south of Aswan.

By the end of January 1898 the Egyptian army was concentrated south of Berber in a fortified camp where the Atbara River joins the Nile, and a British force under Major-General William Gatacre was assembling at Berber. In March the Dervishes tried to outflank the Egyptians, and they established their zariba a few miles away on the Atbara. Kitchener hesitated and did not seem to know what he should do. He worked himself into such a highly nervous state that only through constant effort was he able to present a calm, determined face to the world. On going over his plans, after he had finally decided to attack, Kitchener astonished one of his staff officers by bursting into tears and sobbing, 'I hope everything will go right'.

Like Wolseley, Kitchener was superstitious about Fridays; nevertheless, on 8 April, Good Friday, his Anglo-Egyptian army attacked the Dervish zariba at first light. It was all over within an hour, and the victorious soldiers raised loud cheers for their impassive commander. Kitchener retired with a headache.

Casualties were light: 120 British and 463 natives. Queen Victoria, who always inquired about the wounded, was assured by Kitchener that they were being carefully tended. This was not true. He never evinced much interest in the sick or wounded, and in the interests of economy he had reduced the medical establishment both in personnel and in supplies to the point where even the comparatively light casualties at the Atbara strained resources.

More and more Kitchener seemed to take on the character of Lucius Septimius Severus, the Roman emperor of whom Gibbon wrote that his ambition 'was never diverted from its steady course by the allurements of pleasure, the apprehension of danger, or the feelings of humanity'. He led a triumphal parade through Berber riding on a white horse. The defeated Dervish commander was put in chains and made to run behind the cavalry, driven by hippopotamus-hide whips in the hands of soldiers and pelted with filth by jeering onlookers. Thus did Kitchener carry 'light and civilization to the dark places of the world'. He always maintained that it was the battle at the Atbara that had broken the back of Dervish rule in the Sudan, not the subsequent battle of Omdurman.

Before the campaign continued, the soldiers were put into summer quarters, the railway was completed to Berber, and more British troops were added. By late August, Kitchener had concentrated his forces near Wad Hamed, only about ten miles north of the Dervish capital of Omdurman. Under his command were 8,200 British and 17,600 Egyptian and Black Sudanese regulars, 2,500 friendly irregular tribesmen, ten gunboats on the Nile armed with 36 guns and 24 Maxims, and 44 field guns and 20 more machine-guns on land. On the morning of 1 September 1898 a patrol of the 21st Lancers discovered the massed warriors of the Khalifa, 60,000 strong, moving across the plain of Kerreri about seven miles away. Lieutenant Winston Churchill was sent galloping back to tell Kitchener. Young Churchill found the sirdar riding in lonely splendour; behind him rode two soldiers carrying the Egyptian flag and the Union Jack, and behind them rode his staff.

The Anglo-Egyptian army made camp by the Nile, the troops in a large arc with their backs to the river, where the anchored gunboats opened fire on Omdurman. Several holes were made in the mud walls of the town, and one shot tore a hole in the white dome of the Mahdi's tomb, the gunners' aiming point.

The failure of the Khalifa's hordes to attack that night made the outcome of the battle almost certain. But just when Kitchener thought the battle won and was swinging his army about for a short march to Omdurman, he was attacked by the cream of the Dervish army and was saved only by the brilliance and bravery of Hector Macdonald and his brigade. (The foolish charge of the 21st Lancers, in

The Maxim guns in action at Omdurman *(Photo: Mary Evans Picture Library)*

which Lieutenant Churchill took part and which resulted in the award of three Victoria Crosses, was of no consequence whatsoever to the outcome of the battle.)

When Macdonald was attacked, Kitchener was at first oblivious to the danger, for his view was obscured by a low hill, but as soon as a galloper from General Hunter told him what was happening, he seemed to panic. Ignoring his staff and even his division commanders, he dashed about the plain, throwing out orders to brigadiers and even battalion commanders. When the last Dervish attack had been beaten back, he resumed his cool, imperious manner and, looking out over the field strewn with dead and wounded Dervishes, remarked calmly to an aide that the enemy appeared to have had 'a thorough dusting'.

Kitchener rode through the streets of Omdurman and proclaimed his intention to spare women, children and every man who surrendered his arms. He was then almost killed by a stray shell from one of his own gunboats, a shell that did kill Herbert Howard, correspondent for *The Times* and the *New York Herald*.

News of the victory was telegraphed back to Cairo and then on to London. Kitchener assured the Queen that he had personally made provision for the British wounded. His own Egyptian and Black Sudanese regulars were less well cared for and the enemy wounded scarcely at all. Thousands of wounded Dervishes died from neglect. Three days after the battle, Kitchener arranged for an impressive ceremony amid the ruins of the palace at Khartoum where Gordon had met his end. The Union Jack was hoisted, and a military band accompanied soldiers as they sang 'Abide with Me', Gordon's favourite hymn. Kitchener was much moved: his shoulders were seen to shake with sobs, and tears rolled down his sunburnt cheeks. The strain of the past few years had ended in this glorious victory for which he had so long prayed. Queen Victoria was moved by his account of this memorial ceremony for Gordon, and in her journal she wrote, 'Surely he is avenged!'

It was the wise old Lord Cromer who most accurately assessed Kitchener's victory at Omdurman:

> I have no wish to disparage the strategical and tactical ability which was displayed in this campaign. It is, however, a fact that no occasion arose for the display of any great skill in these branches of military science. When once the British and Egyptian troops were brought face to face with the enemy, there could . . . be little doubt of the result.

Once the difficulties of supply and transportation were overcome, modern weapons determined the outcome, for spears and muskets could not compete with machine-guns and howitzers. What was needed to overcome the only difficulties was, said Cromer, 'a good head for business', and this was found on the sirdar:

The Mahdi's tomb damaged by British gunfire *(Photo: Mary Evans Picture Library)*

> Lord Kitchener won his well-deserved peerage because he was an excellent man of business; he looked carefully after every important detail, and enforced economy.

Kitchener had made little effort to conceal his contempt for the bevy of newspaper correspondents who accompanied his army on this campaign. Just before the battle of Omdurman a group of them had waited for him, standing in the sun outside his tent. When he abruptly strode out, he scattered them, snarling, 'Get out of my way, you drunken swabs!' The reporters retaliated by fabricating reports. (A Reuters correspondent claimed that he was a drunk and that he had 'the other failing acquired by most Egyptian officers, a taste for buggery'.) They stirred up a hornet's nest by reporting his neglect of the Dervish wounded, and created a furore over the desecration of the Mahdi's tomb and the subsequent disposition of the Mahdi's skull.

General Gordon's nephew, Major William Stavely Gordon, RE, was given the task of razing the Mahdi's tomb and throwing his bones into the Nile. This he did, but he saved the Mahdi's skull, which he presented to Kitchener. Some of his staff suggested that he convert it into an inkstand, or perhaps even a drinking cup. Kitchener may have seriously entertained such ideas, but he finally decided to send it to the Royal College of Surgeons. The reporters, British and American alike, made the most of every aspect of this story. There were unkind comments and hostile questions in Parliament; the Queen was shocked by the treatment given to the Mahdi's remains and thought putting the skull on display at the Royal College's museum would do great harm. Kitchener, embarrassed by the fuss, ordered the skull to be properly disposed of, and one night it was buried – no one knows exactly where.

9

On the day after the battle of Omdurman, Kitchener opened sealed orders and found that he was directed to lead an expedition more than a hundred miles farther up the Nile to a place called Fashoda, where the French had established themselves and built a small fort. More than two years earlier, Major Jean-Baptiste Marchand, an intrepid and enterprising man, had set off with a few junior officers and some African soldiers from the Atlantic side of French Equatorial Africa and, travelling largely through wild, unexplored country, had finally reached the Nile at Fashoda with 6 officers and 120 Senegalese soldiers still alive. He planted the French flag there on 10 July 1898. It was in order to eject Marchand that Kitchener loaded up five gunboats with soldiers, field artillery and machine-guns and steamed to Fashoda. On his arrival the two armed groups faced each other uncertainly, Kitchener demanding that the French haul down their flag and Marchand refusing to do so. However, neither side opened fire. Kitchener and Marchand exchanged polite notes and then had lunch together. Wisely, they decided to refer matters to their respective governments.

There was much talk of war in Paris and in London, and in both countries newspapers spewed hysterical nonsense, but in the end France had to back down. Kitchener arranged for Marchand and his men to be carried down the Nile to Cairo and on to France. To please, or appease, French sensibilities, the name 'Fashoda' was wiped off the map and replaced by 'Kodok'; so ended the 'Fashoda Incident'.

On 27 October 1898 Kitchener returned to a hero's welcome in England. W. T. Stead wrote in his *Review of Reviews* that 'not Wellington returning from the Battle of Waterloo could have been accorded more triumphal honours'. Both Cambridge and Edinburgh universities awarded him academic honours, and he was given the Freedom of the City of London together with an expensive, jewel-encrusted sword. When other cities and organizations expressed a wish to honour him, he let it be known that he would really prefer gold plate, furniture and paintings. In spite of his unpopularity with colleagues and war correspondents, he became a hero to schoolboys and the government. He received the thanks of both houses of Parliament (though they were not unanimous), a gift of £30,000 from a grateful nation, the GCB and elevation to the peerage as Baron Kitchener of Khartoum and of Aspall in Suffolk. The press now rechristened him 'K or K', and the Queen welcomed him to Balmoral: 'They say he dislikes women, but I can only say he was very nice to me', she said, and she found him 'very agreeable and full of conversation'. Arthur Balfour told Lady Elcho, regarding Kitchener, 'He seems to have a profound contempt for every soldier except himself, which, though not an amiable trait, does not make me think less of his brains'.

It was while in Scotland that Kitchener made his appeal for funds to build a college in Khartoum in memory of Gordon. Within six weeks he raised £110,000 for what became

Gordon College (now the University of Khartoum). Less than a year later Cromer reported that Kitchener had become 'especially bored with his own creation – the Gordon College – at which I am not at all surprised'.

On 7 December 1898 he left England to return to the Sudan as governor-general of a most peculiar type of nation, a nation such as had never before been conceived. It was called the Anglo-Egyptian Condominium. The two nations were to rule jointly, and the Union Jack and the Egyptian flag were to fly side by side. Since Egypt was supposed to be under the suzerainty of Turkey but was really ruled by Britain, the Sudanese condominium was a bizarre international entity such as only the British could conceive and only the British could make work: an unequal partnership in which the real ruler was and would always be an Englishman. Although Kitchener was supposed to be subordinate to Cromer, he was no longer willing to take orders from him, or even to consult him.

Kitchener wanted to rebuild Khartoum. Even before he left London, he sent orders to Reginald Wingate, whom he had left in charge, to start rebuilding the palace and to 'loot like blazes': 'I want any quantity of marble stairs, marble pavings, iron railings, looking-glasses and fittings; doors, windows, furniture of all sorts'. When he returned, he told his staff, 'Don't dare to quote regulations to me! They are made for the guidance of fools'. Except for his few favourites, he terrified all on his staff. Churchill said of him, 'He is a great general, but he has yet to be called a great gentleman'.

The palace, Gordon College and the Sudan Civil Service he founded, lived long after him. Perhaps his greatest contribution to the country – at least for the next half century – was the civil service, which earned a reputation throughout the Empire as a model bureaucracy. Provincial governors and most key positions in the government were at first held by British officers; then they were replaced by hand-picked young men from the best public schools and universities. The new civil servants were not necessarily those who were best academically (there were no competetive examinations); they were young men in excellent health, of good character, from 'good families', who gave indications of initiative, energy and courage. Because so many were athletes, the Sudan came to be known as a land of Blacks ruled by blues.

10

Kitchener did not long remain a dictator in his new palace. The Boer War, which broke out when the Boers invaded Natal in October 1899, provided new opportunities for glory. In December, after the astonishing series of reverses suffered by the army under Sir Redvers Buller, he gladly accepted the position of chief of staff to Field Marshal Lord Roberts. Kitchener asked for a local rank that would make him senior to the other generals in South Africa, but this was denied him. Undaunted and with little knowledge of staff work, he simply acted as if he were second-in-command, and Roberts permitted him to do so. In spite of the vast differences in personality, character, experience and even physique (Kitchener was a whole foot taller than Roberts), the two men appear to have worked well together.

Roberts's strategy was simple but effective: he planned to march an army through the Orange Free State and the Transvaal, capturing the capital cities, the mines and the railways and defeating any Boer armies that attempted to impede his passage. And that is what he did.

The first major battle took place in February 1900 at Paardeberg, where he trapped the Boer General Piet Cronjé and some 5,000 burghers, together with many of their wives and children. They could not move, but they were not defeated. Their wagons were pulled tight together along two miles of the north bank of the Modder River, in a strong defensive position.

Kitchener, who had been in the lead during the chase of

Cronjé, looked down on the Boers from a *kopje* (hill) with considerable satisfaction. Lieutenant-General Thomas Kelly-Kenny explained to him his plan to mount guns on the *kopjes* surrounding the Boer position to prevent Cronjé's escape. Kitchener thought his plan was imbecilic, and with his usual lack of tact he roughly interrupted Kelly-Kenny and ordered an immediate attack. As a writer of *The Times*'s history of the war said, 'To annihilate Cronjé's force, and then, with the terror of his dripping sword preceding him, to march straight on Bloemfontein, was to Kitchener's mind, the only policy worthy of a soldier'.

However, there arose the question of who was in charge. Kitchener had been three years junior to Kelly-Kenny when both were colonels, but Kitchener had been promoted major-general six months before Kelly-Kenny. In South Africa, though, Kelly-Kenny held the local rank of lieutenant-general, while Kitchener had only his substantive rank of major-general. As chief of staff Kitchener could give orders in Roberts's name, but obviously the orders he was giving were his own. To settle the matter, a galloper was sent pounding off to Roberts, sick in bed in Jacobsdal; a polite message came back, saying that the commander-in-chief hoped to join them the next day but that in the meanwhile all were to consider Kitchener's orders as his own.

Kitchener's reputation for ferocity, ruthlessness and disregard for casualties was now reaffirmed as he threw his infantry in bloody bayonet charges at the entrenched Boers. Kitchener may have known what he wanted his troops to do, but he failed to make his plans clear to subordinate commanders. One brigade commander, Horace Smith-Dorrien, was told to take his brigade and a battery across the river; when he asked how he was to do this, one of Kitchener's 'cubs' airily told him, 'The river is in flood and, as far as I have heard, Paardeberg Drift, the only one available, is unfordable, but Lord Kitchener, knowing your resourcefulness, is sure you will get across somehow'.

The Highland Brigade, led by Hector Macdonald, made

a gallant charge, and it was here that Macdonald was wounded in the foot. Kitchener appeared to be in a frenzy. He galloped about the field, throwing out orders left and right, ignoring the chain of command, just as he had at Omdurman. Kelly-Kenny, watching him, thought he was insane. The Highlanders and all the other British infantry brigades were stopped in their tracks by a hail of musketry. Only a single British soldier penetrated the Boer laager: the ill-fated Colonel Ormelie Hannay.

In the preceding week Hannay, who commanded a mounted infantry unit, had been in a state of near nervous exhaustion, to which Kitchener had contributed by his unmerciful goading. Like the other troops, Hannay's men had been pinned down by the Boer fire; when he sent word that it was futile to try to continue the advance, Kitchener responded with an order to attack anyway, adding, 'Gallop up if necessary and fire into the laager'. On receiving this message, Hannay sent his staff away, hastily gathered up some fifty mounted men and led them in a wild, suicidal charge at the Boer lines. His men were shot out of their saddles, but Hannay dashed on until he fell, riddled with bullets, just inside the Boers' laager.

While the battle was in progress, one of the Boers' best generals, Christiaan De Wet, rode up with 500 men and launched an attack upon Kelly-Kenny's rear. De Wet seized a hill that had been named Kitchener's Kopje and opened fire on the British artillery. This dramatic Boer diversion so late in the day increased Kitchener's frenzy.

The British had suffered 1,262 casualties by the time the sun sank on this mad, bloody day, and all recognized that Hannay's death had been a tragic self-immolation in a desperate protest against Kitchener's ruthless indifference to the lives of his soldiers. Kitchener reported to Roberts, 'Our casualties have, I fear, been severe', but he hoped 'to do something more definite' the following day.

When Roberts received Kitchener's after-action report, he rose from his bed and, at four o'clock in the morning, set off for Paardeberg, which he reached six hours later. He arrived just in time to call off another suicidal assault, which Kitchener, against the advice of all his senior officers, was about to launch. Roberts, appalled by the losses already sustained, did not want 'a further loss of life which did not appear ... to be warranted by the military exigencies of the situation'. Kitchener was sent off to expedite the repairs to the railway and its bridges; Roberts pounded the Boers into submission with his artillery. As long as he remained in South Africa, Roberts never again entrusted Kitchener with a command in battle.

On 11 December, Roberts left South Africa. He considered that the war was won and that the mopping-up operations could safely be left to Kitchener, whom he praised in his final report: 'Kitchener's self-possession, his eagerness to undertake all the hardest and most difficult work, his scorn of notoriety, and his loyalty, were beyond all praise. He was the only officer who shrank from no responsibility, and no task, however arduous'. This was high praise indeed, but the war was not over.

There were still Boers in the field with little clothing on their backs and little food in their stomachs, but with arms in their hands and a fierce desire for freedom in their breasts. They resorted to guerrilla warfare, and they moved among a population that was strongly in sympathy with them. It took nearly two years to crush them even with Kitchener's ruthless methods. He burned farms, killed cattle, destroyed crops and herded women, children and old men into what were called concentration camps in order to deny supplies and aid to the guerrillas. Sir Henry Campbell-Bannerman created an uproar when he spoke of Kitchener's actions as 'methods of barbarism'.

Columns of mounted troops scoured the veld, flushing out Boers; sometimes the columns themselves came to grief. When a mixed force under Lieutenant-Colonel George Benson, one of the best of the column commanders, was attacked and destroyed, Kitchener panicked and telegraphed London that he could not go on unless he was sent 'a large addition to our forces to carry on the war'. But he had plenty of men and arms. There was fear in London that he was losing his grip. Colonel Ian Hamilton was sent out to be his chief of staff, and he was instructed to report privately on Kitchener's health and general condition.

In organized drives using large bodies of troops, Kitchener began sweeps across designated areas, driving the Boers like wild animals against his lines of blockhouses along the railways. He delegated little authority to his subordinate commanders, directing them personally by telegraph wires, which his columns were forced to drag behind them. Ian Hamilton described Kitchener's delight in these drives:

> He was like one of those stage performers who plays six instruments at once. . . . K. worked over the wires direct with the four principal columns, and twice a day, at least, and sometimes half a dozen times a day, gave them his orders. K. was perfectly enchanted with the game of making generals dance at the end of the wires like so many marionettes.

Once, when the telegraph broke and communication was cut, Kitchener 'rose from his chair, went straight to his room, and refused for the best part of two days and two nights to take a bite. Not one single crumb'.

In a letter home, Hamilton described Kitchener to his wife: 'He has character and will like a mountain of granite and his intelligence is notwithstanding as nimble as quicksand. He has faults of course. . . . he is in some ways like a spoilt child for all his greatness and will curl up and sulk over any little trifle that vexes him'. Nevertheless, Hamilton, who was a thorough Roberts man, said of Kitchener, 'He is the biggest and most able man I have ever met, anyway!'

Even near the war's end, the Boers continued to fight with skill and daring. On 7 March 1902 a column of 1,300 men led by Lieutenant-General Lord Methuen was scuppered in the western Transvaal by another famous Boer general, Jacobus Herculaas ('Koos') De la Rey. Methuen was wounded and, with 600 of his men, taken prisoner; the Boers also captured four guns. When news of this stunning Boer victory reached British headquarters, Kitchener took to his bed for thirty-six hours. To Captain Francis Maxwell, VC, one of his favourite aides, he confessed that his nerves had 'gone to pieces'. As Ian Hamilton said later, 'It really almost seemed as if everything might crash back to chaos'. But the Boers had almost come to the end of their tether.

When the Boers were finally ground down and forced to make peace, they still made demands, and Kitchener pleaded with Lord Milner, the British high commissioner, to make concessions. Kitchener had found little glory and much frustration in South Africa; he was tired of the war and anxious to take up a new appointment that he had been promised: commander-in-chief in India. When at last the peace was signed, he sailed for England, taking with him tons of loot, including four statues that had graced the main square of Pretoria (as they now do once again). In England he was given the thanks of Parliament, awarded the GCMG, appointed to the Order of Merit, given a gratuity of £50,000 and created a viscount. (As he was unmarried with no intention of ever marrying, he asked that a special remainder should be settled on his siblings.) Most pleasing of all, perhaps, was his promotion to full general.

11

On 28 November 1902 Kitchener landed in India, where he spent seven years as commander-in-chief. The first viceroy under whom he served was Lord Curzon, a brilliant, ambitious man who was almost as arrogant, tactless and impatient of control as Kitchener himself. He was also quarrelsome, and the pair soon clashed. Initially, the two men liked each other, but Kitchener's experience was a repetition of Charles Napier's: viceroy and commander-in-chief grew quickly to detest each other. Again, like Napier, Kitchener discovered unexpected restrictions on what he could do.

The central problem was that the commander-in-chief did not have charge of what was called the Military Department, which was responsible for all non-combatant army services. The head of the Military Department was only a major-general, but as the military member of the viceroy's council it was part of his duty to advise the viceroy on military policy and to oversee all military expenditures. In short, although in the order of precedence the commander-in-chief ranked second only to the viceroy, the military member was in an ideal position to sabotage any of the commander-in-chief's activities. It was indeed a ridiculous system, and Kitchener considered it unworkable. It had worked for Roberts because Roberts had grown up with the peculiarities of the Indian army and because he had a personality that made it easy for him to like and be liked; he had made a point of working harmoniously with the viceroy and the military member. Kitchener's background and personality were quite different. Curzon was soon comparing him to 'a caged lion, dashing its bruised and lacerated head against the bars' and later spoke of him as 'a molten mass of devouring energy and burning ambition'. He thought he could govern this 'remarkable phenomenon.' He was mistaken.

On 13 November 1903 Kitchener was out riding alone near Simla when his horse shied and threw him. His left leg was broken in two places, and the pain and discomfort did nothing to improve his disposition. He was left slightly lame for the rest of his life. When he recovered, he renewed his fierce fight against the system of dual control of the Indian army. Napier had resigned rather than adapt to the system; Kitchener's response was to fight it.

Kitchener maintained a large correspondence with influential people in London, including Lord Roberts, who, although supporting Curzon in the controversy, maintained friendly relations with Kitchener. Only Roberts could have done it. In this struggle against Curzon and the system, Kitchener even sent secret emissaries to London to explain his problems and to argue that dual control must be abolished. As Churchill said in a private letter to Lady Hamilton, 'It is sad when Empire builders begin throwing brickbats at each other'.

Finally the matter was taken up by the Cabinet, which came up with a comprise that satisfied no one: the military member was to remain, but as a civilian and without authority to interfere seriously with the commander-in-chief. Kitchener got almost everything he wanted, but was still dissatisfied; Curzon felt humiliated and demanded modifications that were not granted. As a consequence, on 21 August 1905 Curzon submitted his resignation. It was accepted, and he was replaced by Lord Minto. Kitchener was now free to organize the Indian army on autocratic and centralized lines. Minto was not a fire-eater. As he allowed Kitchener to do as he pleased and supported him in his quarrels with London, the two men got on well together.

Kitchener was given to dreams of ever greater glory and honours. One evening, at ease after dinner, he remarked that he really should have been given the Nobel Peace Prize* – after all, he had brought peace to both the Sudan and South Africa. A visiting maharaja rashly suggested that it had not been Alfred Nobel's intention that the prize be given to those who created calm through conquest. Kitchener, unaccustomed to contradiction, was enraged. Nobel was a 'weaver of fantasies, a dreamer', he said. 'How could such a man understand what our Empire means for the future of the whole of mankind!'

With Kitchener in India was his 'happy family of boys' – his adoring young aides. They saw a man quite different

---

* The prize was new then. It was first awarded in 1901, five years after Nobel's death.

from the stern soldier the rest of the world saw. Henry Rawlinson, who knew him for eighteen years, wrote of him:

> He was one of the great landmarks of my life, a source from which one could not help receiving many and valuable inspirations. He had a personality in which one could confide one's most secret thoughts without risk of having one's confidence abused. . . . He was a much kinder man than he ever dared admit, even to himself. . . . the qualities I most admired in him were his determination and his imagination.

Chief among his aides in his first years in India was his favourite from South Africa, Frank Maxwell, whom he always called Brat. 'He is awfully shy', Maxwell once said of Kitchener. 'He really feels nice things, but to put tongue to them, except in very intimate society, he would rather die'. Kitchener made the unfortunate mistake of allowing Maxwell to return to England to attend Staff College, and while there Maxwell made the unforgivable mistake of falling in love and marrying. He had promised 'K' that he would return, but Kitchener never permitted married men on his staff. Maxwell was dropped.

Maxwell was replaced by a new favourite: Captain O.A.G. FitzGerald, 18th Bengal Lancers. In 1907 when FitzGerald went home on leave, it was noted that Kitchener was lonely and gloomy until he returned. FitzGerald, like Kitchener, has been called a natural celibate. E.S. Grew, a friend of both, said, 'Never was there a stronger or more loyal bond than that which these two men had for one another'. FitzGerald devoted the rest of his life to Kitchener, who wrote him into his will. The bond endured for nine years, until they died together in the cold waters of the North Sea.

Kitchener never wasted time on what did not please him or what did not fuel his ambitions. He acquired languages with ease, a talent that had advanced his career; he spoke five languages fluently, yet in his seven years in India he made no attempt to learn Hindustani. He saw no need to talk to Indians. He was never known to go out of his way to do a good turn unless it forwarded his ambition. Yet occasionally public interest and humanity coincided with self-interest. He was, for example, acutely aware of the value of healthy troops, and he took pains to keep his soldiers healthy. Evelyn Wood said:

> No one has ever attributed to the present commander-in-chief in India an excess of sentiment, but his reported determination of naming first for employment on service the healthiest corps, irrespective of their peace station, is likely to make all ambitious regimental officers strong supporters of the doctors.

On 10 September 1909 Kitchener relinquished his command in India and was promoted field marshal. At the personal request of the King, he reluctantly agreed to accept the Mediterranean Command, a recently created post that included command of the troops in Egypt. First, however, he was given leave to travel, and with FitzGerald he took a kind of honeymoon at government expense, travelling to China, Japan, Australia, New Zealand and the United States. A cruiser was put at his disposal, and he was given a special allowance of ten pounds a day while on land and three pounds a day at sea. He needed the money, for he spent more than £700 in Shanghai and nearly £1,000 in Peking on *objets d'art*. After visiting New Zealand, they returned to England by way of the United States, where they visited Yosemite in California and West Point in New York State. Kitchener had planned a visit to Civil War battlefields in Virginia, but he hurried home when it appeared from correspondence that he might not be named Minto's successor as viceroy of India, as he had expected.

It came as the biggest and bitterest disappointment of his life when Sir Charles Hardinge was appointed viceroy. For a time he sulked, went on a tour of southern Ireland and refused to take up the Mediterranean Command. If he could not have India, he wanted Egypt and the Sudan, and if not Baring's old post, then he wanted to be ambassador to Constantinople. There were questions in Parliament as to his future employment. He was offered an (unpaid) seat on the recently created Committee of Imperial Defence, but he postponed acceptance.

Richard Burdon Haldane (later Viscount Haldane) was one of the two great secretaries of state for war (1905–12) in the hundred years that separated Waterloo and Mons. He reorganized the army and formed the Territorial Army out of what had been the Volunteers and the Imperial Yeomanry. Kitchener, however, was contemptuous of all civilian schemes, and particularly of Haldane's Territorial Army. The idea of working with Haldane on the Committee of Imperial Defence was therefore not appealing; Kitchener was probably also sufficiently self-aware to know that he was not a team player. Nevertheless, he finally gave an ungracious consent to serve. Perhaps 'serve' is the wrong word. Almost immediately, he left with FitzGerald on a trip to Constantinople, Egypt and the Sudan, then on to Uganda and Kenya, where he shot lions, buffalo and a rare white rhinoceros.

The governor of Kenya was an old Sudan 'cub', Sir Percy Girouard. Kitchener decided that he wanted to own land in Kenya and develop it. He persuaded Girouard to bend the rules – considerably – in order to give him a free grant of 5,000 acres of Crown lands that had been expropriated from the Nandi tribe. A further 2,000 adjoining acres were allotted to FitzGerald and another 2,000 acres to Arthur Montagu McMurdo (another former aide from the Sudan days). The whole was to be administered as the Songhir Estates. In his will, Kitchener left most of his shares in Songhir to FitzGerald.

12

Kitchener returned to England when King George V asked him to command the troops at his coronation. He landed in Dover on 2 April 1911 and four days later bought for

£14,000 a 500-acre estate called Broome Park, near Canterbury. He gutted the seventeenth-century house, reconstructed its rooms and filled it with all the treasures he had acquired in Africa and Asia. Plans for Broome occupied all his spare time until his death, when it was still unfinished. (It eventually became a hotel.)

On 16 July the House of Commons was told that Kitchener would go to Cairo as agent, consul-general and minister plenipotentiary. After a brief stay with the King at Balmoral, he set off for Egypt on 29 September with Fitz-Gerald, a French chef and two spaniels. He was seen off by troops of Boy Scouts, for he was president of the North London Association.

Nationalism was on the rise in Egypt, and Kitchener had been told that a strong man was needed there. Any fear that Kitchener would not be a strong man was risible. One of his first acts was to rip up the Egyptian constitution and replace it with one of his own making. Such democratic institutions as existed were weakened, but he saw the importance of agriculture and devoted much of his energy to improving conditions for the fellahin. He passed laws that protected small farmers from usury, and he gave peasants easier access to the courts; he established rural savings banks; he founded an association of midwives; he initiated policies that encouraged land drainage; he built roads, bridges, railways, dams, hospitals and much else. In the process he alienated lawyers, bureaucrats and politicians, Egyptian and British, but on the whole the Egyptian people found his benevolent dictatorship the kind of personal rule they understood, preferable to the impersonal European system of government, which, however just, they neither understood nor admired.

On 23 June 1914 Kitchener returned to England for his annual three-month leave, which, as usual, he spent directing the work on the house and grounds at Broome Park, shooting grouse and mending political fences. He never returned to Egypt. He and FitzGerald had boarded the

WELCOME TO THE FRIEND OF THE FELLAH

Lord Kitchener honoured in Egypt *(Photo: Mary Evans Picture Library)*

Channel steamer for Calais on 3 August, on their way back to Egypt, when he was asked to go ashore to take a telephone call from H.H. Asquith, the prime minister. Asquith asked him to return to London at once. Kaiser Wilhelm of Germany was about to throw 1,500,000 soldiers against tiny Belgium and the 1,300,000-man French army.

On 5 August the 64-year-old Kitchener, with great reluctance, agreed to serve as secretary of state for war. It was the first time a serving soldier had sat in the Cabinet since George Monck, Duke of Albemarle, had done so in 1660, on the restoration of Charles II. The appointment was greeted with enthusiasm by almost everyone. Soon all Britain was plastered with posters of Kitchener, stern-faced beneath his field marshal's cap, his finger pointing imperiously above the legend 'Your country needs YOU'.

The Committee of Imperial Defence thought, as did almost everyone except Kitchener, that the war would be short and that, since the land force the British could bring onto the field was so small (a contemptible little army, the Kaiser called it), it would be fought primarily by the Royal Navy. Kitchener agreed with the Kaiser's assessment, particularly when applied to Haldane's Territorial Army. He believed that hundreds of thousands of men would be needed to fight a land war destined to last three or four years. Kitchener was not a profound thinker, but he was subject to flashes of brilliant insight. His belief that it would be a long war requiring the deployment of millions of men was shared by almost no one, but he was right.

It was the unanimous opinion of both the British and the French that the British Expeditionary Force (BEF) should be pushed forward as far as Maubeuge on the Western Front. Kitchener strongly disagreed, saying the BEF should concentrate around Amiens. His opinion was overruled, the BEF was pushed too far forward, and within a fortnight it was in full retreat.

On 7 August, he issued the first of his appeals for 100,000 volunteers, and the country's young men responded with such enthusiasm and alacrity that the system for equipping and training them was severely strained. Kitchener simply ignored the fourteen divisions of the Territorial Army; 'Kitchener's armies' were raised, springing like dragon's teeth from the ground and thrown across the seas to France, the Middle East and Africa to fight Germans, Austrians and Turks. To those sent off to France he issued an austere and almost universally ignored general order:

> You are ordered abroad as soldiers of the King to help our French comrades against the invasion of a common enemy. . . . In this new experience you may find temptation both in wine and women. You must entirely resist both temptations, and while treating women with respect you should avoid any intimacy.

At his first Cabinet meeting, Kitchener took the chair on the prime minister's right. He was not trying to make a point; he simply assumed that he was now the second-most-important man in the government – and he was. He never cared for ceremonies or personal publicity; he well understood the difference between honours and power. Asquith said of him, 'He did not pose for posterity; he never laid himself out for either contemporary or posthumous applause'. Even Winston Churchill, First Lord of the Admiralty, sat awed as Kitchener told his political colleagues 'in soldierly sentences' that the conflict would not be won at sea and that they must prepare for a long war.

His colleagues, at first intimidated by his very presence, for some time accepted his pronouncements as gospel. Not until the Ministry of Munitions was instituted in May 1915 was he ever overridden. Without ever directly seeking it or understanding it, Kitchener held enormous political power, for the nation – indeed, the Empire – was solidly behind him. Wherever he led they would follow. The Committee of Imperial Defence was replaced by the smaller War Council in November 1914, but Kitchener remained the warlord.

What was needed was a large, efficient general staff, but this he did not have – and he would not have used one had it been available. Now, as always, he preferred to be his own chief of staff. Any staff officer who ventured to disagree with his policies or lack of policy was instantly replaced. When Field Marshal Sir John French, commanding the BEF, telegraphed his intention of retreating behind the Seine, Kitchener, unable to accept such a move, rushed to Paris to straighten out his thinking and to make sure that the movements of his army did not expose the left flank of the French national army. Later, French complained of 'Lord Kitchener's endeavour to unite in himself the separate and distinct *rôles* of a Cabinet Minister in London and a Commander-in-Chief in France'.

Relations between French and Kitchener rapidly deteriorated, aided by the whispers of the brilliant and witty, but mischievous and scheming, General Sir Henry Wilson. Kitchener was outraged when French, who also had a penchant for intrigue, sent an important appraisal of the situation in France and his objections to the use of British troops elsewhere directly to the prime minister with only a copy to Kitchener. In short, French under Kitchener was behaving much as Kitchener had behaved under Curzon, and Kitchener found this intolerable.

French charged that the 13,000 casualties suffered in the BEF defeat at Neuve-Chapelle were caused by Kitchener, who starved the army of ammunition. Kitchener claimed that the expenditure of ammunition on such an unprecedented scale was irresponsible. Neither was correct. French initiated a press attack on Kitchener, which did no one any good.

Winston Churchill and Ian Hamilton were the scapegoats for the disastrous Gallipoli campaign, but the idea of making an end run around the Central Powers and knocking Turkey out of the war was admirable. It was the poor advance planning, the failure to coordinate the forces and the unfortunate timing that made the campaign such an execrable failure. And for this the blame must fall upon the overburdened Kitchener, who refused to delegate, failed to give Hamilton clear instructions and neglected to provide adequate staff support. When the campaign foundered, he made a special trip to Gallipoli to see if a retreat was called for, but before he could make his report the Cabinet concluded that the Anglo-French force clinging to the shirt-tail of Turkey should be withdrawn. Kitchener could only agree.

By this time Kitchener had lost most of his influence over his fellow ministers, though the general public continued to consider him a leader. Even before his trip to Gallipoli there were rumblings in the Cabinet, and a few members, led by David Lloyd George, began to press for his dismissal. Curzon, behind the scenes, was giving encouragement, and newspapers began to talk openly of his resignation. Kitchener on his return, aware that he had lost the confidence of the government, offered to resign, but Asquith persuaded him to stay on, for he was still the symbol of

A World War I poster *(Photo: Mary Evans Picture Library)*

Britain's determination to win the war. Behind his back Asquith said, 'He is not a great man. He is a great poster'. Kitchener's authority was considerably curtailed, and his activities were limited to recruitment and War Office administration.

In December 1915 Sir Douglas Haig managed to stick the knife into his old friend Sir John French's back and to replace him as commander of the BEF; General Sir William Robertson, the Scottish crofter's son who had risen from the ranks, took charge of a larger, much improved general staff with most of the duties formerly entrusted to Kitchener. Over the next few months Kitchener repeatedly tried to resign but was always persuaded that his name was needed.

In May 1916 he received a personal invitation from the Tsar to visit the Russian front and give whatever advice he could. Kitchener wanted to go, and his political colleagues were not sorry to see his back. In all there were twelve in Kitchener's party when they boarded HMS *Hampshire* for the trip to Archangel on the morning of 5 June 1916. The sea was rough when they set sail, but Kitchener was a good sailor.

At about seven-ten in the evening the *Hampshire* struck a mine that had been laid a week earlier by a German submarine. The warship listed heavily to starboard and then went down, bow first, within fifteen minutes, carrying to the bottom of the sea Field Marshal Lord Kitchener, Earl of Khartoum and Aspall, KG, KP, PC, GCB, OM, GCSI, GCMG, GCIE, together with his intimate friend and personal military secretary, Oswald FitzGerald, CMG.

Kitchener's title passed to his elder brother, Henry, the only Kitchener brother to marry.

Abbreviations

AAG	Assistant Adjutant-General
AQMG	Assistant Quartermaster General
CB	Companion of the Order of the Bath
CMG	Companion of the Order of St Michael and St George
DAAG	Deputy Assistant Adjutant-General
DAQMG	Deputy Assistant Quartermaster General
DSO	Distinguished Service Order
GCB	Knight Grand Cross of the Order of the Bath
GCIE	Knight Grand Commander of the Order of the Indian Empire
GCMG	Knight Grand Cross of the Order of St Michael and St George
GCSI	Knight Grand Commander of the Order of the Star of India
KCB	Knight Commander of the Order of the Bath
KCMG	Knight Commander of the Order of St Michael and St George
KG	Knight of the Order of the Garter
KP	Knight of the Order of St Patrick
NCO	Non-commissioned Officer
PC	Privy Council
RE	Royal Engineers
RN	Royal Navy
VC	Victoria Cross

Glossary

---

batta – an extra allowance paid to soldiers in the field in India

bimbashi – a Turkish and Egyptian military rank equivalent to major

dacoit – a member of a gang of robbers

doab – the area between two rivers

doolie – a kind of litter, usually carried on men's heads

drift – a ford

forlorn hope – a desperate enterprise

gingall – a small cannon or extra-large musket, usually mounted on a tripod

jihad – a holy war

kopje – a hill

laager – a protected camp, often made by circling wagons

mullah – a priest or holy man

pucka or pukka – real, genuine, correct

puggaree – a cloth wound around a hat or helmet

sahib – sir, a general title of respect

sangar – a small breastwork, often of loose stones

sapper – an engineer soldier

sepoy – an Indian infantryman or pioneer

sirdar – Egyptian commander-in-chief

sowar – an Indian cavalryman

veld – South African grassland, often with scattered shurbs or trees

zariba – a fortified camp surrounded by thorn bushes

Select
Bibliography

Anon. *Frontier and Overseas Expeditions from India*, 6 vols., Simla, Government Monotype Press, 1907–.

Arthur, Sir George (ed.). *The Letters of Lord and Lady Wolseley, 1870–1911*, London, Heinemann, 1922.

———. *Life of Lord Kitchener*, 3 vols., London, Macmillan, 1920.

Bates, Darrell. *The Abyssinian Difficulty: The Emperor Theodorus and the Magdala Campaign, 1867–68*, Oxford, Oxford University Press, 1979.

Bruce, George. *Six Battles for India: The Anglo-Sikh Wars: 1845–6, 1848–9*, London, Arthur Barker, 1969.

Burton, Richard F. *Sind Revisited*, 2 vols., London, Richard Bentley & Son, 1877.

Butler, Sir William. *An Autobiography*, London, Constable, 1911.

Campbell, David. *Major-General Hector A. Macdonald*, London, Hood, Douglas & Howard, 1899.

Clements, Lester Louis. 'Hector Macdonald: His Rise through the Ranks and His Contributions to the British Empire, 1853–1903', Ph.D. thesis, St John's University, New York, 1980.

Coates, Thomas F.G. *Hector Macdonald: or, The Private Who Became a General*, London, S.W. Partridge, 1900.

Elliott, Major-General J.G. *The Frontier 1839–1947*, London, Cassell, 1968.

Elton, Lord. *General Gordon*, London, Collins, 1954.

Elwin, Verrier (ed.). *India's North-East Frontier in the Nineteenth Century*, London, Oxford University Press, 1959.

Farwell, Byron, *For Queen and Country*, London, Allen Lane, 1983.

———. *The Great Boer War*, London, Allen Lane, 1981.

———. *Queen Victoria's Little Wars*, London, Allen Lane, 1973.

Featherstone, Donald. *At Them with the Bayonet: The First Sikh War*, London, Jarrolds, 1968.

Germains, Victor Wallace. *The Truth about Kitchener*, London, John Lane / The Bodley Head, 1925.

Hake, A. Egmont (ed.). *The Journals of Major-Gen. C.G. Gordon, C.B., of Khartoum*, London, Kegan, Paul, Trench, 1885.

———. *The Story of Chinese Gordon*, New York, R. Worthington, 1884.

Hamilton, Ian. *Listening for the Drums*, London, Faber & Faber, 1944.

Hanson, Lawrence and Elizabeth. *Chinese Gordon: The Story of a Hero*, New York, Funk & Wagnall, 1954.

Hibbert, Christopher. *The Great Mutiny: India, 1857*, London, Allen Lane, 1978.

James, David. *Lord Roberts*, London, Hollis & Carler, 1954.

Lambrick, H.T. *John Jacob of Jacobabad*, London, Cassell, 1960.

———. *Sir Charles Napier and Sind*. Oxford, Clarendon Press, 1952.

Lawrence, Rosamund. *Charles Napier: Friend and Fighter, 1782–1853*, London, John Murray, 1952.

Lehmann, Joseph H. *All Sir Garnet: A Life of Field-Marshal Lord Wolseley*, London, Jonathan Cape, 1964.

Lloyd, Alan. *The Drums of Kumasi: The Story of the Ashanti Wars*, London, Longmans, 1964.

Macleod, Kenneth I.E. *The Ranker: The Story of Sir Hector Macdonald's Death*, Boonville, New York, privately printed booklet, 1976.

————. *A Victim of Fate*, Boonville, New York, privately printed booklet, 1978.

Macmunn, Lieut.-Gen, Sir George. *The Romance of the Indian Frontiers*, London, Jonathan Cape, 1931.

Magnus, Philip. *Kitchener: Portrait of an Imperialist*, London, John Murray, 1958.

Marlow, Joyce. *The Uncrowned Queen of Ireland: The Life of 'Kitty' O'Shea*, New York, *Saturday Review* / E.P. Dutton, 1975.

Michael, Franz (in collaboration with Chung-li Chang). *Taiping Rebellion: History and Documents*, 3 vols, Seattle and London, University of Washington Press, 1966.

Moore, Doris Langley. *The Late Lord Byron*, London, John Murray, 1961.

Morris, Donald R. *The Washing of the Spears*, New York, Simon & Schuster, 1965.

Myatt, Frederick. *The March to Magdala: The Abyssinian War of 1868*, London, Leo Cooper, 1970.

Napier, Priscilla. *Revolution and the Napier Brothers*, London, Michael Joseph, 1973.

————. *The Sword Dance: Lady Sarah Lennox and the Napiers*, London, Michael Joseph, 1971.

Napier, Lieut.-Gen. Sir W. *The Life and Opinions of Sir Charles James Napier, G.C.B.*, 4 vols., London, John Murray, 1857.

Outram, J. *A Refutation of Certain Calumnies Cast on the Author by Major-General W.F.P. Napier in His Recent Work Entitled 'The Conquest of Scinde'*, Bombay, privately printed, 1845.

Perkins, Roger. *The Kashmir Gate*, Chippenham, Litton, 1983.

Preston, Adrian (ed.). *In Relief of Gordon: Lord Wolseley's Campaign Journal of the Khartoum Relief Expedition, 1884–1885*, London, Hutchinson, 1967.

Rait, Robert S. *The Life and Campaigns of Hugh, First Viscount Gough, Field-Marshal*, 2 vols., London, Archibald Constable, 1903.

Roberts, Field Marshal Lord. *Forty-One Years in India*, 2 vols., London, Richard Bentley & Son, 1897.

Royle, Trevor. *Death before Dishonour: The True Story of Fighting Mac*, New York, St Martin's Press, 1982.

St Aubyn, Geter. *The Royal George*, London, Constable, 1963.

Stanley, H.M. *Coomassie and Magdala: The Story of Two British Campaigns in Africa*, New York, Harper & Brothers, 1874.

Strachey, Lytton. *Eminent Victorians*, London, Chatto & Windus, 1918.

Swinson, Arthur. *North-West Frontier*, London, Hutchinson, 1967.

Trench, Charles Chenevix. *The Road to Khartoum: A Life of General Charles Gordon*, New York, W.W. Norton, 1979.

Watson, Colonel Sir Charles M. *The Life of Major-General Sir Charles Wilson*, New York, E.P. Dutton, 1909.

Wolseley, Field Marshal Viscount. *The Story of a Soldier's Life*, 2 vols., London, Archibald Constable, 1903.

Wood, Sir Evelyn. *From Midshipman to Field Marshal*, 2 vols., London, Methuen, 1906.

———. *Winnowed Memories*, London, Cassell, 1917.

Wrigley, W. David. 'Dissension in the Ionian Islands: Colonel Charles James Napier and the Commissioners', *Balkan Studies* 16, no. 2 (1975), 11–22.

Index